Anticourt Drama in England, 1603–1642

Albert H. Tricomi

Anticourt Drama
in England
1603–1642

University Press of Virginia   *Charlottesville*

To Bet—my partner and my friend

THE UNIVERSITY PRESS OF VIRGINIA
Copyright © 1989 by the Rector and Visitors
of the University of Virginia

First published 1989

Library of Congress Cataloging-in-Publication Data
Tricomi, Albert H., 1942–
    Anti-court drama in England, 1603–1642 / Albert H. Tricomi.
        p. cm.
    Includes index.
    ISBN 0-8139-1200-8
    1. English drama—17th century—History and criticism. 2. Courts
and courtiers in literature. 3. Kings and rulers in literature.
4. Monarchy in literature. 5. Political plays, English—History and
criticism. 6. Politics and literature—England—History—17th
century. 7. Great Britain—Politics and government—1603–1649.
8. Great Britain—Court and courtiers—History—17th century.
I. Title.
PR678.C7T75 1988
822'.3'09358—dc19   88-10187
                                                          CIP

Printed in the United States of America

Contents

Preface

Despite the bewildering variety of subgenres and mixed genres in seventeenth-century English drama, one recurring subject cuts across them all—court life. Courts were, after all, part of the immediate experience of English people. Their own English court helped to define their sense of history, of national identity, of morality in politics; the court also fired the imaginations of gifted poets and dramatists. On the continent as well as in England, courts became the dominant Renaissance institution, the place where all the varied types—the importunate, the ambitious, the melancholy, the sensual, the avaricious, the pious, and the cunning—could and did meet. They were the place where the crosscurrents of the age inevitably converged, where Christian ideals contended with secular imperatives, personal ambition confronted group loyalty, and the authority of state faced its own corrupting potential.

Many of the plays of the late Elizabethan period, including Shakespeare's *Richard II* and Henriad plays, functioned as encomiums to kingship at the same time that they critically examined the nature of kingship and political authority. In the Jacobean period, however, there arose a much more explicit dissentient drama that expressed the countercurrents of the age. The best plays of Marston, Chapman, Webster, Massinger, and Middleton illustrate this preoccupation as do less frequently read plays by Samuel Daniel and John Day. Some of these works—by Jonson, Webster, and Massinger, for instance—were even composed for the Globe theater. Their contribution to the thought and feeling of the English Renaissance has its own permanence, but it is only when we understand the importance of contemporary concerns—the "local habitation and a name"—underlying these dramatists' "timeless" themes that we can properly appreciate this permanence. Examining such concerns requires no special apology. We in the twentieth century have seen in Ibsenian, Shavian, and Brechtian drama a significant modern theater built on the treatment of contemporary issues. This dramatic heritage can in fact provide us with a heightened appreciation of the seventeenth century's anticourt dramas, whose functions were to challenge received values and allegiances, and even to call into question the prevailing values and institutions of an age.

Jacobean and early Caroline drama presented a variety of anticourt and opposition perspectives before divergent kinds of audiences—sometimes even royal ones. This set of theatrical circumstances indicates that the expectations and protocol governing dramatic satire and historical tragedy differed considerably from those governing the royal masque and triumphal entry. The work of Stephen Orgel has helped us to understand the masque as a mystical confirmation of the beneficent, magical powers of royalty. The royal masque appropriated the language and imagery of absolutism in order to represent the king's divinely ordained authority.[1] In a more sweeping application of this view, Jonathan Goldberg finds that the king's relationship to language defines his identity, and his representation of himself through the mystifying language of state, which he jealously guards, manifests his supreme temporal authority.[2] Thus the city pageants celebrating James's accession in 1603 exist "only in and for the king. His presence gives them life; his absence robs them. Their existence depends upon him."[3]

Our readjusted perceptions of the representation of royal authority in early Stuart drama now threaten, however, to blind us with too much light from this regal vantage point. We are in danger of "discovering" the royal perspective, or its mimetic derivatives, as *the* pervasive influence governing the major Jacobean drama as well.[4] Anticourt theater in the early seventeenth century suggests a different field of vision. An absolutist perspective can be used (and was) to propound ideas that in effect subverted Stuart orthodoxy, but such forms of representation need to be seen broadly, in conjunction with other anticourt perspectives. We need a comprehensive view of the anticourt dramatic tradition as well as of explicitly royal forms of entertainment in order to begin to construct an adequate interpretation of the Jacobean-Caroline drama.

There is insufficient space to treat fully the literary expressions of dissident political ideas in the Tudor period preceding, but we can briefly point to works that demonstrate the presence of such a tradition, from which dissentient Jacobeans drew. Anticourt attitudes appear early in the Tudor period with Skelton's poetic satire "Why Come Ye Not to Court" (1522), and then, more prominently, in the last two decades of Elizabeth's reign. Spenser's discursive topical allegory, "Mother Hubberds Tale," with its great passage of complaint on the disconsolate suitors who haunted Elizabeth's court in vain pursuit of rewards, and Donne's Fourth Satire, which elaborates the insight that the court is "A Purgatorie, such as fear'd hell is" (l. 3), are representative poems from each of these decades.[5] The Juvenalian forms of nondramatic satire that flourished at the close of Elizabeth's reign encouraged the expression of numerous but often unfocused anticourt attitudes. Among these nondramatic antecedents, Joseph Hall's *Virgidemiarum* (1598) and Edward Guilpin's *Skialetheia* (1598), with its daring satire on the earl of Essex as the "great Foelix" instructed by Signior Machiavel, were important developments and influenced the early Jacobean anticourt satires produced in the indoor theaters from 1600.[6] More important still are the nondramatic satires of Middleton, Tourneur, Marston, and Chapman, all of whom began their careers composing nondramatic satire before turning to the drama as their prime means of expressing anticourt ideas. The potency of their social-political criticism was surely felt by the authorities, for on June 1, 1599, by order of the bishop of London, T[homas] M[iddleton's] *Snarlinge Satyres,* Tourneur's *Transformed Metamorphosis,* Marston's *Pygmalion's Image* and his *Scourge of Villanie,* in tone and temper the most violent of the group, were all publicly burned.[7]

The dramatic antecedents of Stuart anticourt drama certainly include the politically dissident impulses as expressed in the English history play, especially in its representation of native rebellions and uprisings. These include John Bale's reform-minded *I & II King John* (1538), the heavily censored *Sir Thomas More* (ca. 1596), which explores the social and economic causes of discontent, and *Thomas of Woodstock* (1591–95), which reflects Elizabethan grievances in portraying the problems of Richard II's reign as stemming from the king's arbitrary powers of prerogative taxation and from his elevation of unscrupulous favorites.[8] Marlowe's unique contribution to the development of heterodox political attitudes in the drama, particularly his demystified representation of courts, holds a place of prominence. So too do Marston's *Antonio and Mellida* (1599) and *Antonio's Revenge* (1600) since these initiated the phenomenon of the Italianate anticourt play in England.

Such an inheritance indicates that although Stuart anticourt drama manifested itself in a variety of forms, it nevertheless issued from a well-established literary tradition. In this regard some will immediately recognize that the present study begins chronologically where David Bevington's *Tudor Drama and Politics* ends.[9] Although Bevington's work limits its approach, as its subtitle indicates, to topical meaning, it is cautious in its identifications and adept in its handling of themes—the best we have of its kind. The present study treats topicality in the sections on the contemporary satire of the child actors and on the opposition drama of the 1620s, but it is not limited to this approach. Broader notions of *application,* hortatory *example,* and political *representation*—areas of significant development in the last generation—are equally essential.

No one term, including John Peter's idea of complaint literature (which, in contrast to satire, he defines as impersonal and allegorical), can appropriately convey the variety of anticourt plays produced in the Jacobean and Caroline periods.[10] However, in describing the phenomenon that underlies the creation of these several kinds of plays, I have found the term *anticourt drama* to be the most useful because it covers a range of attitudes to court life and policy that may vary from critical to condemnatory. In this study I have applied the term broadly to those plays that critically depict the political policies and ideology of Renaissance courts and kings, with their absolutist claims and far-reaching authority—Chapman's and Massinger's political plays, for example—and to those that depict modern court *life* as spiritually corrupting—Webster's Italianate court tragedies, for example.

The term is not intended to signify any organized movement toward political or social reform, much less an inexorable development toward any grand historical moment such as the English civil war, but it is intended to reveal the persistence of a dramatic tradition which features the counter-representation of kings and courts and which cuts across class lines. In treating this subject, I have tried to be comprehensive without being exhaustive, to be empirical before being ideological. I have also avoided the older method of trying to make the plays fit into a single cultural overview;[11] this approach is too undifferentiating to provide an accurate perception of the ways that various kinds of plays are tied to more specific, often shifting cultural conditions. The Jacobean and Caroline periods supported a variety of theaters and audiences. I have, therefore, presented plays in groups, generally by genre, with attention in introductory sections to the theaters producing them and the sociological makeup of their audiences.

Such an approach seems to me especially important in treating well-known plays such as *The Revenger's Tragedy, The White Devil,* and *The Duchess of Malfi,* whose significance seems to have been fixed for us (reductively) by the old New Criticism. Even if we praise them for treating universal themes of love, lust, self-affirmation, and self-destruction, we need to view them, not as belonging exclusively to that category of literature Wellek and Warren call "unique," "timeless," works of art,"[12] but as citizen-oriented Italianate tragedies whose social criticism and anticourt perspective help to define their purpose and significance.

One response in the last decade to the old formalist criticism has been to treat Shakespearean and Jacobean plays as ideological tracts, or would-be tracts, reflecting twentieth-century concerns. Jonathan Dollimore's *Radical*

Tragedy is a pertinent example of this approach.[13] This work brings a welcome passion for intellectual history and controversy to the interpretation of seventeenth-century plays, but the experience of the plays themselves as coherent dramatic works is often lost in the search for philosophical cruxes. So too is the distinction between the plays Shakespeare tended to write as compared with those of his more reform-minded competitors. Dollimore's work is perhaps an extreme expression of a corrective movement in Renaissance studies that views literary works as part of a seamless discourse that includes political speeches, sermons, treatises, ballads, and other forms of written expression. This redirection in the focus and method of literary study, which has come to be called "the new historicism," has been accurately summed up by Stephen Greenblatt: "recent criticism has been less concerned to establish the organic unity of literary works and more open to such works as fields of force, places of dissension and shifting interest, occasions for the jostling of orthodox and subversive impulses."[14] My own treatment of the plays within the anticourt tradition places considerable emphasis on "dissensions" or, in my words, "countercurrents," "ambivalence," and even "alienation," but I remain concerned to show the coherence these plays had for contemporary audiences. Toward this end, plays are treated individually, but within generic groups. In my view this method offers the most promising way of demonstrating the ideological, spiritual, *and* dramatic power of the plays constituting the anticourt dramatic tradition.[15]

In the present study I have explored chronologically the related development of the five major expressions, as I have found them, of anticourt drama in the early Stuart period. Each of these groups of plays manifests a view of English or Continental courts that is distinct from the others but also distinctly related to them. Among these several groups, the satiric or tragic points of focus highlight quite different features of court life, varying from government policy to court culture, ethics, and ideology; yet these groups are not only related but united in their critical views of the institution contemporaries referred to by that overarching term "the court." Stated somewhat differently: the five groups of anticourt dramas examined in this study may be viewed as part of a constellation of attitudes toward the Renaissance court in its various functions. Just as the astronomical constellation Saggita (appositely identified in myth as the arrow that Hercules used to slay Zeus' eagle) reveals itself as consisting of five principal stars, each a distinct but constituent part of that configuration we recognize as "Saggita," so too does this study discern a configuration of five distinct but related varieties of anticourt drama. To treat the development of anticourt drama in this flexible way seems to me an appropriate means of recording the dynamic multisidedness the court world signified to contemporaries.

Within each section of this study, I have treated at close quarters the principal plays constituting the particular group, attending at the end of sections to the norms by which Stuart officials variously legitimized and censored such literature. The first group comprises the plays performed by the child actors. At the Blackfriars theater between 1603 and 1608, the Children of the Queen's Revels presented daring topical satires and lampoons on James's court and ministers. Capitalizing on the immunity that child actors traditionally enjoyed until official sanctions humbled them, this company became a center for the expression of anticourt, anti-Jacobean, and anti-Scottish attitudes.

The second group comprises the ideological tragedies of learned writers, both courtly and professional. The philosophical closet tragedies of Samuel Daniel and Fulke Greville, both disaffected Jacobean courtiers who had been preferred in Elizabeth's reign, use court settings in ancient Greece or sixteenth-century Persia to examine absolutist tyrannies while expressing at the same time their disaffection with the contemporary practice of government in England. Among professional dramatists such as Chapman and Jonson, a related form of ideological tragedy developed in which predominantly Roman and contemporary French court settings are used to explore, as in a laboratory, the nature of the modern state. Since these dramatists wrote for gentle audiences, issues of political principle, fealty, and personal honor, often placed in agonizing conflict with one another, make the stuff of their drama.

The popular subgenre of Italianate tragedy, composed for performance before largely citizen audiences in London's outdoor theaters, contrasts markedly with the two prior groups. These tragedies, including some of the most extensively studied of the period—*The Revenger's Tragedy, The White Devil, The Duchess of Malfi* and *Women Beware Women*—are generically anticourt. For the most part, these tragedies were not construed, nor do they appear to have been written, as specific attacks against James or his ministers; they are not topical in so limited a sense. Rather, they employ their nominally Italian settings to present universally applicable themes on the repellent, spiritually corruptive nature of court life. Since their basic concerns are expressed through conventional topoi, which provided a fund of accepted ideas for the edification of citizen, noble, and even royal audiences, such plays could usually be presented with approval. But for the very reason that this kind of theater was so conventionalized, these dramatists had remarkable latitude in presenting the most damning portrayals of modern court life that English theater ever produced—an admonitory mirror for the age.

The fourth group, the dissentient plays of the Buckingham era, 1621–28, are anticourt in a narrower sense. Unlike Italianate tragedies, for example, they offered no wholesale condemnations of court life. But, along with a flood of other literature, these plays opposed recognizable policies of James's and Charles's own courts and championed a parliamentary ideology that directed itself against highly placed court officials and favorites. For this reason this fourth group, which includes the most politically explosive plays of the early Stuart period, warrant the more specific term *opposition drama.* Middleton's transparent allegory of James's proposed Spanish match for his son in *A Game at Chess* and Massinger's more patrician attack on Sir Giles Mompesson's odious monopolies in *A New Way to Pay Old Debts* both exemplify the pattern. Propelled by grievances and apprehensions that England was abandoning its traditional support for the defenders of Protestantism abroad, this politicized drama leaves behind a record of distrust for and disenchantment with crown policy that borders on alienation. In considering in the fifth group the distinctive development of opposition plays from the period of prerogative government to 1642, I have attempted to revise received notions still current that the Caroline drama was politically aseptic, and I have emphasized the emergence in court, city, and country plays of a network of opposition ideas of governance that issue forth from a riveting focus on specific grievances associated with this period.

The social-historical chapters that precede the several parts of this study are not intended to offer definitive renderings of early Stuart history but rather to orient the reader to the selective perceptions among audiences and dramatists in several kinds of theaters of the doings of courts and kings. Readers of the first chapter on the social background to the reign of James I may find, for example, that it highlights the sensational and the scandalous, and they would be right. Such a rendering does not spring from any whiggish distaste for King James—I try to make that point right away—but from the kind of material that the Children of the Queen's Revels at the Blackfriars seized upon for their social satire and, so far as I can tell, from the cravings of that company's more well-to-do, sophisticated audiences. By contrast, the introductory section on the Italianate anticourt tragedies that flourished among citizen audiences in London's outdoor theaters leans heavily on reports from Puritan London and also from parliamentary historians of the later seventeenth century who carried forward early Jacobean anticourt attitudes. These sources offer, it seems to me, our best chance of reconstructing the ambivalence and even hostility to court life that simmered in many of the poorer quarters of London.

Mindful of Foucault's strictures, I do not wish to "privilege" history over literature by rendering the former as a static, linear truth that theatrical representation merely "reflects."[16] To the contrary, my purpose is to exhibit the dramatic and the political as a mutually constitutive dynamic expression of culture. Nevertheless, history is for me event-centered as well as language-centered. I do not exclude from consideration concrete events as they affect the drama—acts of licensing and censorship, political addresses and contemporary perceptions of foreign and domestic policy; but the more inclusive kinds of explanation are to be found in the appearance of several varieties of anticourt drama composed for distinctive audiences and theaters throughout the early Stuart period. From these kinds of evidence, I am interested, finally, in exploring the articulation and dispersion in the drama of what we may call an ideology and rhetoric of opposition, an ideology that was in the later seventeenth century to become part of mainstream political discourse.

In offering this study, I have labored to build on past research, documenting amply. My aims, I would simply say, are to provide the cultural perspectives that enable us to better understand the homiletic component in the art of early Stuart anticourt dramas, to demonstrate through analysis of the plays themselves that they indeed constitute a major dramatic tradition, and to show how this tradition contributes to our understanding of the countercurrents in early Stuart England.

Acknowledgments

This study began in 1977 as a response to the dominance of formalist studies of the Jacobean-Caroline drama and took its present shape as a social-political-critical study of the dissident and lost voices in seventeenth-century drama. Over the years I incurred many debts and am pleased, finally, to acknowledge them in print.

Roger Lockyer was of signal assistance during my stay at the London Historical Institute in 1977, directing me to numerous historical texts I might otherwise have overlooked; later, he read with incisiveness several sections of the manuscript. Moody E. Prior, Professor Emeritus at Northwestern University, read numerous parts of the manuscript and provided encouragement and wisdom at every stage of my work. In him I have learned how mentorship and friendship may grow together. The late Walker Cowen, director of the University Press of Virginia, championed this study; I am sorry that he did not live to see this work in print and that I never met him in person.

I am grateful to Annabel Patterson for reading the entire manuscript and suggesting important changes. Christopher Hill offered crucial suggestions on the treatment of the Caroline drama. At least two anonymous readers for the University Press of Virginia provided searching analyses that led to substantial improvements. Gerald Trett, an editor at the press, provided a thorough technical reading and helped to speed the publication process after Walker Cowen's death.

A two-month Folger Shakespeare Library Fellowship, a Huntington Library summer fellowship, and an American Philosophical Society travel grant in 1977 enabled me to consult original manuscripts and important secondary materials during the initial stages of this study. I am also grateful to the State University of New York for a summer research fellowship in 1982. A Dean's Research Semester awarded by SUNY-Binghamton enabled me to produce the initial draft of this study. The staff of SUNY-Binghamton's Manuscript Center prepared several drafts of the manuscript. The university's library staff, particularly Harold Geisse, Jr., and Michaelyn Burnette, have been unfailingly generous in helping to locate source materials.

Many members of the English department read parts of the manuscript at one stage or another. I wish to thank them publicly: David Bartine, Norman Burns, Michael Conlon, Richard McLain, Bernard Rosenthal, Elias Schwartz, Melvin Seiden, Patricia Speyser, and Susan Strehle. Wilhelm Nicolaisen interpreted problems related to English manuscript practice. Grant Webster read the manuscript, providing advice concerning critical theory, and William Spanos, in his commitment to postmodernism, urged the importance of scholarship that seeks to make a difference in the world.

Finally, I wish to acknowledge the assistance of my colleague of twenty years, Alvin Vos, who read the manuscript in at least two drafts, considering with me every important critical problem I faced. The one person who knows this book best and who sustained me through each stage of its making is my wife, Bet. During the writing and revisions, our children, Al, Will, and Eebie, were to me more than a discipline of humanity: I acknowledge the many times that they called me to join them in play while I chose to continue punching letters in front of a tinted screen under fluorescent lights.

I

TOPICAL DRAMATIC SATIRE

1603–1608

1

The Social Background

The Reign of James I

      The picture of the court of James I, and of the king himself, as drawn in contemporary histories of the reign is so negative as to verge on caricature. Anthony's Weldon's depiction of James as having large eyes "ever rowling after any stranger that came in his presence," a "tongue too large for his mouth," spindlelegs, and a "circular" walk, "his fingers ever in that walk fidling about his cod-piece," provides such an example.[1] Other reports have come down to the effect that the king so loved hunting he would relieve himself on his horse rather than dismount and that at his court the excess was so great "the most luxurious tyrants" did not rival it, for "dishes, as high as a tall man could well reach, [were] filled with the choycest and dearest viands sea or land could afford: And all this once seen . . . was in a manner throwne away, and fresh set on to the same height, having only this advantage of the other, that it was hot."[2]

    These several accounts display an untrustworthy pattern of historiography fostered by Parliamentarians who, without exception, composed their histories after James's death. Similar patterns of analysis have survived into modern times through whig historians. Even the monumental work of S. R. Gardiner, whose exhaustive analysis of the events of the reign is still unrivaled, reveals a teleological conception of English history (reminiscent of such great system-perceivers as Spengler and Hegel) as moving inevitably away from absolutist and monarchist governments to the more advanced liberal or democratic forms.[3] To correct Gardiner's inveterate bias, twentieth-century historians have approached the contemporary accounts of the early Stuart period much more cautiously. They have paid more attention to the information of diarists writing in the first decades of the reign as well as to the social documents of the period. Others such as Joel Hurstfield and Conrad Russell have reexamined James's reign using the more objective data from government inventories and account books, and virtually all have taken account of the tolerance of official corruption experienced in other reigns or in the Continental monarchies.[4]

These approaches have tended to curb the formerly prevalent view of James as a foolish statesman and a drunkard, prematurely senile and presiding over a thoroughly corrupted court.[5] More appreciative evaluators of monarchical government have also helped to rehabilitate the reputation of James and his court.[6] The traditional view is not dead, however. Menna Prestwich's controversial analysis of William Cecil's ministry has thrown the focus once more upon the wastefulness and fiscal corruption of James's court, and David H. Willson's standard study of James has been justly described as a "biography of a king whose financial irresponsibility and political ineptitude have been generally conceded."[7]

But whether or not the early assessments of James and his court are accurate is not so crucial for our purposes as that burlesque, even caricaturist representations of James and his court were made in the early seventeenth century by satirists composing for largely elite audiences in the indoor theaters. A sinewy thread thus connects the savage representations of king and court by mid-century Parliamentarians and Jacobean dramatic satirists. But whereas the Parliamentarians often wrote satire and called it history, the Blackfriars satirists, by lampooning the authorities in their topical plays and savaging James's court, created their own brand of social history. For readers unfamiliar with the social causes of James's unpopularity, this chapter sets forth the issues that contemporary dramatists seized upon in fashioning their anticourt plays. In describing the import of these issues, I have drawn as much as possible from the accounts of Jacobean observers, particularly of the drama.

England had never seen James, nor he the fair demesnes that lay south of Scotland, but the leisurely progress he began in Edinburgh on April 5, 1603, through the countryside to Cecil's magisterial estate at Theobalds gave his subjects their opportunity. Everywhere the new king was wildly acclaimed. Elizabeth was still being mourned, of course, but she had achieved the biblical ripeness of three score and ten, and after a decade of recurring plague, inflation, and famine, people looked ahead to a new era of prosperity. Fifty-six years after the robust Henry VIII had died, England was again given a mature male sovereign, with two male heirs to insure a continuous succession that Elizabeth, for all her diplomacy, had not provided.

Then too, the transition to James had been achieved, thanks to Cecil, without struggle. As a prince of thirty-six, a Protestant, a statesman well versed in the arts of government, an intellectual, and an author of avidly read treatises on poetry and political theory,[8] James appeared to many to be an ideal prince for England, a genuine philosopher-king whose coming seemed to validate the theory of Divine Right.

But the actual appearance of the king brought disappointment and consternation. At Newark-upon-Trent, James, forgetful of English positive law, ordered a cutpurse summarily hanged.[9] Ominously, the king, a practiced horseman, fell from his horse just as he was arriving at his destination of Burghley House, breaking his collarbone.[10] Even more ominously, the plague began to increase in virulence. Everywhere it seemed to follow him. The more crowds gathered to greet him, the greater the incidence of disease became. For a people who saw the hand of divinity in all such inexplicable phenomena, this turn of events did more than any other to change exuberance to apprehension. By the time James arrived at the outskirts of London, the city was so overcome with pestilence it could not permit a public entry. Even the king's scheduled Coronation, on the feast of St. James, was for a time cast in doubt. In the face of the most serious outbreak of plague since the Black Death, all show of state was forbidden by royal proclamation. By the end of the year, over 38,000 had been recorded on the death rolls, taking a full fifth of London's regular inhabitants.[11] For James it was bad luck; for others it was, possibly, a judgment.

James was, of course, not responsible for the plague's outbreak, but as crowds gathered round him, he and his magnificent entourage unintentionally helped it to spread. The measures taken to combat the outbreak are pitiable to a modern eye. No one knew that the black rat carried the infection; to an alert eye it seemed that the frothy-mouthed dogs who preyed upon the rats were responsible, and so, wholesale slaughter of the domesticated animals was undertaken in an effort that succeeded only in spreading the plague as the natural enemy of the rats was ignorantly removed.[12]

Those futile prophylactic activities provide an emblem for James's wellmeaning but ineffective social and economic policies. If his original hope of establishing a strong bond of affection with his new people had been thwarted by plague, he found himself lucky enough to have a second chance. By March 1604 the plague had disappeared as quickly as it had arrived. For the first time in a year the theaters hummed with activity. And James had his triumphal entry. Virtually every guild member and writer of note involved himself in pageants, spectacles, and musical salutes. Triumphal arches were erected after the Italian manner for the royal procession to pass through. The city again thronged with spectators who awaited their king in expectation that he would make as much of the occasion as they had for him.[13]

But they were again disappointed. James was not a lover of pretty pageants in the open air, nor did he enjoy the fanfare of the state occasion. Unlike Elizabeth, the Stuart king was really a retiring man who felt a distaste for crowds; they reminded him of more tempestuous days in Scotland when conspirators had made attempts upon his life.[14] Although he loved the flattery he heard, James was unable to establish, even on his own terms, a personal rapport—as Elizabeth had—with the people. Actually, the situation was worse than the absence of good feeling, for James could or would not attempt to conceal or tone down his aversion to public appearances. Rather than be a leader of his people, James preferred to be himself. Sir John Oglander recalls how the king, informed of the people's desire to see him, waxed wroth, crying, "God's wounds! I will pull down my breeches and they shall also see my arse."[15]

At the Hampton Court Conference James so mixed his disquisitions with coarse language that Sir John Harington quipped, "The bishops . . . said his Majestie spoke by the power of inspiration . . . but the spirit was rather foule mouthede."[16] The Venetian ambassador, coolly observing the progress of events, remarked that the English "like their King to show pleasure at their devotion, as the late Queen knew well how to do; but this King manifests no taste for them but rather contempt and dislike. The result is he is despised and almost hated."[17]

Courtiers who had looked with eagerness toward the dawning new reign began to look back with nostalgia on Elizabeth, not one year in her grave. And on James they now looked with newly criticizing eyes. So long as James remained a vague ideal, he could be acclaimed, but as soon as they had firsthand experience of the man, enthusiasm diminished quickly. As early as 1603, one of James's own councilors who gained preferment under him, Sir Roger Wilbraham, reported that whereas the old queen was "solemne and ceremonious, & requiring decent & disparent order to be kept . . . the King . . . who altho he be indeede of a more true benignitie & ingenuous nature, yet the neglect of those ordinarie ceremonies, which his variable & quick witt cannot attend, makes common people judge otherwise of him."[18] Many observers charted a great falling off from the standards set by Elizabeth. So offended was Arbella Stuart by the court's indecorum that she wrote, "But if ever there were such a virtue as courtesy at the Court, I marvel what is become of it, for I protest I see little or none of it but in the Queen [i.e., Anne]."[19]

Had this plain-speaking king created a plain-speaking court in his own image, English courtiers might well have accepted, even preferred it, as in Henry VIII's day, but James, a man who had been starved for affection and recognition throughout his youth, encouraged his court to offer him the most groveling flattery. According to D. H. Willson, "No adulation was too gross, no praise too strained or fulsome for the taste of their new monarch."[20] Such criticisms merged with distaste for the king's personal style—his table manners, his habit of dress, his Scottish brogue, and his vulgarity. These sat peculiarly beside his Divine Right pretensions. Although these flaws made the monarch an easy target for humorists, they would have amounted to very little were they not also joined to a conception of kingship and of courtly rewards that repelled his English subjects.

Having endured in Scotland a rather shabby life for an anointed king, James waited covetously, and after much grooming, for his Elizabethan inheritance. When it came, he spent in a manner befitting the splendor of his new titles. When James ascended the throne of England, he established the royal households with an extravagance out of proportion even to the expectations of the times. Royal household expenses immediately doubled from £40,000 to £80,000 and continued to soar.[21] A frugal Elizabeth, with no family, had accumulated total ordinary annual expenditures of between £225,000 and £300,000; James in the same account soon ran up a bill of half a million each year.[22] The figures do not, however, convey adequately the conspicuousness of his expenditures, which satirists repeatedly lampooned. By 1611 James's country residences had proliferated to include estates at Windsor, Hampton Court, Greenwich, Etham, Richmond, Nonsuch, Enfield, Royston, Newmarket, and the fabulous mansion at Theobalds, which James had acquired from Cecil (in exchange for Hatfield House) in 1607. Since each of these estates had to be maintained in a condition of perpetual expectancy, they duplicated many times over the expenses of maintaining a royal household, for entire staffs, from the stablekeepers, the gardeners, maidservants, cooks, foresters, and housekeepers to the petty officials and stewards, had to be kept in readiness.[23]

More threatening than this "Asiatic" style of magnificence was the enormous entourage of Scottish courtiers who expected to bask in a warmer English sun of preferment. These fellow countrymen James neither could nor wished to deny. With them, like them, he traveled to what he believed would be a fabled land of plenty. What he found were great numbers of English courtiers starved for preferment.[24] These reward-hungry Englishmen then beheld James's solicitous treatment of the importunate Scotsmen who, without having toiled before in the English court, were showered with the coveted prizes and appointments Englishmen had sought unsuccessfully for years to attain. The rewards were conspicuous, as so many of these foreign tatterdemalions began to sport hose and doublets of satin and velvet. Their cash awards were astounding. A state paper drawn up in 1610 lists the king's awards to his Scottish brethren from the date of his accession. It records £10,614 in annual pensions, £88,280 in "ready money," and £133,100 in "old debts."[25] Early in 1607, after Englishmen had become fully aware of the government's need to curb runaway expenses, the king undertook to pay the

debts of two of his most spendthrift Scottish retainers, Lord James Hay and
Viscount Haddington, in addition to those of the English earl of Montgomery.[26] At a stroke the burden to the treasury increased by £44,000. Such gifts,
McElwee estimates, amounted to more than 25 percent of James's total
indebtedness in 1610, and his annuities to about 6 percent of his yearly
expenditure.[27] A stronger king might have lived more frugally. As it was,
James became the object of a parasitism which, although odious to those
outside the court, he interpreted as loyalty. Among Scotsmen, not surprisingly, an exhilarating spirit of predation prevailed, but many Englishmen, as
Jacobean dramas attest, felt like virtuous servants shut out from the banquet.
To them, these rewards to the Scots meant a loss of recompense for years of
service and diminution of their own status, since in a hierarchical society
such as England, the offices, titles, and pensions a man received defined his
place. Nor could they have been mollified by a state of affairs in which "no
Englishman, be his rank what it may, can enter the Presence Chamber
without being summoned, whereas the Scottish Lords have free entrée of the
privy chamber."[28] Francis Osborne's recollection of these come-lately Scotsmen as a horde of "locusts [come to] devour this kingdome" and as "hors-
leeches" who hung onto James "till they could get no more, falling then off by
retiring into their owne country," illustrates the persistence of this resentment.[29]

Not that James wished to deny his new countrymen. On the contrary, the
king had need, like the feudal sovereigns depicted by the Beowulf poet, to be
his own kind of ring-giver, to distribute rewards broadly in order to establish
new loyalties among the English nobility. James was, after all, a new king in a
strange land bent on building a new dynasty. Were there money enough,
offices, and sinecures enough—that is, had James come to rule a land of
fabulous wealth—he would have satisfied all. Unfortunately, he had little
capital to bestow upon deserving Englishmen and not nearly enough offices,
grants, or pensions.

But he could bestow knighthoods, and this he did exuberantly and unreser-
vedly, collecting at least £30 per head for the honor. In the entire course of
Elizabeth's reign, forty-five years, 878 knights had been created, a figure that
includes the wholesale knightings performed by Essex during his Rouen and
Irish campaigns against the queen's explicit wishes. James had not trod on
English soil six weeks before he had dubbed 237 new knights, and 432 more
in a single day. One morning at Belvoir, the king, to the disgust of most
onlookers, created 46 knights before breakfast. Such knighthoods would
also help to diminish the national deficit by exposing those knighted to feudal
dues. With this in mind, the king, on July 17, 1603, enforced a statutory
requirement that all freeholders with land yielding £40 a year come to be
knighted.[30] By the end of James's first full year, 1604, the number of knights

who roamed the country demanding obeisance had trebled. James had created 1,161 knights. None was created for military achievement. For the *ancien* nobility who retained some sense of the ideals of chivalry, there could be only contempt for these mere "carpet" knights. Even for members of the aspiring gentry, who ached to bend their knees so that their merit might be recognized, the honor had been tarnished.[31]

No less provocative of contempt was the king's own conduct in office and the character of the court he organized around him. It took less than a year for the English to realize that they had "an hunting King" with little love of London or of the serious business of state. Thus, in addition to proliferating his estates, the king projected an image, which he did little or nothing to correct, of a sovereign who had abandoned the ship of state for a life of aristocratic leisure. Of this royal indolence the Venetian ambassador, a shrewd observer of the new scene, wrote, "[He] seems to have almost forgotten that he is a King except in his kingly pursuits of stags, to which he is quite foolishly devoted."[32] Commoners too discerned a pattern, and by 1604, began to express openly their sense of grievance. During one of James's hunting vacations at Roystan, a now celebrated event occurred. The king had lost one of his prize hounds, Jowler, in the hunt. The next day the animal suddenly reappeared with a letter attached to its neck: "Good Mr. Jowler, we pray you speak to the King (for he hears you every day, and so doth he not us) that it will please his Majesty to go back to London, for else the country will be undone; all our provision is spent already and we are not able to entertain him longer."[33] What had begun as a prerogative of kingship had become for the English a question of ethics, of good government.

Back at Whitehall, what had begun as a matter of style was fast becoming a matter of morals. A vulgarity and rowdiness unknown in Elizabeth's court colored the festivities. The more restrained gentlemen, dressed in the height of ostentatious fashion, gathered in the events at the gambling tables where reports of high wagers became commonplace. Cardsharping and dicing became synonymous with self-indulgent courtiership. Both became easy marks for Jacobean satirists. Similarly, the less restrained younger courtiers gave themselves over to adolescent displays of ruffianship, such as playing at horse racing by riding on one another's back. The king, for his part, sipped his heavy wine from a goblet and sometimes dozed off.[34]

At the banquets thrown by the most eminent courtiers, James allowed the court to indulge its aristocratic predilections for competitive displays of wealth. The seemingly endless courses of rich food at Lord Hay's banquets are perhaps the most memorable, but they were in keeping with James's extravagant practice of ordering feasts of a minimum of twenty-four courses.[35]

These lavish displays were spurred on by the example of Queen Anne, whose love of fashionable dresses, rich jewelry, and courtly entertainments prompted the court ladies to embark on a spree of ostentation. In 1604, at one of the great masques that all London was beginning to buzz about, the queen appeared wearing jewelry appraised at £100,000.[36] In a letter of January 8, 1608, John Chamberlain wrote to Dudley Carleton that "one Lady . . . [has been] furnished for better then an hundred thousand pound, and the Lady Arbella goes beyond her and the Quene must not come behinde."[37] At the court masques especially, which were themselves aristocratic celebrations of power and status, the court ladies found the occasion to indulge their tastes in finery as never before. While some entered the competition with alacrity, others, feeling a vulgarization of Elizabethan manners, looked on reprovingly as Anne's ladies appeared for court masques in gowns costing £50 to the yard.[38]

Rumors also began to circulate about the court's scandalous moral standards. In particular, the infidelities of some of the great ladies and the kept mistresses of the great lords became a source of contemptuous gossip in the early years. Lady Anne Clifford wrote in her diary that the ladies of the court had gotten "ill names," that the court "was grown a scandalous place," and that the queen's own reputation had fallen sadly.[39] At another remove, courtesans and procurers found business brisk in this lax court filled with newcomers.[40]

This spectacle of extravagance and sensuality at court, and the evident inattentiveness to pressing matters of state, provided surefire matter for dramatic satirists who sought to highlight the decline of the age. At the same time, James's wholesale creation of knights, his inveterate preference for hunting rather than governing, and his encouragement of the Scottish parvenus who had followed the new court to London provided the hot matter from which dramatists forged a genuine drama of protest in London's indoor theaters.

Only in recent years has serious consideration been accorded to the theaters that produced this drama. Alfred Harbage's *Shakespeare and the Rival Traditions* drew attention to Shakespeare's Globe as a national theater and to the children's companies as a rival repertory catering to a well-to-do coterie.[41] However, Harbage's denigration of the playwrights who composed for this coterie—Chapman, Day, and especially Marston—is a bias still in need of correction, for their drama constitutes a valuable countertradition, critical of court and country. Equitable treatment involves something more than merely adjusting attitudes, however. The distinctive dramatic tradition of these indoor theaters, their political outlook and art, and their unique repertory all need to be more widely understood and appreciated.

Of the two indoor theaters, by far the more audacious was the Blackfriars. To Londoners this theater must have gained an identity early on for the expression of attitudes antagonistic to James and his court. For one thing, the company, by the patent of February 4, 1604, was called the Children of her Majesty's Revels and was placed directly under the patronage of the queen,[42] who was known to feel isolated from the king and to resent his dalliance with male favorites and his repeated excursions into the countryside to hunt. The king, although generous in providing for his wife's expensive tastes and respectful of her in public, created separate living arrangements for her and from 1606 forward lived apart from her. James's abandonment of Anne for homosexual partners is now generally conceded, and, certainly, Anne's resentment and loneliness were well-established facts of court life.[43]

For the Blackfriars theater, all this would have meant very little were it not that the queen began to attend performances there, responding enthusiastically to the satiric jibes at James's court. A striking measure of the notoriety Anne's presence lent to the Blackfriars' performances, to say nothing of the license taken in the plays themselves, is provided by the captious wonder of the French ambassador, Beaumont, in his dispatch of June 14, 1604: "Consider for pity's sake what must be the state and condition of a prince, whom the preachers publically from the pulpit assail, whom the comedians of the metropolis bring upon the stage, whose wife attends these representations in order to enjoy the laugh against her husband."[44] As Beaumont's letter implies, Anne's attendance at such performances was an acute embarrassment to the government, especially since it gave informal sanction as well as encouragement to the company's topical satires on king and court.

The queen's involvement with this company apparently amounted to a passion. She must have attended often, for so infatuated with their satires did she become—although not always with their political content—that she involved her entire household in imitations of plays she had seen. Lady Arbella Stuart, one of her more reluctant recruits, wrote the following wry account to her uncle:

Will you know how we spend our time at the Queen's side. Whilest I was at Winchester there were certain child plays remembered by the fayre ladies, viz. "I pray my Lord give me a course in your park," "Rise pig and go," "One penny follow me!" etc. And when I came to Court they were as high in request as ever cracking of nuts was. So I was by the Mistress of the Revelles not only compelled to play at I know not what (for till that day I never heard of a play called Fior) but even persuaded by the princely example I saw to play the childe again. This exercise is mostly used from 10 at the clocke at night till 2 or 3 in the morning.[45]

The queen was, however, only the most illustrious of the Blackfriars' auditory. The backbone of the audiences at these indoor theaters was made up of the professional classes, as well as gentry and lower nobility—groups with money and status that felt acutely the social turmoil caused by James's reckless knightings and his largesse to the Scots. In these respected and influential groups of theatergoers, London dramatists found audiences eager to applaud ever more disrespectful and satiric representations of the time's decay.

How much the dramatic expression of anticourt sentiment persisted and how daring their political and personal satire became is indicated by still another missive—that of Samuel Calvert, March 28, 1605, to the future secretary of state, Ralph Winwood: "The plays do not forbear to present upon their Stage the whole Course of this present Time, not sparing either King, State or Religion, in so great Absurdity, and with such Liberty, that any would be afraid to hear them.[46]

These reports on the dramatic satires of the period were entirely political in nature and, since written by career diplomats, censorious, even contemptuous in tone. The artistic merit of these satires at Blackfriars and Paul's and their place in the history of the Jacobean period were not addressed by early seventeenth-century commentators and in our time have been only cursorily. These are matters that will be treated in the following pages.

2

Warnings for a New King

The Disguised Duke Play

In the very year in which James saw himself hailed during his triumphal entry into London as England's Solomon, its Astraea, its reincarnated Augustus Caesar, a countercurrent of dramatic criticism was being directed at him and his new court, mainly in the indoor theaters where the child actors performed their satirical comedies. One voguish form these early Jacobean presentations took was the disguised duke play.[1] By portraying the awakening of a ruler to the rank abuses within his own court and society at large, these plays aimed at alerting the new king to grievances and at quickening expectations for redress. To this subgenre belong Marston's *Malcontent* (1602–3; rev. 1604) and *The Fawn* (1604; rev. 1606), Shakespeare's *Measure for Measure* (1603–4), Middleton's *The Phoenix* (1603–4), and Sharpham's *The Fleer* (1606).

To a modern eye, such a grouping may appear to be the product of hindsighted analysis; yet even in 1606 a wry Francis Beaumont clearly perceived something of the pattern, for in the prologue to *The Woman Hater*, itself an indoor comedy that satirizes, notably, the activities of professional informers, he could comment, "A Duke there is, and the Scene lyes in *Italy*, as those two thinges lightly wee never misse" (ll. 17–18).[2] In sharp contrast to the triumphal entry, these plays reveal that other occasions permitted a great deal more than uncritical praise of the new regime; several, in fact, probe the acceptable limits of irreverent, reproving representations of court life, Jacobean and otherwise.

The Malcontent, The Fawn, and *Measure for Measure* all employ Continental settings to depict broad problems in the art of governance. The anomalous *Measure for Measure,* the only adult-company play of the group, focuses less on the need for reform than for a merciful ruler, especially in matters pertaining to regulation of the passions. *The Malcontent,* the most influential of the group, makes the twin appetites of courtly ambition and lust its subject and establishes a paradigm for the unstinting representation of debased court life. The revised *Fawn* treats more explicit Jacobean issues, in places even satirizing James's complacent self-regard. More daring than Marston's early satires, *The Phoenix,* produced by Paul's Boys, and *The Fleer* are set in London and explicitly call for relief of grievances and reformation of the court.

By 1604, when *The Malcontent* was published, Marston surely knew that he had not only perfected his experiment with anticourt satire in *Antonio's Revenge* (1600) but had also engendered a triumphantly successful species of drama. Originally produced at the Blackfriars, *The Malcontent* was subsequently augmented by Marston and then in 1603 stolen by the King's Men, endowed with an induction by John Webster, and again produced in 1604.[3] This theft of what the newly written induction calls a "bitter play" illustrates how the appetite for social satire was spreading to the adult theaters. The preface to the printed edition (1604) illustrates, furthermore, that Marston knew he was straining against the limits of acceptable representation. "*Vexat censura columbas*" (Censorship disturbs the doves), it admonishes. Similarly, the address to the reader cagily broaches the threat of censorship, the author protesting that his "supposed tartness" is "so general and honest as may modestly pass with the freedom of a satire" (ll. 24–26). The prologue, written in the same vein, demands that readers not take "each hurtless thought to private sense," and since the satire is general, the poet should be allowed the "old freedom of a pen," to "write of fools, whiles't writes of men!" (ll. 1, 13–14). By this appeal to the example of Rome and to universal human nature, Marston in effect claims that contemporary conditions are unavoidably reflected in his satire, and thus he ought not to be hampered by censors.

This justification for satire was strongly endorsed by anticourt dramatists. Some, indeed, claimed it as their right to compose such drama and appealed to England's own literary heritage. Middleton is an excellent example. His reformist orientation is evident both from the condemnation and burning of his nondramatic satire in 1599 and from his 1604 tract, "Father Hubburd's Tales," by whose title he revealed his sympathy with Spenser's great poem of complaint, "Mother Hubberds Tale" (pub. 1591). Like this Spenserian satire, *The Phoenix* depicts its leading figure wending his way through the various strata of English society, uncovering abuse after abuse. Within this satiric perspective, the corruption of government and of men in high places, including judges, courtiers, and nobility, looms large.

High up on the social scale is Justice Falso, who manipulates the two great arms of Elizabethan-Jacobean government, the courts of justice and the Court of Wards, to his own scandalous ends. As his name suggests, Falso abuses the trust of his office by accepting bribes and appropriating the dowry of his female ward, whose body he also abuses. His boast, "I can behave myself courtly, though I keep house i' th' country" (2.3.25–26) illustrates the anticourt theme.[4] In the courts of law, the complement to Falso is Tangle, who in his twenty-nine pending lawsuits fleeces yokels unfamiliar with judicial procedures. A punishment he reports having received in 1588 indicates that he is a knight of the post, that is, one whose business is giving false evidence in court. This abuse, closely associated with that of government informers, eventually became a revolutionary issue and was cited by the long-lived dramatist Thomas Heywood in a pamphlet in 1642.[5]

Repeatedly using the term *abuses* to describe the conditions he witnesses, Phoenix, the disguised prince and duke-to-be, laments that kings seldom see the corruption in their midst. With pithy explicitness he describes the operation of the corrupt patronage system as contemporary Englishmen knew it:

> For oft between king's eyes and subjects' crimes
> Stands there a bar of bribes; the under office
> Flatters him next above, he the next,
> And so of most, or many.
> Every abuse will choose a brother:
> 'Tis through the world, this hand will rub the other.
>
> (1.1.118–23)

The indictment has a modern ring, for Phoenix recognizes that the system itself fosters venality.

The exposé of justice's rape accompanies a still more savage attack on the corruption of eminent noblemen within the royal court. Allegorically named, Infesto and Lussurioso "riotously consume their houses in vicious gaming," causing their inherited estates to be mortgaged to merchants (5.1.81–98). A third, Proditor, meaning "Treason," conspires against the aging Duke until a resplendent, *undisguised* Phoenix denounces him as "The unswept venom of the palace" (5.1.158–60).

Since the Duke is made to have ruled for forty-five years, precisely the number Elizabeth had before her death, and since Essex in 1600 and Ralegh in 1603 had stood trial for treason, "to deprive the king of his Government," there is good reason to suspect allegorical intentions at work.[6] How specific Middleton's allegorical intentions were with respect to Proditor's treason is difficult to know. This is not to say that the notion of topical allegory is ill-conceived,[7] for it may safely be said that no thinking audience in 1604 could have witnessed Proditor's unfolding conspiracy without recalling that such treasons *had* been hatched, not once but several times in recent years. Proditor's threat to the kingdom should thus be seen as summoning Renaissance habits of application and as offering its audience an admonitory homiletic.

The militancy of *The Phoenix* is vouchsafed by its tactic of educating the new prince. Such a move places the prince beyond the bounds of satire while still allowing him to uncover the abuses in his father's realm. Yet "Phoenix" (after the unique mythological bird) is a royal epithet that devolved to James upon Elizabeth's death, and Middleton's recourse to it illustrates his expectation that James would rise out of the ashes of the old regime to bring forth a new dispensation. Such an orientation reveals how Middleton could articulate an anticourt position without being anti-James, for the satire was performed before the king, evidently without incident, on February 20, 1604.[8]

The Phoenix directs its savage satire toward the city and, in its frame story, the court. By contrast, the predominant setting of *The Malcontent* is the court at Genoa. The most powerfully conceived of the court satires among the disguised duke plays and a very influential one, *The Malcontent* presents its disguised (and here outcast) duke, Altofronto, reentering his own court to discover the vermin and abuses therein. Furthermore, since the deposed duke takes on the role of the spitting critic Malevole, he attains (as does Marston himself) the "free speech" that renders his tongue "as fetterless as is an emperor's" (1.3.160–62).

One of the signal features of *The Malcontent* is that despite the nominally Italian setting, Malevole's invective is broadly anticourt. The satire, we quickly notice, employs dramatic conventions in ways that permit the playwright to express his ideas freely. For instance, one of the more feverishly imagined depictions of vice is the court masque:

> When in an Italian lascivious palace, a lady guardianless,
> Left to the push of all allurement,
> The strongest incitements to immodesty,
> To have her bound, incens'd with wanton sweets,
> Her veins fill'd high with heating delicates,
> Soft rest, sweet music, amorous masquerers,
> Lascivious banquets, sin itself gilt o'er[—]
> Thus being prepar'd, clap to her easy ear
> Youth in good clothes, well-shap'd, rich,
> Fair-spoken, promising-noble, ardent, blood-full,
> Witty, flattering—Ulysses absent,
> O Ithaca, can chastest Penelope hold out? (3.3.33–49)

A Spenserian luxury of detail reveals the true topos of Malevole's censure, the fair-seeming temptations of the courtly garden of delights. Of course, the setting is explicitly labeled an Italian palace, and for Englishmen such a setting would have been apposite because Italian courts were popularly perceived as the epitome of vice. But the Elizabethan George Gascoigne had even rebuked his own court in "The Steele Glas" for falling under the corrupt influence of these "newe Italian sportes" in their courtly entertainments, and the same kind of complaint echoed in the early Stuart period.[9] Marston's satiric target is, however, not at all limited to Italian courts. He knew little about them, and his plot follows no known Italian history or novella; his critique of the court masque expresses eminently English concerns, for this form of entertainment was just beginning to flourish in the English court and had a bad reputation in some quarters. Edward Peyton, for example, labeled the masque a sinful enticement where "holiness of life" was "devoured" because the "masks and playes at Whitehal were used onely for incentives of lust: therefore the courtiers invited the citizens wives to those shews, on purpose to defile them in such sort."[10]

Other details demonstrate more certainly that the artistic imagination draws on English life and concerns. Malevole sarcastically reasons that he must be noble because "I find myself possessed with all their qualities: love dogs, dice, and drabs; scorn wit in stuff-clothes; have beat my shoemaker, knock'd my seamstress, cuckold' my 'pothecary, and undone my tailor. Noble! Why not?" (3.3.53–57). Similarly, Malevole alludes to English problems when he declares that "sects, sects" have made "piety change her robe" many times (1.3.10–12). In a nation divided as England was into factions that included Puritans, Separatists, Catholics, Calvinists, Anglicans, and familists, such a speech could hardly be taken to apply to Catholic Italy. Then too, Malevole's complaint about the tacking of religious sails—"I have seen Piety change her robe so oft that sure none but some arch-devil can shape her to a new petticoat" (1.3.10–12)—is clearly prompted by England's rocky religious history, as Protestant Edward, Catholic Mary, and Protestant Elizabeth charted their distinct religious courses. In those days, to be a conformist was no easy matter.

Marston's wish to reform the court world results from his perception of the emerging Renaissance state as exhibiting its own raison d'être, that is, as being shaped according to wholly secular principles in which religious scruples are only encumbering superstitions. Such a calculation of means to ends, without regard to normative ethical principles, excites what we may call Marston's Reformation imagination, which hypercritically fixes on the court world as exhibiting the most advanced forms of destructive individualism.[11]

This outlook is epitomized in the satiric cry "insatiate impudence of appetite!" (4.5.47). The epithet explicates the motives of each of the court figures who excite Malevole's ire and unites the satire's dual concern with the great worlds of political and sexual corruption at court. The former is dramatized by the ambitious upstarts, Bilioso and Pietro, the latter by the licentious Ferneze and the loose ladies of the court, including Aurelia. The farcically treated archvillain Mendoza, who heralds the ethics of self-advancement, is appropriately driven both by inordinate sexual and political desire and so becomes, unforgivably, both cuckolder and usurper.[12]

Despite the plenitude of melodramatic incident in Marston's play, the presentation of this array of vice and vicelike figures is quite close to the kind of nondramatic satire which prevailed at the turn of the century and which Marston himself composed. By parading as he does these characters across the stage, Marston manages to create a panoramic vision of debased court life. This visual dimension of *The Malcontent* is an undervalued aspect of its meaning.

On the ladies' side, "the old cunnycourt" as it is called, walks Macquerelle, the wrinkled agent of lust's business who carries possets to quicken the blood and plaster-casts to preserve beauty. As the mother of deception, Macquerelle moves in dark corners, carrying the nostrums that cover up not only nature's true face but every human feature. Her art is a kind of witches' brew, the poetic expression of her moral deformity: "By this curd," she says, "[Dr. Plaster-face] is the most exquisite in forging of veins, spright'ning of eyes, dyeing of hair, sleeking of skins, blushing of cheeks, surfling of breasts, blanching and bleaching of teeth, that ever made an old lady gracious by torchlight" (2.4.26–32). Behind her follow the most beautiful, eminent ladies of the court—Aurelia, Emilia, and Biancha, who under her tutelage have learned to "thank advice and practice" in the art of seeming honest (2.4.25). The magnitude of the appetites to which Macquerelle caters is figured in her swelling purse, as young gallants of the court—most notably Ferneze, Aurelia's lover—find their passions translated into equivalent cash value. Of Macquerelle's art, with its love philters and aphrodisiacs, the English nation was to learn much in sensational trials and firsthand confessions of the adulterous Lady Essex and her pander, Mrs. Turner.[13]

Near the center of the court's state business is marshall Bilioso, whose name denotes both his choleric humor and the ever-shifting allegiances that Dante depicts in the despised trimmers who chase the ever-shifting, wind-blown banner of the moment. An egregious bootlicker, Bilioso sells his integrity for profit and as the male counterpart (in spirit) to Macquerelle is a catamite of state. Married to the loose Biancha, who has ever counseled him to flatter royalty, he is a politic wittol whose banquet table and whose wife lie open to invited guests. Commissioned as an ambassador, he jubilantly resolves to perfume his jerkin, spit frowns, and surround himself with fifty gentlemen attendants and his own fool in velvet (3.1.50–108). The burden of the expenses, in what is an unmistakable application to a notorious English abuse, will be borne at Christmas time, ironically, by rackrenting his tenants in lease renewals of two manors. Bilioso's politic self-interest is really a spiritual choice, and the satire so renders it. "What religion will you be of now?" taunts Malevole. "Of the [new] duke's religion," comes the response, "when I know what it is" (4.5.92). Politics, in short, becomes religion in *The Malcontent,* self-advancement the only sacrament. Appropriately then, the judgment Malevole passes upon him is a spiritual one. Bilioso is "a fellow to be damned," for he is like bawds who "go to church—for fashion's sake" (4.5.101–5).

Accompanying this parade of court figures is Marston's burlesque of the ideology of self-advancement, which in turn is closely identified with Machiavellian wisdom. Particularly noteworthy is a series of Machiavellian axioms (enunciated according to the prevailing stereotype), which sprinkle the play:

> No band of nature so strong,
> No law of friendship so sacred,
> But I'll profane, burst, violate.
> > (2.1.14–16)
> We that are great, our sole self-good still moves us.
> > (4.3.130)
> Mischief that prospers, men do virtue call.
> > (5.4.73)
> The chiefest secret for a man of state
> Is to live senseless of a strengthless hate.
> > (5.4.78–79)

All of the foregoing tags are enunciated by that would-be deep-seeing master of statecraft Mendoza. The energy Mendoza devotes to his own self-magnification, originally conveyed by a boy actor who very likely hammed up the role, reveals how fully the satirist's object, ridicule—here of a current political philosophy—is embedded in the dramatic design. Ultimately it is not political philosophy but Mendoza himself who is the object of the satire. In Marston's satire, as in *The Phoenix,* government is the product of the monarch's character; it is a personalized conception of state. This outlook explains why so much of the political satire expresses itself in a lampoon of court personality types. Most notably, Marston's hybridization of Mendoza as a Machiavel and fool burlesques the psychology of the aspirant, which is epitomized in Mendoza's wish to have "petitionary vassals licking the pavement with their slavish knees . . . ! O blessed state!" (1.5.27–32). By contrast, Altofronto provides the paradigm of a ruler who seeks to exercise power for the good of the commonweal.

Given the farcical self-exposure Mendoza provides his audience, Malevole is really not needed to reveal the self-evident ethics of the play. Nevertheless, by speaking in a voice poetic and cruel, Malevole deepens the play's sense of moral outrage. Furthermore, his frequent colloquies with his prototypical

opposite reveal in elliptical ways the ideological nature of the struggle between them. Thus, when Mendoza promises to reward his would-be hench-
men for murder by making them "emperors," Malevole rejoins with frenzied
emphasis, "Make us Christians, make us Christians!" (4.3.76–77). The
Christian perspective with which Marston surveys the political world underlies the issue of events, as well as much of the satire.[14] Self-abnegation and
repudiation of political desire for gain provide antidotes to the disease of
courtly appetite in their several incarnations. Thus, the salvation of the
usurping Pietro depends on his achieving an inward transformation in which
he "renounce[s] forever regency," while his erring wife, Aurelia, appearing
"in base mourning attire," must renounce "masques, / Music, tilts, tourneys,
and such courtlike shows" (4.5.119,s.d.0.2,12–13).

The issue of events clearly shows that the stance from which *The Malcontent* launches its incessant assaults on the new political philosophy, and on
courtly aspiration and culture, is profoundly conservative and traditional.[15]
Marston himself abandoned his worldly ambitions as dramatist when he
took holy orders in 1609.[16] Right religion and right politics are both affirmed
in the awe-filled moment when Pietro, Aurelia, and Ferneze all kneel in fealty
before their proper sovereign lord, the miraculously uncased Altofronto.
"Who doubts of Providence / That sees this change?" Altofronto asks rhetorically (4.5.137–38).

Such an epiphany, characteristic of the disguised duke play, may make the
play appear as an argument for absolutism, for "the true monarch, and only
the true monarch . . . [is] absolutely devoted to the law and absolute manner
of it."[17] This is the conclusion that Leonard Tennenhouse draws when
surveying the phenomenon of the disguised duke play. But not all the plays in
the group work with this emphasis; *Measure for Measure* is not *The Malcontent*. Altofronto takes on a new name and identity as Vincentio does not, and
he resides at court (as Vincentio does not) in order to rail, thereby showing
Marston's much greater interest in satirizing courtly abuses than in glorifying
true royalty—although he does that too, finally. But even with respect to its
posture pertaining to "true monarchs," *The Malcontent* contains a kind of
solemn warning that is absent from either *Measure for Measure* or even *The
Phoenix*. Marston spells out his position in the final scene. The return of
legitimate authority does not mean acceptance of the status quo or the ruler
himself. His very subservience to God's law, the only restraint on his temporal authority in Marston's play, is invoked in the augmented 1604 version
of *The Malcontent* as a rationale for the deposition of rulers: "Yet thus much
let the great ones still conceive: / When they observe not heaven's impos'd
conditions, / They are no kings, but forfeit their commissions."[18] Through
this rhymed admonition to princes, *The Malcontent* concludes by reaching

beyond its fictional world, just as its prologue does, to address a fundamental issue of absolute law.

By such methods as these, Marston offered a means of making his imaginative Italianate satire speak to important contemporary issues. Other Blackfriars dramatists eagerly strove to apply Marston's anticourt perspective to more radically topical ends in their disguised duke plays. Moreover, the revised version of Marston's *The Fawn* (1606), also produced by the Children of the Queen's Revels at the Blackfriars, shows how the rage for political satire carried Marston's own dramatic work to more daring ends.[19]

Although it is usually viewed as a romantic comedy or satire, *The Fawn* trades on the *Mirror for Magistrates* tradition of advice to princes. In a variation on disguised duke plots, the satire pits one duke against another, making the Duke Hercules of Ferrara disguised as the Fawn, the seer who enters the neighboring kingdom of Urbin to discover in Duke Gonzago a complacent, unseeing ruler puffed up by flattery. By this technique Marston ingeniously uses one prince to criticize the doings of another. Then, in another strategic move, he composes a prologue that blurs the distinction between the fictive world of his satire and the real world of Jacobean England. Donning the persona of an ingenuous writer, Marston denies that any "rude disgraces / Shall taint a public, or a private name" (ll.5–6),[20] a disclaimer absolutely de rigueur at this time. But when read in the context of the entire prologue, the disclaimer appears to be artful equivocation, for Marston lards his address with fulsome compliments to his readers, makes unctuous protestations of innocence, and ends by declaring, "Now if that any wonder why he's drawn / To such base soothings, know his play's—*The Fawn*" (ll.34–35). This couplet-closing volta throws the entire passage into ironic relief, undermining the professed disavowals and providing a real-life induction to the issues of stifled free speech that are subsequently treated in the court of Urbin. It also adeptly connects the world of *The Fawn* with its reprehensible love of flattery to that of the Jacobean court.

Within this satiric-romantic framework Marston works his political themes. Awakened to the enormous wrong done to majesty through flattery, Hercules determines to reform the ill-run court of Urbin by donning the disguise of a court parasite. Through his disguise he will oversee his son Tiberio's wooing of Duke Gonzago's daughter and, pointedly, makes his especial object of reform Gonzago himself:

> Thou grateful poison, sleek mischief, flattery,
> Thou dreamful slumber (that doth fall on kings
> As soft and soon as their first holy oil),
> Be thou forever damn'd.
>
> (1.2.313–16)

The soliloquy sounds a political theme that recollects the lost *Cradle of Security* (1565–75). According to Robert Willis's account, the king, kept in "pleasure and delight" by easeful counselors, lies down in a cradle where his false lady counselors rock him to sleep with sweet song.[21] Then too, Marston, employs the structural device of David Lindsay's *A Satire of the Three Estates* (1540), in which one sovereign brings another to reformation. In Lindsay's satire, once King Correction enlightens Rex Humanitas, the latter establishes a Parliament which brings to judgment Flattery and Folly. This movement of course parallel's that of *The Fawn*, which ends with "Cupid's Parliament."

Awareness of these earlier dramatic renderings helps to establish Marston's contribution to the sleeping prince motif. In contrast to Lindsay's satire, which places the blame on Rex Humanitas's ill-chosen advisors, Marston, much more pungently, attributes the originating cause of Urbin's troubles to the adulation-seeking Duke Gonzago himself.

This political perspective prepares for a point of view that has been gaining ground, that Marston's portrayal of Gonzago as a vain and pedantic king is a personal satire on James I.[22] The counterview that Marston could be criticizing pedants per se and not royal pedantry will not do since the satire on Gonzago's rhetoric burlesques a prince's discourse—"I think we yet can speak, we ha' been eloquent." "When I was eighteen old such a pretty toying wit had I, but age hath made us wise. Hast not, my lord?" "We have been a philosopher and spoke / With much applause; but now age makes us wise" (1.2.85–86, 107–9, 171–72).

The proclamations of wisdom, the claim to be a philosopher, to having been trained up as a wit, and the inveterate use of the royal "we" all take Gonzago's folly into the realm of political satire and so provide an unexceptionable context for the argument that James I is shadowed in the figure of Gonzago. The undeniable caginess in Marston's presentation *ought* to make it impossible to identify absolutely Gonzago's vanity and pedantry with James's. But the implications of such a guarded position are tantamount to a recognition that the play does indeed broach personal satire. Acutely sensitive to his audience's habit of making topical identifications, the dramatist could hardly have failed to recognize the many parallels between his characterizations of Gonzago and James, any or all of which he could have removed had he wished. And once it is acknowledged that these tantalizingly suggest a personal satire on James, the connection has in fact been made. In the seventeenth century there was only a hair's breadth of difference between an admonitory satire that benignly holds up a mirror for magistrates—all magistrates—and a personal satire whose application ensnares the reigning monarch. Such distinctions meant a great deal. In the case of *The Fawn*, the satire does not appear to have been censored in any way, an unusual outcome for

Marston. But the theme of the sleeping prince, adapted as it had been to James's court, was not forgotten, for in the Commonwealth period, in 1651, a pamphlet highly critical of James's reign appeared displaying a picture of James lying asleep, unaware of the evils of his reign, including, as the picture shows, the murder of Thomas Overbury.23

Sensational as the disguised duke plays had been when the augmented *Malcontent* appeared in 1603–4, their satire was evidently not sensational enough by 1606. William Sharpham's *The Fleer,* a rank imitation of *The Malcontent,* leaps to outdo its model in topical daring. In imitation of Marston's "Alto-front," it gives us a dethroned duke, from Florence this time, named Anti-front, who in disguise appropriates the satiric name (compare Malevole) of Fleer (i.e., Scorner). However, in a daring innovation on the disguised duke plot, Sharpham has the deposed Duke Antifront appear not in his native city to anatomize it, but in London. The shift demonstrates the startling direction topical anticourt satire was taking by the third year of James's reign. *The Fleer* shows itself to be reflexively aware of its tactics. "Why camst thou out of *Italy* into *England?*" a lord asks, and Fleer ripostes, "Because *England* would not come into *Italy* to me" (1.458–59).24

Unfortunately, the play is unable to develop its satire into a coherent vision of life or to manage its tragicomic genre. There are unexplored possibilities in Sharpham's decision to organize his satire around the promiscuity of Fleer's two daughters who, courtly in Italy, become courtesans in London, and the play lurches in arbitrary, unmotivated alternations of sentiment and satire. Yet for all these limitations it contains one extraordinary scene in which Fleer reports what he saw at the English court. Fleer's depiction of the court is perhaps the most vivid and censorious of any in the period: "I saw a Farmers Son sit newly made a courtier, that sat in the presence at cardes, as familiar as if the chayre of state had bin made of a peece of his fathers Barne-doore: O tis a shame: I would haue state be state in earnest and in game, I like your Courtier for nothing but often saying his praiers" (2.249–54).

Sharpham's anticourt viewpoint, it is clear, is traditionalist, the playwright decrying the disorderly Jacobean court and, just as significantly, the corruption of the simple virtue of country gentlemen and their progeny. The slovenly conduct of the English court, it will be noted, is emphatically linked to James's cronyism, which reliable prose sources also confirm, and to the King's unkingly familiarity with handsome young men.25 Fleer's account of the cardplaying at court transparently alludes to the unstately Jacobean court, where gaming tables with wagers at high stakes were permanent features.26 The indecorum of it all is neatly expressed in the perceived equivalency between the regal "chayre of state" and the farmer's "Barne-doore." The same kind of criticism of the king's indecorum and cronyism lies behind Fleer's denunciation of James's preferment of his beggarly Scotsmen

(2.160–70) and Sharpham's wry burlesque of the proposed union between England and Scotland (2.258–64), one of the prominent features in 1605–6 of James's domestic policy.

Inconsiderable as *The Fleer* is as drama, its scattershot satiric blasts, like those of the revised *Fawn,* demonstrate the widespread disrespect, even contempt, for James's regime that was being disseminated at the Blackfriars theater by 1606. Stronger dramatists than Sharpham, such as Chapman, Jonson, and John Day, produced sustained topical satires of Jacobean politics and society. As part of their "platform," they also dared to lampoon individuals in high places, and this brought the Children of the Queen's Revels (also known as the Chapel Children, the Children at Blackfriars, and the Children of the Chapel) to a peak of notoriety and danger.

3

The Growth of Anti-Scot and Antiministerial Satire

Between 1605 and 1608 virtually all the theaters in London became caught up in a craze for topical matter. At the Fortune, Prince Henry's Men produced Dekker and Middleton's collaborative depiction of the London eccentric Mary Firth, nicknamed "Moll Cutpurse," in *The Roaring Girl* (ca. 1608). At the Red Bull, Queen Anne's Men commemorated the commercial adventures of Thomas, Anthony, and Robert Shirley in John Day's *The Travels of Three English Brothers* (1607). At the Globe the sensational chronicle of Walter Calverly was put into dramatic form by George Wilkins in *The Miseries of Enforced Marriage* (1606).

At the Blackfriars, however, topicality was presented with a difference. There, Francis Beaumont could mock this unsophisticated craving for topical matter in his *Knight of the Burning Pestle* (1607), a rollicking burlesque of citizen achievement and the low-brow expressions of nationalism that were the fare of the open-air theaters. At the same time, other Blackfriars dramatists could and did present topical plays with sophisticated, even contemptuous satire aimed at the Jacobean court. By 1605, despite the dangers of censorship, the Children of the Queen's Revels were performing personal political satires.

The only two Jacobean comedies George Chapman composed, *The Widow's Tears* (1604) and *Monsieur D'Olive* (1605), illustrate how even this philosophical dramatist became caught up in the rage for topical satire.[1] Having explored in his earlier plays the doctrine of native noblesse and the disjunction between goodness and greatness, Chapman created in *The Widow's Tears* a searching satire on the degeneracy of the Jacobean age. In its alienated Jacobean outlook and anti-Scots perspective, this early Blackfriars satire may be viewed as a powerful forerunner of the burlesques of James's ministers and court that appeared in 1605 and 1606, one of which Chapman himself composed.

Chapman's prime agent in revealing the debased nature of contemporary society in *The Widow's Tears* is Tharsalio, the play's true-seeing antihero, who delightedly revels in the corruption he uncovers.[2] Through Tharsalio's competition with Lord Rebus for the hand of the Countess Eudora, one of the play's two supposed paragons, Chapman presents an effete aristocracy that is made to resemble not the Cypriots Chapman's setting might suggest but James's own Scottish retinue.

Pedigrees drawn "from *Lycurgus* his great Toe" (2.4.163) do not make a noble man, Tharsalio asserts.[3] Idle great men live off "the lard of others" (1.2.105). "Choose a Man," he urges, "and not a Giant, as these are that come with Titles, and Authoritie" (1.2.76–77). Lord Rebus is himself a transparently disguised Scottish retainer, whom Tharsalio denounces as "a very hault-boy, a bag-pipe; in whom there is nothing but winde" (1.2.118). Likening Rebus's retinue to the one that followed James to Whitehall, Tharsalio denounces all of them as "Whores-sonne bag-pipe Lords" (1.2.102). An enterprising director might easily present Rebus in kilts or Scottish plaid without violating Chapman's satiric intentions.

The attack upon Rebus presages a ferocious satire on the smug virtue of leading citizens, whose character has never been tested. The dramatic form of this satiric exposure is shaped by the testing of the two chaste widows, Eudora and Cynthia, but the philosophic outlook moves broadly to indict an entire society. Tharsalio's metaphors repeatedly recollect a lost golden past that has become counterfeit coin in the fallen present.[4] His specific projects he describes in terms of reformation, the reform and readvancement of his own noble house and the reformation of Eudora's, with its affectations of modesty and decorum.

In sharp contrast to the earliest Jacobean satires, *The Widow's Tears* offers no true reformation at all, for the imposture and deceit of society is beyond reformation. For these reasons *The Widow's Tears* celebrates an inverted heroism, enacts an inverted reformation, and then satirically commemorates both. The satiric culmination of this Jacobean vision takes place in the fifth-act trial scene, when the new governor of Cyprus attempts to unravel the play's mixups, boasting, "In matters of iustice I am blinde" (5.5.191). Inaugurating what he calls "a new discipline" that will "turne all topsie turuie" (5.5.209–10), the upstart governor winds up ushering in a mad world where the last are become first. He himself appears to prove the case, for being "at a non plus" (5.5.288), he can resolve nothing. Tharsalio, in a mocking aside, welcomes this new order as "a wholsome reformation" (5.5.232), thus reminding us that the newly instituted rule of misrule will guarantee the debasement of all genuine social values.

This virtually apocalyptic vision of an inverted society is Chapman's artistic response to his own society, which in the space of two years had witnessed a bewildering set of social changes. Not only had the city and the court become overrun with Scotsmen, but Scottish courtiers and would-be courtiers had begun to take on airs. By the date of Chapman's satire, late 1604 probably, James had dubbed over a thousand carpet knights and had attracted hundreds of upstart courtiers eager to cash in on the largesse of the new Golden Age.[5] For Chapman, who revered aristocratic values when they were expressed in aristocratic actions, these events must have been appalling. *The Widow's Tears* is his monument to English society in one of its most visible eras of social mobility and, from Chapman's perspective, degenerative instability.

In a continuing attempt to expose the shamlike quality of James's court, Chapman in *Monsieur D'Olive* (1605) ridiculed the ambassadorial pretensions of one of the king's most senior officials, the earl of Nottingham, whom James had appointed to sign a treaty of peace with Spain in Madrid in 1605. Nottingham's expedition, the most expensive and elaborately prepared in James's reign, confirmed a new but unpopular policy of friendship with England's Catholic nemesis. Through the ambassadorial activities of the vainglorious Monsieur D'Olive, technically a subplot figure who gradually becomes the play's center of interest, Chapman shadowed the preparation of this great lord admiral and at the same time developed a comprehensive satire on what may be termed "the imitation of greatness."

The elevated serious action offers the antithetical example of the authentic man of noblesse, Count Vandome. This man is one of Chapman's herculean heroes, which is to say that his greatness, following medieval and Renaissance interpretations of Hercules' mythic career, inheres in his moral strength rather than in brute physical prowess.[6] In Chapman's play Vandome faces two seemingly insurmountable tasks, both of which are treated with a lofty Neoplatonic idealism.[7] The first pertains to Vandome's platonic mistress, who shuns society because her husband, Vaumont, has misconstrued her chaste admiration for Vandome. To restore Marcellina to her rightful position as a reflection of the form-generating beauty of nature, Vandome successfully undertakes the labor of returning her to the light of day and reconciling her to Vaumont. In a second, similar labor Vandome undertakes to free Count St. Anne from his strange vow to worship the embalmed cadaver of his wife, in brief to return him to the active life of service. These are acts of genuine heroism for a modern age.

Satirically counterpointing Vandome's lofty endeavors are those of the topical, nominally subplot-figure of Monsieur D'Olive, who volunteers to undertake a great embassy on behalf of Duke Phillip to the king of France, entreating him to command St. Anne to bury his wife. Affecting a rhetoric of modest disregard for greatness, D'Olive is in fact moved solely by an unquenchable desire for recognition. D'Olive's degenerative pattern of courtiership unfolds in his resolve, farcically rendered, to imitate Duke Phillip's "place and power" (2.2.32). This he demonstrates with a blithe impudence by kissing the duke's wife as if she were his own.

D'Olive repeatedly lays claim to a nobility of spirit that rests on ability, not titles, but in Chapman's rendering even this assertion proves vacuous. Thus, when the bemused Duke Phillip bestows a commission on D'Olive, the latter immediately exploits the privileges of his new office, swearing to pay no creditors and to take on religion for fashion's sake "as it becomes great personages to doe" (2.2.323), and for adulation's sake to surround himself with a popular following. This theme of ersatz greatness culminates in D'Olive's encomium to his own embassage: "The Siege of *Bullaine* shall be no more a landmarke for Times: *Agencourt* Battaile, *St. Iames* his Fielde, the losse of *Calice* [i.e., Calais], and the winning of *Cales*, shal grow out of vse: Men shal reckon their yeares, Women their mariages, from the day of our Ambassage: . . . [it] shall be helde sacred to immortalitie" (4.2.98–115). The passage, as I have established elsewhere, echoes Henry's St. Crispin's day speech in *Henry V*.[8] The details of the parody need not concern us; what should command our attention is that D'Olive's encomium in effect burlesques itself by invoking patterns of genuine achievement and by exalting itself through a rhetoric of vainglory, not valor. The absurd theatricality of it all is then tied to a specific Jacobean context.

General topical satire becomes personal satire, for the earl of Nottingham's celebrated embassage to Spain was taking place just months or even weeks before *Monsieur D'Olive* was produced, and although the earl was no upstart, his embassy exhibited all the qualities of ersatz greatness that Chapman satirizes.[9] To the peace conference between England and Spain in 1604, Spain sent such a magnificently attended embassage, headed by Juan de Velasco, duke of Frias and constable of Castile, that England felt obliged to reciprocate with an even more dazzling embassage to Spain.[10] Charles Howard, earl of Nottingham and lord high admiral of England, the very man who had presided over the defeat of the Spanish Armada in '88, was commissioned "ambassador extraordinary" to head the costliest mission ever undertaken in James's reign.

But the mission was controversial. Jingoistic Protestants, of which party Chapman may be counted one, vehemently opposed embassage on the ground that peace with papist Spain was an abomination because it would effeminize a great warlike nation.[11] Even merely nationalistic Englishmen, which included almost everyone, felt that the country was going to excessive lengths of obsequiousness to achieve a risky, questionable end. Yet England was making a great display of its peaceful intentions. From the very first report of this extraordinary embassage in Winwood's *Memorials of Affairs of State*—"My *Lord Admirall* prepareth against *March* to go with very great Magnificence" (p. 39)[12]—the ostentation of the expedition attracted notice, the more so because the admiral "carries with him *the Title of Excellence*" (p. 41) and because "all his Gentlemen shall have black Velvet Cloaks, and what else I know not" (p. 39). In addition to Nottingham's huge allotment of £15,000, Prince Henry's royal gift "of certaine Horses and hunting Geldings" must surely have become an object of pleasantry since these horses, like the lord admiral's gentlemen, came bedecked in velvets "valued at eight hundred Pounds a piece," all in magnificent inappropriateness to the hot Spanish climate (p. 41). In this manner the pomp of state began to reveal itself as verging on the ludicrous.

Comedy can bloom out of such circumstances as these, especially if it can center on some stunning public event. Just such a series of catalytic events did transpire, throwing the entire enterprise into a perspective so ridiculous that Chapman could not resist lampooning it. A letter of February 26, 1605, reveals that the mission had begun to attract too large a retinue. Part of the lord admiral's "great Preparations," it seems, entailed his retention of "*six Lords* . . . and 50 Knights" (p. 50). By March 10, the ever-growing retinue had gotten out of hand: "My *Lord Admiral's* Number is 500, and he swears 500 Oaths he will not admitt of one Man more" (p. 52). By this time the mission had become a pilgrimage to Mecca. To be permitted to participate, as enterprising Englishmen understood it, was tantamount to making one's fortune. No wonder the expedition raised an army of fortune's happy followers!

In addition to the sensationalism aroused by the assigning of so many men to this ambassadorial mission, a second series of stunning events occurred. The circumstances surrounding Nottingham's preparations had apparently become so humorous that Stone the Fool made "a blasphemous Speech, *That there went sixty Fools into* Spaine *besides my Lord Admiral and his two Sons*" (p. 52). Provocative in itself, this jewel of a quip was uttered by a man so familiar to Londoners that Jonson comically eulogized him for sixty lines in *Volpone* (performed late 1605).[13] The combination of the man and the quip must have thrown the lord admiral's enterprise into the most mirthful of perspectives. But Stone suffered, for he was "well whipt in *Bridewell*" (p. 52), a sign that the speech had been so effective it required an official refutation. But even the welts of official disfavor were insufficient to silence this famous Stone, for the tart rejoinder he made after his release from custody survives by report: "[Stone] *gives his Lordship the Praise of a very pittifull Lord*. His Comfort is, that the News of *El Senor Piedra* [i.e., Stone] will be in *Spaine* before our Ambassador" (p. 52).

Chapman's parody of Nottingham's embassage makes the most of the mad clamor that the venture excited among elements of London's citizenry. Indeed, nearly all of act 3, scene 2, act 4, scene 2, and the last forty lines of the play depict the ambitious followers who hound D'Olive. So important to the comedy are these swarming recruits that the word *followers* occurs over twenty times in the course of the satire. As the comic situation develops, it recapitulates and parodies the situation recorded in the *Memorials*. Just as Nottingham swore "500 oaths . . . not [to] admitt of one Man more" (p. 52), so D'Olive declares, "I am so haunted with Followers, euerie day new offers of Followers: But heauen shield me from any more Followers . . . Ile no more Followers, a mine honour" (3.2.36–45; cf. 148–55).

This parody of entourage and admiral soon expresses itself in resplendent topical detail. If the horses Nottingham received from Prince Henry were bedecked in richly embroidered velvets "whereby they are hot and heavy, and so, very improper for that Place" (p. 41), D'Olive, outfitted in "compleat Satten of some Courtly cullour" (3.2.104–5; 57–59, 87–88, 163–77), demands that his entourage follow suit and "load euerie day a fresh Horse with Satten suites, and send them backe hither," since "'tis like to be hot trauaile, and therefore t'wilbe an ease to my Followers to haue their cloathes at home afore 'am" (3.2.174–76). In addition to these parodic parallels, there may even be a topical mimicry of Stone the Fool's well-known rebuke of the lord admiral as another fool. D'Olive, who has himself enjoyed the title of "lord," has by the last scene learned his comic lesson and declares: "And a man will play the foole and be a Lord, or be a foole and play the Lord, he shall be sure to want no followers, so there be hope to raise their fortunes" (5.2.101–3). Certainly, Chapman's satire on the foolishness of great lords hits the topical bull's-eye.

D'Olive's embassage differed from that of the earl of Nottingham in one singular respect, however. Whereas Nottingham set sail from England on March 28, 1605,[14] D'Olive never does embark. This predicament provides the occasion for a not very subtle warning to those who thirst for the glories of court life. Although he has been exposed as without substance, D'Olive remains besieged by the tribe of fortune hunters, who now clamor for hard coin. Encircled by the very men he supposed would enhance his glory, D'Olive experiences poetic justice and for the first time perceives the dangers of courtly greatness. He exits hounded by creditors, inveighing against court parasites and cursing his employment.

The spectacle of a man who has put on a mantle of herculean greatness too large for his small soul provokes an easy mirth, but the underlying gravity of

Chapman's theme of inauthentic greatness in the Jacobean age pulls powerfully. Considered in the sweep of Chapman's dramatic development, *Monsieur D'Olive* illustrates Chapman's retreat from the vision of herculean
reform exhibited in his pre-Jacobean comedies and his increasing preoccupation with the misdirection of heroic ability in the false great man.

Finding a ready audience for their views, Chapman and his colleagues
grew more daring as they satirized the Jacobean age, its officials, and its ill-
suited aspirants to courtly privilege. In the same season that *Monsieur
D'Olive* was performed, Chapman joined with Jonson and Marston to create
in *Eastward Ho* (1605) one of the most successful collaborations of the
decade as well as one of the most notorious satires acted by the Children of
the Queen's Revels to that date. The play itself and the events surrounding
the imprisonments of its authors provide priceless data on the kind of
political satire that most provoked official retribution.

In recent years *Eastward Ho* has attained prominence as a citizen comedy
that plays ironically on the prodigal son theme.[15] This perspective, while
helpful in its way, throws the play somewhat out of focus. The parody of
citizen-longing for the courtly life is one side of a zestful satire that also
dispraises the Jacobean court as an inappropriate model for imitation. The
debased Jacobean court makes citizen imitation of it debased.

The tongue-in-cheek prologue, which is usually interpreted as an induction to a citizen satire and as a recollection of *Eastward Ho's* relation to
Dekker and Webster's *Westward Ho* in the so-called War of the Theaters, is
much more as well.[16] Since eastward is preferable to westward movement,
the audience should, the poets observe wryly,

> Honour the Sunnes faire rising, not his setting;
> Nor is our Title vtterly enforste,
> As by the points we touch at, you shall see;
> Beare with our willing paines, if dull or witty,
> We onely dedicate it to the Citty. (ll. 10–14)[17]

The images of the rising and setting sun convey a complex symbolism that
not only touts the superiority of the new offering to the old but, more
significantly, alludes with affected admiration to the splendor of the Jacobean court—situated *east* of the city at Greenwich during the king's sojourn
there in the spring of 1605.[18] The court outshines the city, and the behest to
honor the new sun—with an anticipation of the notion of "Roi soleil"—
cheekily advises Englishmen to put aside nostalgia for Elizabeth in welcom-
ing James's "brilliant" court. The brilliant Jacobean court signifies opportunity, indeed opportunism, for would-be courtiers. An anonymous ballad
captures the spirit of the time: Honour invites you to delights— / Come all to
Court, and be made Knights."[19] The scramble eastward is for gold and

advancement. But the dramatists' refusal to endorse the mad pursuit of courtly ways is revealed in their half-serious, half-mocking dedication of the satire to the city.

The rising sun is the comedy's governing metaphor for misplaced aspiration and courtly imitation. Thus, Quicksilver must abandon his tradesman's identity to become a court gallant so that he can live "like a gentleman, be idle" (1.1.118). Gertrude must put on courtly airs, requiring for a start a velvet gown, a coach, a chambermaid, and a castle. Ironically, she settles on Sir Petronel Flash, a thirty-pound knight with flashy looks and no prospects, to realize her dreams. This parody of citizen-aspiration must be apprehended as including the kind of court to which Londoners aspired.

The representation of Gertrude and her knight, for example, eventually ridicules James's court. Dressed in a citizen's gown with a "courtly" French headdress, Gertrude cuts a ludicrous figure that is only topped by the broader representation of her along with her court-attendant Poldavy, dressed in a Scotch farthingale, and her maid Beatrice, who leads a monkey across the stage (1.2.0.1.s.d.). Although the text has been censored by nine lines, in which Beatrice's monkey probably performed "some trick" on the word "Scotch,"[20] the essence of the joke remains: "Is this a right Scot?" Gertrude exclaims, bawdily referring to her farthingale. "Does it clip close? and bear vp round? . . . I protest you Tailers are most sanctified members, and make many crooked things goe vpright." And Poldavy agrees, asserting that Gertrude, "now you are in the Lady-fashion" must "doe all things light. I, and fall so: that's the court-Amble" (1.2.49–61).

The dance, the sexual encounter, the Jacobean Scotch fashions, are all subsumed in "the court-Amble." The monkey too, kept as a pet by dapper courtiers, symbolizes the idle life, the apish fashions of courtiers, and sexual promiscuity.[21] The satire pursues these suggestions in other places, as when Gertrude asks Sir Petronel whether they will "play at *Baboone* in the countrey." Her assertion that they can play "With arme, or legge, or any other member, if it bee a court-sport" (1.2.81–85) illustrates the corruptive example the court provides her.

In *Eastward Ho* corruptive examples become topically explicit. The moralism of the play must in the Renaissance manner be applied, and so the anticourt parody quickly holds James and his court up to ridicule. In a fantasy about utopian government in the New World, Seagull imagines a life free from corruption and work, except for "a few industrious Scots perhaps." And on reflection he observes it would be better if they were in Virginia rather than England, for "wee shoulde finde ten times more comfort of them there, than wee doe heere" (3.3.41–48). The same passage pokes fun at the perceived absurdity of making the Scots "all one Countreymen" with Englishmen. Elsewhere, *Eastward Ho* derides James's Scottish grooms for obsequiousness, "that by indulgence and intelligence crept into his fauour, and by Panderisme into his Chamber" (2.2.82–83). These lines, presumably, were the ones that prompted Sir James Murray, whose brother John was groom of the King's Bedchamber, to report Jonson to the king "for writting something against the Scots in a play Eastward hoe."[22] Such mockery of the groom-pander need not have been aimed at Murray, of course, but it was quite sufficient to slander the office he held.

In this same jeering vein is the famous passage that combines the ubiquitous ridicule of James's new-made knights and the king's sale of honor with an impersonation of James himself, speaking in his thick Scottish brogue: "I ken the man weel, hee's one of my thirty pound knights." The perception is asserted to be mistaken; the man in question "stole his knighthood . . . for *foure pound*" (4.1.177–80). Such dialect humor, we must note, is written into the script and requires the actor for the nonce to *be* James. Such purloining of royalty's representation, along with the attack on the king's grooms, is what brought James's wrath upon Jonson and Chapman, threatened as they were with having their ears clipped and noses slit.

The conclusion to be drawn from such evidence is surely not that *Eastward Ho* presents a normative citizen comedy with a few daring topical jibes. This view must be replaced by one that integrates the offending passages, so-called, into an interpretation of *Eastward Ho* as a sweeping critique of Jacobean society. The referentiality to the court must in turn be seen as lampooning James's Scotch courtiers, as violating the rules forbidding personal satire, and as mocking the prodigal values of the Jacobean court, which erring citizens desire to imitate. Jonson, Chapman, and Marston's kind of topicality is the concrete expression of their social criticism in what we may describe as their satire of the two estates, city and court.

The topically applied satire that we see in *Eastward Ho* is, however, of a different order from full-scale personal satire. This latter *Eastward Ho* edges into—arguably, only backs into. The satire cannot be said to inhere in a full-dress portrait of James, for example. But a full-dress satire on the royal person was taken on by the Children of the Queen's Revels the next season in John Day's *The Isle of Gulls,* a play whose performance cost them dearly.

4

An Antiroyal Satire Too Daring

The Isle of Gulls

More than any other Blackfriars satire, John Day's *Isle of Gulls* (1606) illustrates the dramatic license Samuel Calvert complained of when he described the practice of representing on the stage "the whole Course of this present Time, not sparing either King, State or Religion."[1] The play also marks a turning point in the fortunes of the Children of the Queen's Revels, who produced it. Sir Edward Hoby's letter of March 7, 1606, to Sir Thomas Edmonds reads, "At this time was much speech of a play in the Black Friars, where, in the 'Isle of the Gulls,' from the highest to the lowest, all men's parts were acted of two divers nations: as I understand sundry were committed to Bridewell."[2] Following as it did the presentation of the peccant *Eastward Ho* in the previous year, *The Isle of Gulls* brought about decisive government action against the offending company. In addition to the imprisonments Hoby reports, the company was deprived of its royal patronage for two years and its management reorganized.[3]

Through its title Day's satire claims descent from Thomas Nashe and Ben Jonson's *The Isle of Dogs,* a play that so offended the authorities in 1597 that the players, who included Gabriel Spencer, Robert Shaw, and Ben Jonson, were committed to Marshalsea prison. Two letters from the Privy Council dated August 15 and October 8, 1597, describe *The Isle of Dogs* as a "lewd" satire "contanynge very seditious and sclanderous matter" and reveal that Nashe's lodgings had been searched for incriminating papers.[4] These letters, first ordering imprisonment for the players and then releasing them, suggest that the offenders remained incarcerated for seven weeks. All known copies of *The Isle of Dogs* were confiscated and destroyed. Mute testimony to the rigor of the suppression is that the play has not survived. The whole episode provides an instructive example of the fate that could befall the dramatist and company that presented outspoken political satire. Day's titular echo of the censored *Isle of Dogs*, combined with the presentation at Blackfriars of his own topical satire *Isle of Gulls* only months after the imprisonments of Jonson and Chapman for *Eastward Ho* (alluded to at 3.3.86), thumbs the nose at the authorities.[5] The play, in fact, reveals itself to be reflexively aware of its hypercritical, anticourt orientation, for its induction broaches the subject by having a gallant ask, among other questions, why the author has chosen such a title—"it begets much expectation" (ll. 36–37).[6]

These topical expectations are indeed satisfied, but deftly, wittily. Using Sidney's *Arcadia* (rev. ed. 1598) as a foil, Day juxtaposes his Arcadian setting with a provocative personal satire on James and his chief minister. The ironic interplay between the play's satiric elements and the romantic surface it continually burlesques is the uncelebrated achievement of this neglected work.

Like *The Isle of Dogs*, *The Isle of Gulls* is plainly about England. The "two divers nations" referred to in Hoby's letters, the Arcadia and Lacedemonia of the play, are England and Scotland, respectively.[7] This burlesque of the entire nation is considerably more rash than the attacks of earlier plays on James's court. In fact, Day's personal satire on James I comes closest to deserving the designation that Philip Finkelpearl attributes to *The Fawn*—"the only full-length portrait of the ruling sovereign in the Elizabethan drama."[8] Although issuing out of the fashion for topical satires that produced *The Fawn*, *The Isle of Gulls* is much more brazenly, unequivocally, modeled on James.

In *The Isle of Gulls*, the prologue's bland disclaimer that the play does not "figure anie certaine state, or private government: farre be that supposition from the thought of any indifferent Auditor" (ll. 39–42) ironically calls attention to the prospect. And it protests too much, for when one of the gallants presses for an admission that perhaps lawyers, citizens' wives, or even a "great mans life [is] charactred int" (l. 56), the prologue begins with a firm denial, but then politely draws attention to the one character in the play who modern readers generally agree is modeled on a living person: "None I protest sir, only in the person of *Dametas* he expresses to the life the monstrous and deformed shape of vice" (ll. 57–60).[9] Although this example of vice may indeed be a composite one, "resembling one or more of James's favorites,"[10] the principal model for the character was certainly Robert Cecil, a matter to which we will return.

Conspicuous in its absence is any mention of satire on King James himself. Vestigial evidence of the printer's decision, not Day's, to tone down the personal satire on James is apparent, however, from the inconsistent replacement in the quarto of the titles "King" and "Queen" with the more remote ones of "Duke" and "Duchess."[11] Unchanged from Day's prose source is the Duke's Christian name "Basilius" (meaning "kingly, royal, regal"), which just happens to recall the most widely read political work by King James, *Basilikon Doron* (first public edition 1603).

As the play proper commences, Basilius is revealed as having just removed "our princely government," as James often did, from the court to a country residence in Arcadia. The major interest of the play quickly reveals itself not so much in the imitation of Sidney and in the attempts of two pairs of disguised princes to woo ladies (here the daughters of Basilius), but in the counterpointing satire on James and his chief courtiers, which repeatedly pierces the Arcadian surface.

Basilius' joyous retirement to the country to avoid the importunity of suitors—in the play, the love-suitors—was James's habitual response to the pressures of court life. In his country retreats James spent months at a time. There he principally hunted. The Venetian ambassador's observation that the king was "foolishly devoted" to the activity has already been noted.[12] Others reported the king's "proclamation that none shall presume to come to him on hunting days," and when a petition was, in fact, pressed upon him by his own lord treasurer, he is reputed to have answered "in some wrath, 'Shall a King give heed to a dirty paper, when a beggar noteth not his gilt stirrops?' "[13] Members of the court who sought to defend his behavior—John Hacket for example—left behind an apology that only proves the case, for Hacket writes, "The King went not out with his Hounds above three Days in the Week."[14]

This mania of James for the hunt becomes a focal point for the personal satire. At the mere mention of a hunt Basilius becomes enraptured: "*Dametas,* were thine eares ever at a more musicall banquet? how the hounds mouthes like bells are tuned one under another, like a slothfulnes, the speed of the cry outran my sence of hearing" (2.2.21–24; cf. 2.2.150–57). In another manifestation of this idée fixe, Basilius, like James, is made to call each of his hounds by name, as if they were people. Contrariwise, people are addressed as if they were dogs, just as James did in his "beagle" letters to Cecil.[15] Because of Basilius' obsession, the crafty Dametas is able to distract the Duke (originally the King) by calling his attention to his best hunting hound: "Did you observe that my liege, that *Melampus* as a true hound is ever horce cheerd or hollow [i.e., halloed], yet he kept time to[o]" (2.2.99–101). This discourse succeeds in engrossing Basilius' interests so much that he neglects to take action against the cries of "treason and murder" as his daughters are abducted.

The inductions to *The Taming of the Shrew* and *Titus Andronicus* (at 2.2.1–26) reveal the dramatic conventions of the hunt—the barking, the music of the chase, a pastoral setting—but *The Isle of Gulls* turns these to topical ends because Day makes the hunt convey contemporary complaints about court policy and lifestyle. Violetta, for example, feelingly describes the object of the hunt, the deer, as being the victims of impost, or impositions, a form of taxation to support the court; and in a similar vein Hippolita likens the royal hunt of "harmelesse beastes" to "the tyrannie of greatnesse without pittie" (2.2.45–59). In this manner the "recreational" royal hunt, with its barking dogs, emblematizes royal disregard for the country's pain.

The play demonstrates its protesting perspective through the romantic action as well. In the midst of the romantic mixups and mistaken identities of New Comedy, the issues of topical complaint keep breaking in upon the leisure-seeking Duke. Chief among these is the grand petition of grievances reported by the Lacedemonian messengers. As a means of gaining access to Basilius' daughters, Aminter and Julio, suitors in a double sense, present the Duke with an urgent request for the immediate redress of grievances in Arcadia. In what must have been a moment of hushed expectation at the Blackfriars, the Duke asks the inevitable question, "What grevances oppresse them? briefly speake" (3.3.93). The pointed topical detail of their response is unique in the drama of the time:

Aminter. Marchandise (my Ledge) through the avarice of purchasing Officers, is rackt with such unmercifull Impost, that the very name of Traffique growes odious even to the professor.

Julio. Townes so opprest for want of wonted and naturall libertie, as that the native Inhabitants seeme Slaves, & the Forrayners free Denizens.

Ami. Offices so bought and sould, that before the purchaser can be sayd to be placed in his Office, he is againe by his covetous Patrone displac't.

Julio. Common Riots, Rapes, and wilfull Homicide in great mens followers, not onely, not punished, but in a manner countenaunced and aplauded.

Ami. Indeede since your Majestie left the Land, the whole bodie of the Common-wealth runnes cleane against the byas of true and pristine governement.

Julio. And your honorable Brother, like a Shipp toste upon the violent billowes of this Insurrection, by us intreates your Majesties Letters of speedy reformation, for feare the whole kingdome suffer inevitable shipwracke.

(3.3.94–113)

For the purposes of the romantic action, the petition is a mere ruse, yet its topical specificity quite exceeds the functional requirements of the scene—to get the suitors admitted to Arcadia. To begin with, the presentation of the petition appositely mimics the well-known manner in which state business intruded itself upon James, for as Chamberlain relates, "The Kinge . . . findes such felicitie in that hunting life . . . he desires . . . that he be not interrupted nor troubled with too much busines. . . . Though he seeke to be very private and retired where he is, yet he is much importuned with petitions."[16] The suitors' list of grievances also recalls grievances currently under consideration by James's first Parliament in 1606.[17] Chief among these, as in the Lacedemonian petition, was impost, an onerous form of taxation that was exacted by the crown without the consent of Parliament. The issue touched on traditional English notions of liberty and is raised in just those terms in the petition. Although the crown's decision to have a syndicate collect the taxes it could not efficiently collect itself was reasonable enough, the system was abused and became a grievance. The "Great Farm," as it was called, hurt the producers of goods, the carrying merchants, and finally the consumers.[18] In practice, the system impeded England's commercial development (a fact that may be gleaned from the passage above), and at the same time hurt the entire populace by virtue of the inflation such a system of tax collection engendered.

Complaints against the scandal of office-buying also appear in the petition as the grievance of an entire nation. Dametas' boast, "An other Milion ile lay to bestow in Offices. I wil have welth or ile rake it out ath kennels else" (4.5.56–57), underscores this issue. The Lacedemonians' report of the oppression felt in towns "for want of wonted and naturall libertie" does not specify the problem leading to the complaint, but the petitioners' righteousness appears to be based on an appeal to their inalienable rights, the same appeal that parliamentary leaders increasingly made in their conflicts with James. A more explicit expression of English resistance to the unruliness of the Jacobean court lies behind Julio's reference to "common Riots, Rapes, and wilfull Homicide in great mens followers." This complaint reflects the widespread perception that members of the peerage in violation of their feudal obligations had ceased to exercise control over those in their patronage, "murder it selfe," in Osborne's words, "not being exempted."[19]

The most serious warning of all, the Lacedemonians' report of imminent insurrection, accurately reflects the concerns of a jittery English populace after the Gunpowder Plot and an alleged plot to put Arbella Stuart on the throne of England. These apprehensions illustrate the conservatism of the petition. In their fear of civil disorder, most Englishmen, along with their Parliament, fervently wished no more than that James would reform court and government, setting the wobbly ship of state aright again. To this urgent petition, the Duke responds with bland courtesy. Yes, he will answer all grievances after "short deliberation"; any proud rebellion will be put down with a princely "frowne." "In the meane time," the unperturbed Duke announces, "let 'em [these Lacedemonian passengers] taste the best entertainment of our Court" (3.3.114–18). With these quieting words, urgent matters of state are laid aside unredressed and the burlesque Arcadian romance allowed to proceed as the suitors gain access to Basilius' daughters.

Juxtaposed to the waggish satire on the hunting sovereign is a detailed exposé of the venal activities of the Duke's minister, Dametas. His loathsome influence over the Duke is revealed by his boast of having obtained a letter of patent that gives him life-and-death power over the people. The lethal potency claimed for this unspecified patent is surely hyperbolic, but the circumstances by which it was obtained accurately reflect early Stuart conditions. To the dismay of Parliament, the king (who alone had the power to grant such patents) all too often conferred them as political spoils upon those (like Dametas in *The Isle of Gulls*) who supported crown policies.

Invested as he is with "offices, titles, and all the additions . . . of a man worshipfull" (1.2.35–36), Dametas is depicted as the primary dispenser of the patronage system. In this key role he introduces himself: "What an excellent trade it is to be an office maker, Ile have more officers, and one shall be to keepe schollers and souldiers out of the Court" (1.3.65–67). Dametas would thus deprive these traditionally loyal but neglected groups of the courtly rewards of service. Furthermore, Dametas delivers the petitions of the suitors to a bureaucratic fate that was habitual in Tudor-Stuart England—"Fellowes, deliver your peticions to my scribe *Major*, and dost heare, put em up *Manasses*, they may be wrongs to us" (1.3.21–23). The term *put up* can mean both to "hand up to a superior for consideration" and to "stow away" or lay up.[20] Given Dametas' allegation that the petitions may "wrong" (i.e., harm) those in his office if heard, the second (here satiric) meaning of his order to "put em up" assumes special prominence.

Equally true to the conditions of contemporary life is Day's depiction of Dametas' greed in exacting a gift of bribe from every petitioner who comes his way. The ritual is daringly dramatized when Dametas' secretary, Manasses, who may be modeled on Robert Cecil's undersecretary, Sir Michael Hickes, refuses to grant the disguised Demetrius and the disguised prince Lisander an audience with Basilius without a bribe.[21] "Your onely way to moove a sute by," he cautions, is "humbly complayning to your good worship, O tis most pathetick, and indeed without money, can doe just nothing with authoritie" (2.1.116–19). When, in an earlier scene, Lisander objects to such bribery, the lackey Manasses patiently informs him of the political facts of life, saying, "Tis my maisters pleasure, and [the] usuall fashion" (1.4.57–58). Constrained either to abandon his suit or to compromise his principles, Lisander with gracious speech produces a jewel that Dametas with pretended diffidence accepts saying, "Well Madam, tho I hate nothing more then a man that takes brybes, yet prest by your importunitie, and that you tender it in love, least I might seeme too nice to withstand a Ladies favour, Ile wear it for your sake, and if the Duke be not too busily imployed, worke your accesse" (1.4.66–71).

Dametas' speech accurately reproduces the candied rhetoric that sweetened the ritual by which Elizabeth-Jacobean suitors were compelled in effect to beg court officials to accept precious gifts they did not wish to bestow. This pseudo-Arcadian surface is then stripped away as Day exposes a new layer of corruption. Despite having paid his bribe, Lisander is soon informed that there is still no assurance he will receive an audience with the Duke. Hearing this, Lisander breaks into the tirade that the scene has previously refused to make, calling Dametas "the Court spaniell with the silver bell" and "you unnecessarie mushrump" sprung out "in one night" (1.4.101–10). Undeterred, Manasses reveals in an orgy of hyperbolic self-congratulation that he has taken advantage of his position in the chain of command to enjoy not very forbidden fruits of office: "He [Dametas] puts mee in trust with his whole estate: he buyes Maners, I purchase Farmes: he buildes houses, I plucke downe Churches: he gets of the Duke, and I of the Commons: he beggers the Court, and I begger the whole Countrey" (4.1.117–21).

This satire on the operation of the patronage system is notable for its attack upon the court official Dametas. Although Day's depiction of him may well be a composite one, the man principally satirized in him is James's chief minister and privy councilor, Robert Cecil, before whom Jonson appeared for writing *The Isle of Dogs* and to whom he wrote when imprisoned in 1605 for *Eastward Ho*. As evidence of a sharply focused anticourt outlook, this unusually specific identification merits close attention.

The play emphasizes, as we have seen, Dametas' bribe-taking, his acquisition of others' lands, his role of advisor to the sovereign, his participation in his master's hunting pursuits, his quick elevation, his self-interest, and, above all, his control of the patronage system. Bullen's suggestion that this lord is the Scottish George Home, the earl of Dunbar, is plausible if one looks at only a few details in the satire and ignores the others.[22] Dunbar was for a time chancellor of the Exchequer and, according to David Willson, "omniprevalent with James," conditions that fit the play; however, Dunbar's most conspicuous success was not in this office but in that of master of the wardrobe, where he sold off Elizabeth's gowns and dresses for a small fortune.[23] However, neither of these men were conspicuous in his rise to power or acquisition of new offices. Robert Cecil was.

A trusted advisor to Elizabeth, Cecil rose immediately and conspicuously under James. Dubbed Viscount Cranfield and, about six months before *The Isle of Gulls* appeared, earl of Salisbury, Cecil pocketed large sums of money and achieved control with Lord Sackville (sometimes referred to as "Lord Fill-Sack") of the custom farms, thereby procuring "gifts" and private loans.[24]

Cecil's father, it is true, was a great minister in Elizabeth's time, but to noblemen who counted pedigrees in hundreds of years Cecil was a rank upstart, a point made several times in *The Isle of Gulls* (see 1.3.126–35) and documented by contemporary jingles about him.[25] Born with a hunched back, Cecil was commonly satirized with punning references to his "natural" deformity.[26] The same sort of unkind humor may well underlie the description of Dametas as "the most mishapen sute of gentility that ever the Court wore" (1.1.57–58). This same Cecil, whom for his avarice and cunning contemporaries dubbed "the fox of Hatfield Chase," is four times referred to as "the olde foxe" or "slye foxe" (4.1.277–80, 293; 4.5.122), and if contemporary reports may be credited, Cecil accompanied James to many of his hunting lodges and took an active interest in hawking.[27]

Audacious as its personal satire on Cecil and James is, *The Isle of Gulls* must also be credited with dramatizing the ruinous national effects of a brutalizing patronage system. Although historians sometimes trace the origins of this kind of opposition politics back to the late 1620s, when an anticourt—sometimes rendered "country"—opposition developed to the "court" government installed in London,[28] *The Isle of Gulls,* along with *The Fleer, Bussy D'Ambois,* and *The Revenger's Tragedy,* demonstrates that such anticourt attitudes were spreading outside Parliament a generation earlier. In fact, *The Isle of Gulls* employs the terms *court* and *country* contrastingly—the former as a synonym for a self-interested and corrupting coterie, the latter as a synonym for the national interest, and sometimes more narrowly for country innocence. In addition to Manasses' self-satirizing speech about beggaring the whole country while Dametas beggars the court, there is a passage in which Dametas declares, "Ile put on wings and flie," and the virtuous Violetta remarks contemptuously, "Out of the Court, and the whole Country shall have a good riddance" (2.2.81–83). Here the court's corruption is seen as infecting the nation. The same idea underlies Dametas' wife's complaint that the court fashion is for husbands to pay attention to other women. "And [if] this be the Court fashion," she concludes, "would I were an honest woman of the Countrie againe, be Courtiers who list" (4.1.269–71).

The latter passage is a wonderful example of how the political satire exploits its romantic materials. The blending of the two elements helps to explain the sardonic tone of parody that ultimately undercuts the play's imitation of Sidney's pastoral. Pastoral romance though the play purports to be, its topical satire keeps shattering the Arcadian idyll. The Children of the Queen's Revels produced several other accomplished satires, but none more wittily dramatizes the abuses and grievances of Jacobean court life and governance—and then calls for their redress. Such artfulness, however, was not appreciated by Jacobean officials. The very effectiveness of the satire provided reason to censor it and to punish the company by depriving it of royal patronage.

5

Suppression of the Satires of the Children of the Queen's Revels

If governmental sanctions against the Children of the Queen's Revels are the measure of the vigor of anticourt drama, the company was the most offending one in England. The King's Men, it is true, had on two notable occasions performed plays subsequently forbidden—the enactment of *Richard II* on the eve of Essex's rebellion and in 1604 *The Tragedy of Gowry*.[1] However, as Chambers observes, these plays were performed "probably without any intention to offend."[2] The 1600 performances of *Richard II,* undertaken for a fee by private individuals, was particularly anomalous for the Globe.[3] But at the Blackfriars not a year went by between 1603 and 1608 without the Children of the Queen's Revels falling afoul of the authorities.[4] Approximately one in three of their plays in these years drew some form of official sanction against the performances or playwrights or both.

Whereas the King's Men offended by presenting histories on the touchy subject of conspiracies—dangerous by example or analogy—the Children of the Queen's Revels made their bread by transparent personal attacks against James, his court, and his ministers. Such a record corroborates the impression that their anticourt satires were not a matter of accidentally produced peccant plays but of a repertory substantially comprised of controversial, even subversive satires.

The notion of a Jacobean theatrical company with a politically daring repertory is a peculiar one, for the existence of such a company seems to require its suppression in an age where political tolerance of dissent was unknown. There ought not to have been a significant drama of protest, and yet there was. Strange as it may appear, the history of the Children of the Queen's Revels underscores *both* the threat the company posed and its ability to thrive, at least for a time, in the face of governmental sanctions and suppression of its plays. The explanation for this bizarre set of circumstances lies partly in the decentralized exercise of Jacobean censorship, partly in the inconsistency of James's own policy toward the offending company, and very substantially in the fact that the company capitalized on its relationship with the well-to-do courtly audiences, relentlessly carrying the license it enjoyed in satire to unacceptable limits.

As England's new king, James was eager to support the revival of London's theaters after a year of plague. Yet the king himself did not love the drama to the degree Elizabeth had, preferring to spend his time away from the city in his hunting lodges. The consequence of this pattern of behavior was that the king was either unconcerned or unmindful of the increasingly bold satires on his court and policies that Calvert so complained of in his missive to Winwood in March 1605.

When the king was moved to action, invariably it was because others had provoked him. James's great anger against the Children of the Queen's Revels in Marston's lost play of the mines and in Chapman's Byron tragedies was engendered by the strictures of the French ambassador, who lodged an official protest.[5] Similarly, his stern moves against the dramatists of *Eastward Ho* were apparently provoked by the complaints of the Murray brothers.[6] Whether a different sovereign could have avoided seeing his court become a subject of derision in the private theaters is uncertain since any new king would have inherited the problems James faced, but for the vehemence of the reaction and its continuation James must be held in significant measure responsible.

James's evident inattention to the anticourt dramas were not, however, the only reason for their continued production. Imprecise and overlapping divisions of responsibility among other governmental agencies or officials charged with regulating the drama also played their part.[7] Unlike all the other companies, the productions of the Children of the Queen's Revels were licensed, not by the master of the revels, but by an especially appointed censor, Samuel Daniel, who seems to have looked on this office as a sinecure.[8] From him the company appears to have had only pro forma supervision. After Daniel, authority for regulation passed to bodies which had much other business and which made decrees pertaining to the drama only when special problems were forwarded to it. Among these, the Privy Council had supreme authority over the drama (next to the king) and especially concerned itself with treasonous matters of state or religion. The order for suppression of *The Isle of Dogs* in 1597, for example, originated in the Privy Council.[9] Ecclesiastical authorities could also step in on occasion, as could the lord treasurer, who was particularly concerned with the patents and publication of plays. As an ex officio member of the Privy Council and a great peer of the realm, the lord chamberlain sometimes played a mighty role in approving particular plays and in hearing appeals from offending dramatists or actors. Thus, when Chapman and Jonson were imprisoned, they addressed letters of apology to the lord chamberlain, to the king, and to James's chief minister, Robert Cecil, earl of Salisbury.[10]

The lack of any consistent pattern in the supervision and control of productions of the Children of the Queen's Revels is reflected in the sanctions brought against their offending plays. In his prose pamphlet of 1606, *The Black Year*, Anthony Nixon records that Marston brought "in the *Dutch Courtesan* to corrupt English conditions, and [was] sent away *Westward* for carping both at Court, Cittie, and countrie."[11] Nixon does not cite particular verses from *The Dutch Courtesan*. At worst, the play offers isolated lines that poke fun at the Scots for "shaving" and "polling" their English countrymen. Similarly, there appears in the first quarto of *The Malcontent* (at 5.3.112) a disrespectful allusion to James's Scottish ancestry that is deleted from subsequent editions.[12]

These matters of touching up texts for publication were nothing compared to the shocks to come. Early in 1605 the king's official censor for the Children of the Queen's Revels was called before Cecil's Privy Council for having had produced (by the very company he was charged to oversee) his *Philotas*. The close resemblance the tragedy bore to Essex's controversial trial and execution clearly angered Cecil, who had played an unpopular part in Essex's conviction. The degree of Daniel's culpability is problematic;[13] his abrogation of his official role as censor and his use of his position to air his own political views are not. No doubt the matter distressed Daniel sorely, but it did not touch the company as a troupe.

When the wrath of royalty did break out over *Eastward Ho* in the following year, the magnitude of the official response must have appeared incomprehensible. Marston, Jonson, and Chapman were all sentenced to have their noses slit and their ears clipped. Marston may have escaped, although if Nixon's statement that he was "sent *Westward*" for carping at city, state, and country wittily alludes to his part in *Eastward Ho,* then Marston too was detained or imprisoned, albeit elsewhere.[14] Not surprisingly, the first of several management shake-ups ensued.[15]

It is easy to undervalue the significance of the punishment the offending dramatists faced since, after all, the sentence was not carried out. However, the survival of ten manuscript copies of letters sent by Jonson and Chapman to virtually all the great nobles in the court testifies to the darkness of their prison experience. Jonson's moving appeal to the earl of Suffolk explains that they have been committed thither, "vnexamyned, nay vnheard (a Rite, not commonlie denyed to the greatest Offenders) and I made a guiltie man, longe before I am one."[16] He terms the prison "vile" (1.195) and laments to the countess of Bedford that he is forced to "prophane" his appeal by writing "with prison polluted Paper" (1.197)—perhaps foul-smelling paper—in "bondage and fetters" (1.198).

To Chapman was assigned the task of appealing directly to the king. His abject penitence is pitiable. The letter ends, "In all dejection of never-enough iterated sorrow for your high displeasure, and vow of as much future delight as of your present anger; we cast our best parts at your Highness' feet, and our worst to hell" (p. 126). The more robust-spirited Jonson, with growing connections at Whitehall, stood on his dignity, but in his letter to the earl of Pembroke voices the fears he and Chapman must both have felt: " 'The Anger of the Kinge is death,' (saieth the wise man) and in truth it is little lesse with mee and my friend, for it hath buried vs quick."

Years later, in his conversations with Drummond, Jonson related how grave his situation was thought to be, for at a banquet held at his deliverance "his old Mother" "shew[ed] him a paper which she had (if the Sentence had taken execution) to have mixed in ye Prison among his drinke, which was full of Lustrie strong poison & that she was no churle she told she minded first to have Drunk of it herself" (1.140).

The rigor of the official sanctions against those involved in the writing of *Eastward Ho* must be weighed against the government's failure to respond to the topical matter in *The Fawn* and to the satires on Nottingham in *Monsieur D'Olive* and the "courtly" Scots in *The Widow's Tears*. The persistence of a relish for muckraking criticism, even after the *Eastward Ho* imprisonments, is evident from the title of a lost play, *Abuses,* produced by Paul's Boys in 1606 and played before James, as well as from the authorial prefaces to such plays as *Volpone* (published 1607) and the *Fawn* (published 1606).

The government's failure to exercise control over other topical satires by the Children of the Queen's Revels must have fostered in those dramatists who had not been singed by *Eastward Ho* a sense of daring or exhilaration. The company's production of John Day's *Isle of Gulls* only several months after the *Eastward Ho* imprisonments shows that some such attitude must have been present. If there was indeed a sense of daring, it was short-lived. For producing *The Isle of Gulls,* the company was not to get off so easily this time. It was, first of all, deprived of the queen's patronage, forbidden thereafter from using her name as part of its official title. As a consequence of this loss of patronage, Samuel Daniel appears to have lost his position as censor of the company (he was the queen's appointee). Thereafter the master of the revels apparently took up the task of licensing the plays. Numerous members of the acting company were, by Hoby's report, committed to Bridewell.[17] And once again the management of the company was reorganized as Edward

Kirkham retired from the business and the Children themselves became joint masters of the company.[18]

In the wake of these profound changes, the government issued an edict of restraint aimed directly at the company. The decree, dated November 7, 1606, disassociated the Chapel from the Blackfriars theater. This action, along with the company's changed title, put the troupe on a new footing with the government, reducing its degree of protection or immunity. Another presumably unintentional effect of the decree was that it made easier attempts by other, more favored companies to rent or buy up the very premises where the children customarily performed. Also, a codicil to this same document expressly revokes a chief part of the authority of Nathaniel Gyles, the officer commissioned with recruiting for the company, noting, "It is not fitt or decent that such as shoulde singe the praises of God Allmightie shoulde be trayned vpp or imployed in suche lascivious and prophane exercises [as stage plays]."[19] The decree thus permitted the continued impressment of children for singing in choir—but no longer for acting in plays. The effect of the decree was simple and, to the future of the company, devastating.

Along with the special decree directed against the Children of the Revels came greater rigor in the regulation of the drama generally. In May 1606 was published the Act to Restraine Abuses of Players—a title aptly revelatory of the government's attitude toward the players at this time. This act forbade the use of "the Holy Name of God," the Holy Ghost, Jesus, or the Trinity by any stage player under the stiff penalty of 10 pounds. Although directed at the production of plays in the theater, its practical effect was to prompt a revision of blasphemous language in the printing of plays subsequent to 1606.[20]

This weight of evidence indicates a turning point in the government's relationship to the London theaters, but especially to the offending Children of the Revels, which now became the object of harsh governmental sanctions. The surviving documents corroborate the supposition that James and his counselors would not tolerate long the performances of a theater given to social protest.

Subsequent events brought the company to the brink of extinction. Early in 1608 the Children of the Revels, still unchastened, twice more produced seriously offending plays. One of these was Chapman's two-part *Conspiracy and Tragedy of Charles Duke of Byron,* which depicted among other topical matters the current queen of France, Marie de Medici, slapping the mistress of Henry IV. The other was a play of "The Silver Mines," a personal satire directed against James, said to have been composed by Marston. Although the satire is now lost, its subject was James's ill-fated venture to recover silver from mines discovered near Linlithgow, Scotland, in 1607. Of this satire, the French Ambassador complained, "Un jour ou deux devant ilz avoient dépêche leur Roi, sa mine d'Escosse, et tous ses favorits d'une estrange sorte; car aprés luy avoir fait dépiter le ciel sur le vol d'un oyseau, et faict battre un gentilhomme pour avoir rompu ses chiens, ils le dépeignoient ivre pour le moins une fois le jour."[21]

To this protest the government reacted swiftly, reporting, "His majesty was well pleased with . . . the committing of the players that have offended in the matters of France, and . . . that for the others who have offended in the matter of the Mynes . . . his Grace had vowed they should never play more, but should first begg their bred and . . . therefore my lord chamberlain . . . should take order to dissolve themn, and to punish the maker besides."[22] As a result of these offenses the king went so far as to close for a time *all* of London's theaters, reopening them only after receiving a substantial bribe from the theaters—James's insolvency was such that he could virtually always be brought to a cool view of matters with coin—and only then by extracting a promise that no current events or living personages ever again be represented.[23]

In all of these events the Children of the Revels were at the center of the controversy and its direct cause. The growing severity with which the government reacted to its productions demonstrates the threat the company posed to government officials. But as the king's threat to close all the theaters indicates, by 1608 the notorious Children of the Revels had endangered the position of the adult companies as well. Thomas Heywood's *Apology for Actors* (published in 1612) was composed during just this period of turmoil. As a dramatist employed by the adult companies, Heywood testifies not only to the anxiety felt in the other theaters but also to the distinctiveness of the children's repertory and by implication to the heterodox ideology then prevalent at the Blackfriars:

Now to speake of some abuse lately crept into the quality, as an inueighing against the State, the Court, the Law, the Citty, and their gouernements, with the particularizing of priuate mens humors (yet aliue) Noble-men, & others: I know it distastes many; neither do I any way approue it, nor dare I by any meanes excuse it. The liberty which some arrogate to themselues, committing their bitternesse, and liberall inuectiues against all estates, to the mouthes of Children, supposing their iuniority to be a priuiledge for any rayling, be it neuer so violent, I could aduise all such to curbe and limit this presumed liberty within the bands of discretion and gouernment.[24]

Heywood's description is specific enough to indicate that he is referring to the Children of the Revels, not Paul's Boys. The composition date of his treatise, 1608, confirms the impression. For reasons that remain obscure, the Children of Paul's had ceased to perform after 1606. It is known that the company's announced intention to reopen its theatrical doors prompted the managers of the Blackfriars theater to buy off the impending renewed competition from this indoor theater for a dead rent of £20.[25] This seemingly extreme action was very likely prompted by the dire straits in which the Children of the Queen's Revels found itself from early 1606. In any event, this preemptive action left London with *one* children's company in 1607.

A year later the managers for the Children of the Revels began negotiations to renew their lease at the Blackfriars theater, which was expiring in 1608. But to the misfortune of the company, the lease was awarded upon its expiration to the Burbage brothers of the Globe. In his reply to a suit pursuant to these events, the lessee, Henry Evans, revealed a major reason why he did not renew his contract: after the king had prohibited the performing of plays at Blackfriars, there was "little or no proffitt made of the howse." This evidence is consistent with the still more revelatory deposition Evans made when he testified that "by his Maiesties speciall commaundement" the Blackfriars managers were "prohibited to vse any plaies there, and some of the boyes being committed to prison . . . no proffitt [could be] made of the said howse but a contynuall rent of ffortie powndes to be paid for the same." The image of the empty theater with its lack of income is a silent reminder of the real cost to the Children of the Revels of its satirical practices.[26]

A month or so after the events of the spring of 1608, preparation was made by the managers of the Blackfriars theater to vacate, and an appraisal of all its goods and properties was made. Evans quotes the disheartened Kirkham as saying that after the imprisonments of the boy actors, "he would deale no more with yt" and that he had "delivered up their commission, which he had vnder the greate seale aucthorising them to plaie, and discharged divers of the partners and poetts."[27]

Chambers believes that the king's anger proved only "a flash in the pan" because the company was later rehabilitated in another theater.[28] But the evidence warrants a stronger judgment. The sanctions of the government against the theater had affected every aspect of its operation, from the imprisonment of its actors to the temporary closing of its theater, which cost it its Blackfriars lease, to the withdrawal of its managers, to the imprisonment of its dramatists. These were disabling events for the company and the dramatists. After his imprisonment for his part in the *Eastward Ho* affair, George Chapman, the dramatist associated the longest with the company, ceased to write the comedies and satires that had flowed so easily from his pen until that time. For two years after his imprisonment, he did not write and his plays were not produced. As for the king's vow to punish the maker of the mines play—John Marston in all probability—it is known that Marston was in fact imprisoned in Newgate on June 8, 1608, a little over a month after La Boderie delivered his letter of protest to James. After these events Marston sold out his one-sixth share of the ownership of the Children to Robert Keysar, one of the new managers. He then left London without his unfinished *Insatiate Countess,* abandoning forever his spectacular playwrighting career. After being ordained in 1609, he never again composed political satire (despite a tradition to the contrary), dwelling, after 1616, in Christchurch, Hampshire, in obscurity.[29]

It is true that James did not go so far as to "dissolve" the Children of the Revels. His best interests lay, after all, not in destroying a company he had created by royal patent but in regulating it effectively so that the company no longer performed offensive plays. To this end he was successful, for the company was forced to reconstitute itself. After the company had been deprived of its former name and its boy actors designated merely as the Children at Blackfriars rather than the Chapel Children (all relationship to the Chapel being denied them), fresh managers, unassociated with the offensive policies of the company, were brought on in the persons of Robert Keysar, a respected London goldsmith, and Philip Rosseter, a lutenist, well respected in court circles. By Christmas 1608 the reorganized company had made its peace with James, for it performed at court for the first time since January 1605. By 1610 it even received its old name back, "The Children of the Queen's Revels."[30]

But the company was never to be the same or ever to regain its pride of place. Jonson, the only upwardly mobile dramatist of the group, conveniently repudiated the satirical methods of the children's companies in his preface to *Volpone.* Marston, its chief satirist, had been driven out, and Chapman, its principal dramatist from 1600, reappeared again after a two-year silence to present probing tragedies of stoic individualists in corrupt French courts—but no more political satires. As daring lampooners of the king and court, the Children of the Queen's Revels were finished.

The activities of the Children of the Queen's Revels may be viewed as one of several vigorous expressions of Jacobean anticourt drama. Their topical brand of satire, which struck at reputations, at the sacred word *honor,* was too direct, too personal, to be tolerated for long. There were, however, safer modes of dramatic expression. All along, Jonson and Chapman had also been composing historical tragedy. Chapman particularly continued to tilt a dramatic lance toward issues of royal authority. In tragedy he could probe issues of courtly reward and punishment, personal liberty and fealty, from an explicitly philosophical perspective.

Indeed, all the dramatists who composed the ideological tragedies that I examine next were intimately involved with one or more children's companies. The connections between these two modes of drama were thus considerably closer than is currently recognized. Samuel Daniel, the appointed censor of the Children of the Queen's Revels, used the very Blackfriars stage to present his political tragedy *Philotas,* and Fulke Greville, a disaffected Jacobean who suffered under Robert Cecil's ministry, helped to sustain members of the Children of the Queen's Revels, even as he composed in private his philosophic assessment of modern kingship and politics in *Mustapha.*

Such weighty drama had its own risks, of course. As Stephen Greenblatt observes, Elizabeth's pique over the 1600 production of *Richard II,* by numerous reckonings a paean of orthodoxy, must alert us to the subtleties of subversive representation.[31] The very publication of an account of Richard's deposition could be construed as an assault on kingship itself, and was. By one report, Elizabeth is said to have responded to Sir John Hayward's *Life of Henry IV,* which offered the unwelcome example of the deposition of Richard II, with the words "I am Richard II, know ye not that?"[32]

We may take the argument a step further: the representation of kingship presupposes an examination of its practice. In the Jacobean period such representations contained a potentially irresolvable clash between two value systems, both of consummate importance to courtiers—the fealty subjects owed to their sovereigns and, as Chapman might have put the case, the honorable sovereignty of the noble self. In comparison with the indecorous topical portrayals of authority in dramatic satire, these tragedies frequently offered respectful, formal, full-dress treatments of kingship and authority. Subversion was not the aim of representation; yet, for dramatists and for the gentlemen, knights, and courtiers who frequented London's theaters, the ideological clashes between subjects and sovereign were ineluctable issues in an age of courts and kings. To scrutinize the uneasy relationship between these two estates was to interrogate the received orthodoxies, and of their relative freedom to depict such issues, using historical, non-English settings, dramatists of an intellectual bent availed themselves fully.

II

IDEOLOGICAL TRAGEDY

1603–1612

6

The Political Background

Divine Right Kingship and the Ministry of Robert Cecil

The early years of James's reign brought to the forefront as many political and ideological issues as social ones. All the unsolved problems of Elizabeth's reign lay before the new king, who was expected to bring redress. This James attempted to do in 1604 by calling what proved to be the longest Parliament of his twenty-three-year reign, lasting, with recesses, until 1610.

Since James involved himself in the proceedings of his first Parliament, dramatists had plenty of opportunity to assess the king's conception of kingship. Moreover, as the House of Commons debated grievances, it dealt with several bills that required interpretation of the limits of the king's authority, a theme that politically minded playwrights quickly took up. Thinking of himself as a philosopher-king, James for his part dealt with Parliament from principled positions. Whereas Elizabeth maneuvered for specific political ends and usually succeeded, James lectured on principles of Divine Right, admonished, and usually aroused an active opposition, which then sermonized on *its* own conception of principles. These circumstances created an intellectual climate upon which dramatists such as Chapman and Beaumont could (and did) draw. Even tragedies that were created during the transition period of 1603-4, such as Jonson's *Sejanus* and Chapman's *Bussy D'Ambois,* appear to have been inspired, at least in part, by the copious political commentary that accompanied the installation of the new dynasty.

The issues that proceeded from James's pronouncements on kingship and from Parliament's debates were one by-product of the early years of the reign. A second was the displacement of former Elizabethan officials and courtiers.

Of signal importance in this latter development was the emergence of Robert Cecil as James's chief minister and the sole dispenser of patronage. Courtiers such as Fulke Greville, Samuel Daniel, and John Harington, who had allied themselves in Elizabeth's time with Cecil's principal rival, the earl of Essex, found themselves sadly unprotected.[1] As Cecil consolidated his base of power, each of these figures saw his career suffer a grave setback.

However, through it all these men retained their allegiance to an aristocratic ideal of service (as against what they perceived to be cronyism) and to an idealized conception of right government. For them the memory of Sir Philip Sidney and the earl of Essex provided nostalgic rallying points in the new Jacobean age. Despite Essex's execution in 1601, the circle of Essex's followers, which also included parliamentary historians and antiquarians, the painter Marcus Gheeraerts, numerous MP's, and Essex's distinguished son, Robert (later, the parliamentary general), continued to keep the spirit of Essex alive in the Jacobean period. In later years the circle provided the nucleus of the aristocratic opposition to the early Stuarts.[2]

Two literary members of this group, Daniel and Greville, gave voice to their aristocratic ideals in the political closet tragedies they wrote for Sidney's sister, the countess of Pembroke. In the revised Jacobean versions of Daniel's *Philotas* and Greville's *Mustapha*, they also expressed their disillusionment with the Jacobean political scene. Jonson, another member of the circle, pursued similar ends while composing for the public stage. Each of these developments—on the one hand, philosophical concerns with principles of kingship and subjects' rights and, on the other, practical concerns with the actual exercise of power under Cecil's ministry—considerably affected the tone, perspective, and context of early Jacobean political drama. Because of their powerful influence on the drama, we will consider each of these political developments in turn.

Having been schooled in Roman, not English constitutional law, and having composed several works, such as *The Trew Law of Free Monarchies* (1598) and *The Basilikon Doron* (priv. pr., 1599; public ed., 1603), James awakened suspicions early on that he had little regard, foreigner that he was, for English rights and liberties. In practice, it must be said, he used his authority with moderation and often backed away from confrontation. Nonetheless, his public pronouncements had the very real effect of provoking a vigorous airing of these great issues.

To appreciate James's knack for making momentous issues out of lesser ones, we may examine the early conflicts between the king and his Parliament.[3] The commencement of the 1604 session was immediately marked by a dispute over who was to judge parliamentary election returns. The Court of Chancery had refused to seat Sir Francis Goodwin on the grounds that he was an outlaw. Parliament voted to seat Goodwin, but James, who would not stay out of the fray, announced for Goodwin's opponent, Sir John Fortescue, couching the crown's position in terms of the supremacy of royal privilege. Although the issue was resolved happily in conference, James conceding that the Commons was "a proper, though not the exclusive, judge" of election returns,[4] this first clash raised the question of the proper limits of the royal prerogative.

Such disputes as these precipitated the first constitutional document of the Jacobean period—*The Form of Apology and Satisfaction* (1604). It asserted, "The prerogatives of princes may easily, and do daily grow: the privileges of the subject are for the most part at an everlasting stand. They may be by good providence and care preserved, but being once lost are not recovered but with much disquiet."[5] The signers even charged that James's speeches were tending "to the utter overthrow" of "fundamental" House privileges and "of the rights and liberties of the whole Commons of your realm of England, which they and their ancestors from time immemorial have undoubtedly enjoyed" (p. 287). The issue of absolutism they addressed directly to James, asserting that he had been "misinformed" if he had heard that the kings of England held absolute power in themselves (p. 287).

It may indeed be true, as increasing numbers of historians have concluded, that this document deserves only a small place in parliamentary history—the document was later rejected as too extreme[6]—but parliamentary history is one thing, political consciousness another. As a mark of the latter, *The Apology* reveals a zeal to safeguard the English political inheritance, a notable apprehension of despotism, and a disenchantment with James that is also evident in Jacobean satire and tragedy. The values of "Ancient Liberty," and especially freedom of speech in representative bodies were also major concerns of Greville and Jonson. These dramatists, like so many MP's, were serious readers of history who brought to contemporary political issues a historical perspective that emboldened them with a sense of righteousness. The factiousness of a significant segment of the Commons (in a cause that could only have brought them profitless confrontation) and the dramatized political concerns of intellectuals in the theatrical world reveal a society that was finding the means to disseminate its ideas (however unfounded historically) about England's unique heritage of subjects' rights.

The apprehension of tyranny that underlay these constitutional issues kept returning, even on peripheral issues. The king did his part to exacerbate the friction. In 1608, for example, when the crown decided to increase the book of rates on impositions, James addressed the issue in terms of a prince's "special power and prerogative," and further asserted that the House was "not to dispute of the King's power and prerogative" on these matters.[7] In its several clashes with the king, Parliament never challenged the idea of Divine Right. Divine election was not the issue. Right up to 1642, and even later, most English subjects believed in the sanctity and divine origin of kingship. Believing that God provided a model of monarchical supremacy, they held that monarchy, supported by a healthy aristocracy, was the best form of government and that hydra-headed democracy (akin to mobocracy in our parlance) was the worst. Then too, the English welcomed the Divine Right doctrine in their religious controversies with the papacy: election of princes came directly from God, not from Rome.[8] Seen from this contemporary vantage, Divine Right was a bulwark of nationalism, a doctrine essential to the operation of the English nation-state.

But because the king's Divine Right authority was closely associated with his royal prerogative, the House argued acrimoniously over the extent of the king's absolute powers. More and more insistently the question became, What prerogatives belong to the monarch absolutely and what freedoms and liberties belong to subjects inviolate? When the judge Sir Henry Finch wrote that the king "hath also a prerogative in all things, that are not injurious to the subject"[9] (by which he meant, personal and property rights), he gave felicitous expression to this broad, if ill-defined, system of belief.

English kings, everyone understood, enjoyed vast prerogative powers, but they were still the servants of the law. That is to say, seventeenth-century Englishmen believed both that their king enjoyed absolute authority in governing and that he was subject to the law and to his oath of allegiance.[10] Furthermore, English kings could not by law create law, for to do so would contravene the principle that they were subject to it.[11] Hence the need for Parliament. When grievances arose or old laws became outmoded, the crown's responsibility was to summon Parliament to propose new laws or to withdraw old ones. As Greville's *Alaham* and *Mustapha* illustrate, England despised the Persian form of government because the monarch ruled by whim, corrupting both his ministers and the state. In him authority was tyranny because the sovereign had unlimited power (a key phrase) and no oath of obligation to uphold established law.

Whatever the faults of his administration, James was no tyrant. He never levied taxes without parliamentary consent and he refrained from imprisonment without trial. What James did do was to make pronouncements inconsistent with his practice. Not the least of these was the claim he made in *The Trew Law of Free Monarchies* (1598) to "make daily statutes . . . without any aduice of Parliament or estates."[12] The problem then appears to have been that the king, by his theoretical positions and his defensive aloofness, inspired fears that he might become tyrannical, or had tyrannical designs.

This fear of unlimited and hence tyrannical power found a focus in Dr. Cowell's *The Interpreter* (1607). The treatise defined such terms as "*Subsidie,*" "*Praerogatiue of the King,*" "*Parlament,*" and "*King*" in ways that demonstrated the writer's belief that English kings were above the law absolutely.[13] In 1610 an aggrieved Parliament asked that the book be condemned. The king, fearing a deterioration of his position in the Parliament, promised to suppress the book, and did. The crown's action defused a potentially explosive confrontation, but once again attention had become riveted on the fundamental issue of the king's relationship to the law.

In asserting his Divine Right powers, James only perpetuated a Tudor doctrine, but his pronouncements were couched in such august terms that many Englishmen came to mistrust and doubt his allegiance to English law and tradition. In fact, by 1610 Parliament was filled with whisperings that the king, wearying of the challenges the Commons had put in his way, meant to rule like a tyrant without it.[14]

These fears the king answered in a major address to Parliament on March 21, 1610. Although he loved his subjects and would not rule by whim, he was *"Parens patriae"* and responsible for his people (p. 307).[15] Recalling the origins of laws in settled kingdoms such as England, James acknowledged that kings set down laws "at the rogation of the people" (p. 309). But despite James's manifest acknowledgment of his duty to uphold the laws, his phrases exude the odor of absolutism. His opening paragraphs advance the proposition that "Kings are justly called Gods" because their power resembles divinity (p. 307). The metaphors suggest that omnipotence is the alluring attribute of kings. Kings "make and vnmake their subiects: they haue power of raising, and casting downe: of life, and of death: Iudges ouer all their subiects, and in all causes, and yet accomptable to none but God onely" (p. 308). James continues, "They haue power to exalt low things, and abase high things" (p. 308). This is the poetry of absolutism. All these powers (James wished his listeners to remember) kings possessed in their original glory. For James this brief history lesson had the further virtues of making the king's subsequent acknowledgment of his responsibility to uphold English law the more magnanimous and unassailable.

The notion voiced by some historians, that James's speech is in reality "moderate" and "constitutional," quite underestimates its tonal impact in at least two ways.[16] First, James's speech *is* symbolism; that is part of its meaning. Second, despite James's recognition of positive law, he still chose to present himself as lofty and untouchable. The opening section of his address concludes with the warning that it is "sedition in Subiects, to dispute what a King may do in the height of his power," and again, "I wil not be content that my power be disputed vpon: but I shall euer be willing to make the reason appeare to all my doings, and rule my actions according to my Lawes" (p. 310). These pronouncements aim at inspiring, even through fear, something of the awe that belongs to majesty. Soon thereafter James forbad Parliament to debate any further the grievance of impositions.

Had his speech been delivered to a parliament of princes, the king's absolutist rhapsody might have played to greater applause. As it was, frightened sailors on the ship of state sought to steer clear of this would-be siren's song. Chamberlain, an astute observer, remarked that James's speech "bred generally much discomfort; to see our monarchicall powre and regall prerogative strained so high and made so transcendent every way, that yf the practise shold follow the positions, we are not like to leave to our successors that freedome we receved from our forefathers."[17]

Chamberlain correctly gauged the pulse of James's audience, for the king's address to Parliament led directly to the Petition of Right (May 1610) in which Parliament answered with *its* mythic account of the "ancient liberty of your realme, and of your subjects' rights and proprieties."[18] As he had done in the Cowell controversy, James again moved away from confrontation, observing that he had put forward claims *in abstracto* and that he had never intended to abridge the liberties of his beloved subjects. Yet this "Great Debate" brought to a culmination all the prior concerns about the relationship of subjects to kings, and the difference between royal authority and tyranny, even if *in abstracto*. As it turned out, the issues of royal authority and subjects' liberty provided such spade-digging professional dramatists as Jonson and Chapman with fertile ideological fields to till.

However, not all drama of political disaffection in the period was composed by middle-class professionals, not all of it was satiric, and some of it was not even meant for public performance. During the same years that the Children of the Queen's Revels were drawing large audiences at Blackfriars to witness the decay of the present times, several learned writers were composing political tragedy for noncommercial, aristocratic consumption. Following principles of dramatic composition that Sir Philip Sidney would have admired, the group, which originally met at Mary Sidney's estate at Wilton, dedicated itself to an aesthetically refined didactic tragedy of state. As political drama the early compositions of the group—those before 1600—belong to the *Mirror for Magistrates* tradition and illustrate unexceptionable themes such as the baneful effects of tyranny, flattery, and bad counselorship. The later tragedies of the Wilton group—the *Four Monarchic Tragedies* of Sir William Alexander, the *Alaham* and *Mustapha* of Greville, and the *Philotas* of Daniel—all abandon reheated Roman subjects (Alexander's *Caesar* excepted) for fresher Persian and Mohammedan ones. In such Eastern settings representations of social oppression and absolutism could be treated forthrightly.

Among these later dramatic compositions those of Alexander display little advance over the methods used by the group before 1600. Of Scotch origin, Alexander dedicated his facilely versified *Four Monarchic Tragedies* to James with fulsome flattery in hopes of preferment.[19] Of a different order, however, are the revised versions of both Greville's *Mustapha* and Daniel's *Philotas*, which use their Near Eastern subject matter to make closely drawn political parallels to England and, by implication, to the Jacobean political system. Their final Jacobean versions express a common outlook of political disaffection and even protest. This outlook no longer found its inspiration in the politicized historical tragedies of Robert Garnier, their French contemporary and early model but in the allegiances Greville and Daniel had developed to the faction of the earl of Essex.[20]

Fulke Greville, first Lord Brooke, was a cousin of Essex's and a highly regarded dignitary in Elizabeth's court. In 1581 he was elected to Parliament, became clerk of the signet and secretary of the council in the Marches of Wales in 1590, was appointed treasurer of the navy in 1598, and rear admiral in 1599. He became the patron of musicians and writers, including Samuel Daniel. A follower of Essex in all but the ill-conceived rebellion in 1600, Greville avoided disgrace during Essex's fall and at the time of Elizabeth's death was enjoying one of the most visibly successful court careers.[21]

Daniel too had allied himself with the Essex faction. He wrote verses of commendation to Essex and to his noble followers, the earls of Southampton and Devonshire. After accepting the patronage of Essex himself, whom it is said Daniel grew to love, Daniel sought and received the patronage of Essex's cousin Greville, to whom he dedicated *Musophilus* (1599). By 1599–1600 the queen herself had become his patron, and a legend soon developed that Elizabeth made Daniel England's first poet laureate.[22]

The recognition and rewards these men received in Elizabeth's court provided the perspective from which they judged James's. Not that their prominence under Elizabeth need have compelled their disapproval of James. To the contrary, Daniel prepared an elegant "Panegyrike Congratulatorie" for the new king while the cautious Greville sought to smooth his own way diplomatically. The underlying source of trouble came not from James but from Cecil, longtime opponent of the old Essex faction.

After James's installation, Cecil's vise-grip over their fortunes became unbreakable. The fate that overtook them helps to explain their dark Jacobean outlook. In April of 1603 Greville was "withered" of £500 and then stripped of his Welsh offices, which had provided the foundation of his income. Although James raised him to knight of the bath in July of that year, Greville discovered his true position when he was stripped of his office as secretary of the navy. By mid 1604, at almost fifty years of age, Greville moved into forced retirement, where he remained until after Cecil's death in 1612.

Untitled and without an estate, Daniel escaped Cecil's displeasure and for a time he fared better. In 1604 he composed the first masque of the reign and was appointed licenser of the Children of the Queen's Revels at the Blackfriars.[23] These preferments were attributable not to Cecil but to the queen, who championed him. Nevertheless, within fifteen months of his appointment Daniel too fell afoul of Cecil, who accused him before the Privy Council of making seditious commentary on Essex's rebellion and trial in his *Philotas*.[24] As a result of this affair, Daniel, it appears, lost his office as licenser and saw his career suffer a stultifying setback.[25] A record of Daniel's feelings may be found in his dedication of the published edition of *Philotas* (1605). Although still young, Daniel described himself in the dedication of *Philotas* as "the remnant of another time" (l. 65) and as having "out-liu'd the date / Of former grace, acceptance, and delight" (ll. 99–100).[26]

For Fulke Greville the years of forced retirement provided opportunity to meditate on the inner workings of government and to compose. This he did by revising *Mustapha* and by composing his famous *Life of Sidney,* both of which express Greville's disillusionment with the Jacobean political scene. Of the two, *The Life of Sidney* is the more patently topical and the one that shows most clearly Greville's embittered relations with Cecil. Surveying the decay of the Jacobean age from his lifelong Calvinistic perspective, Greville saw Elizabeth's reign as a sparkling interlude amidst the spreading darkness. Seeking to express his sense of the splendor of the former age, Greville set about to compose a Life of Elizabeth, but Cecil, fearful of its political point of view, denied him access to the state papers.[27] Thwarted even in this scholarly task, Greville abandoned the project and composed instead *The Life of Sidney* (ca. 1610), which, like the proposed project, proved to be a paean to an earlier age—and an anatomy of the present one.

Despite its title, approximately one fourth of the *Life* is devoted to an analysis of Elizabeth's foreign policy, her commendable relations with Parliament, and her superior management of the royal household. Absent for the most part in the *Life* are the detailed reminiscences of Sidney we might expect. Instead, Sidney's virtues are depicted in a generalized way as a model against which men of the present time could measure their deficiencies. In this way the *Life* becomes a didactic work.

Seen in terms of its larger purposes, the *Life* amounts to the very indictment of Jacobean government that Cecil had feared. Like Greville's plays, the work was for reasons of prudence never intended for publication during the author's lifetime. Significantly, the *Life* was finally published in 1651, after the parliamentarian cause had triumphed. Posthumously, Greville had been taken into the fold of the parliamentarian cause, as the erring ascription to him of other vituperative treatises attacking James's ministry also demonstrates.[28]

The *Life* proceeds by a cunning principle of comparison. Instead of merely praising Elizabeth, it reckons all the problems she avoided or forestalled. Any contemporary would recognize that these were the great dilemmas of James's reign. If a work of indictment by innuendo is possible, this is it. Greville observes that Elizabeth never burdened her yeomanry "with extraordinary

Taxes out of the course of Parliaments," never "stir[red] up the Nobility" by trying to rule absolutely, and used "the safer medium of State-assemblies" as "the only judicious, faithfull, and industrious Favorites of unincroaching Monarchs" (pp. 189–91). Furthermore, in her state councils she never propounded "any prejudicate resolution, which . . . suppresseth the freedome both of spirit and judgment" (p. 188). Elizabeth, he remembers, "forced every man to beleeve his private fish-ponds could not be safe, whiles the publique state of the Kingdome stood in danger" (p. 188). For Greville, Elizabeth was the provident reconciler of "these wildernesses of will, and power" (p. 190). As such, he eulogizes her (with implied, prejudicial comparison to James) as "this homeborne Princesse of ours" (p. 190).

In the same period that he composed the *Life,* Greville thoroughly revised *Mustapha* to make it an attack on political conditions in Jacobean England and, at the same time, a philosophic treatise on the nature of declining kingdoms. In respect to Greville's anti-Jacobean political perspective, and particularly to his pro-Essex outlook, his drama closely resembles Daniel's *Philotas.* Although both plays are usually called academic and therefore by definition isolated from the cultural mainstream, that label is quite inaccurate when applied to *Mustapha* and *Philotas.* These tragedies were part of a cultural phenomenon that reveals itself in several other arts. Not only in literature, but also in ballads, madrigals, lute songs, and paintings, the spirit of Essex remained alive. Opponents of James's policies and of his ministers made Essex's life into a legend, his death into a martyrdom, and his opposition to the Cecil-dominated Privy Council into a charter for fuller parliamentarian government. Among older nobility who had seen their traditional powers whittled away under the Tudors and the Stuarts, he represented a cause that was not to be forgotten. Thus, members of the Parliament and of the nobility undertook to secure their vested interests by hiring historians and antiquarians, such as John Selden, George Hakewill, and John Cotton, to prove to English precedent their birthrights. This movement, if we may call it one, found its living symbol in Essex's son, the third earl of Essex, who labored to regain his father's lands and clear his attainted title. By the late 1620s, his presence in Parliament had helped to provide the beginning of the first organized "country" opposition to the court.[29]

The Essex subject matter of *Philotas* and Greville's *Antony* was part of this phenomenon, and it may be expressly linked with the pro-Essex compositions of lute song composers in the late Elizabethan and early Jacobean period. Many of these somber lyrics express sentiments of regret and consolation for Essex's plight and, later, for the fate he was made to suffer. Even more to the point, Greville became a leading patron of these composers. In one of these collections "fourteen poems of Fulke Greville were set to the twenty-one pieces by Martin Peerson."[30] This record of politically oriented artistic activity puts the trouble Daniel faced with the Privy Council over his

Philotas in a fuller cultural context. Far from being a musty old work whose subject was outside the mainstream, Daniel's *Philotas* was one of numerous examples of a flourishing kind of dissident literature.

The lutenist composers with whom Greville was identified also had a special relationship to the Children of the Queen's Revels at Blackfriars, where musical composition played so important a role in dramatic performance. In 1601, for example, Phillip Rosseter, a very talented composer among the pro-Essex lutenists, published his appealing *Booke of Ayres*.[31] His patron for this work was Sir Thomas Monson, whose brother, Admiral William Monson, was knighted by Essex at Cadiz and who in his position in the navy was closely associated with Greville.[32] Thomas Monson, like Daniel, was a member of Anne's household and was instrumental in helping the Children of the Revels to regain the name "Queen" in their title and the royal patent (restored January 4, 1610) they had lost because of their offensive performances.[33] The respected Rosseter, a member of the royal household, became a manager of the Children of the Queen's Revels in 1606 or so, following one of the several organizational shake-ups.[34] Also associated with this circle of composers was Daniel's brother, John, who composed in 1606 *Songs for the Lute, Viol, and Voice.* This book contains two of Samuel's own lyrics and several with the "style, mood and imagery" of Greville's, but also displays a number of songs that "fit Fulke Greville's new [i.e., Jacobean] relationship with the all-powerful Cecil after the Queen's death."[35] In due course John too became associated with the Children of the Queen's Revels, although years after the company's heyday.[36]

We may note that Jonson, an occasional composer for the Children, was, like Daniel and Greville, a member of the Essex circle, and that he engaged in the practice, as they did, of interpreting Roman history for the parallels it offered to contemporary political affairs.[37] Chapman, Jonson's close friend and the chief tragic dramatist for the Children of the Queen's Revels, was not a member of the group, but he espoused similar aristocratic ideals, and he dedicated both his "Achilles Shield" and the first seven books of the *Iliad* to Essex.[38]

These data establish a series of mutual links among the activities of the Essex circle, the pro-Essex lutenists, and dramatists for the Children of the Queen's Revels at Blackfriars, and the academic drama of political disaffection that Greville and Daniel composed. Indeed, the Jacobean closet drama of Greville and Daniel may be viewed as the aristocratic counterpart of the anticourt satires and political tragedies that professional playwrights were presenting to select audiences at the Blackfriars. But in whatever theaters aristocratic audiences gathered in this period of Parliaments, Jacobean dramatists composed tragedies that probed the proper limits of aristocratic fealty to overbearing, frequently villainous kings.

7

The Not-So-Closeted Tragedies
of Daniel and Greville

In the same year that Greville went into forced retirement, 1604, Samuel Daniel was summoned to appear before the Privy Council to answer charges of sedition concerning his *Tragedy of Philotas* (rev. 1604). Daniel's letters, addressed to the earl of Devonshire and to Robert Cecil, and several reports in the *Calendar of State Papers* reveal the political matter of his offending play.[1] The letter to Cecil shows Daniel trying to put the most innocent construction upon his motives in penning the fourth and fifth acts of *Philotas*. Had not necessity driven him to the vulgar stage, Daniel protests, he would never have had his play performed, and he certainly had never intended any modern application of his ancient subject. That is not to say Daniel denied the pertinence of his play to his own age. Like Marston before him and Greville after him, Daniel protested that the affairs of men in every age bear the same resemblances, "the like supplantations, rysings & overthrowes, so yt there is nothing new vnder the Sunne" (Daniel to Cecil, p. 38).

It is, however, hard to credit Daniel's account of his motives. To suppose that a man in Daniel's position might launch a stage play wholly unaware of the treacherous currents around him is to ignore the very reason why he was appointed licenser of the Children of the Queen's Revels. His position becomes virtually untenable when it is recalled that his fellow dramatist Greville had so feared that *his* tragedy of *Antony and Cleopatra* (ca. 1601) might be construed as a comment upon Essex's conspiracy that he cast it into the fire.[2] But given Daniel's difficult circumstances, it is not reasonable to expect his reply to have been candid.[3]

Laurence Michel's comparison of the last two acts of *Philotas* with the court records of Essex's trial has demonstrated that Daniel followed it closely, drawing from it several of the issues of civil liberty Essex had raised in his own defense. Many of these details, Michel shows, cannot be found in Daniel's source, Quintus Curtius' *De Rebus Gestes Alexandri*.[4]

The prototype for Daniel's dramatic treatment of the Essex legend was in all likelihood Greville's *Antony*. Greville's own account of the tragedy makes plausible the hypothesis that Antony's amorous relationship with Cleopatra could easily have been woven to adumbrate Essex's relationship to Elizabeth, with Cleopatra's advisors standing for Cecil, and so forth.[5] If this is so, Greville's play stood in some kind of informing relationship to Daniel's; just how, we do not know. What is certain is that *Philotas* works the Essex material toward two principal ends—to depict the corruption of bureaucratic government, which observes the forms but not the substance of liberty, and to impersonate the liberty-destroying machinations of Cecil in the figure of Alexander's advisor, Craterus.[6]

Unfortunately, the same data that show Daniel's political motives in composing the last two acts also reveal a vitiated artistic structure. Whereas the first three acts seem to establish *Philotas* as a study in the frailty of greatness, achieved by emphasizing Philotas' ambition, the completed Jacobean version, with its Essex-Philotas connections, reverses this trend as the Chorus begins to treat Philotas as the victim of the state's oppression.[7]

Despite its structural inconsistency and its rhetorical, Senecan conception of character, the tragedy does achieve surprising power in the last two acts. This result is in part due, oddly enough, to the introduction in the first part of the play of a subsidiary action that enlarges the scope of the political theme. There, Philotas' concubine, Antigone, is interrogated by Craterus and threatened with torture if she does not reveal Philotas' privileged conversation with her. Presaging Philotas' own subsequent interrogation and torture, this development has the effect of creating a fine sense of the tyrannical procedures absolute governments regularly employ. During his interview with Antigone, Craterus alternatively appeals to her sense of duty, interrogates, flatters, and terrifies her. In comparison to Daniel's other figures, Craterus is drawn with greater realism and depth. Aware of how much Alexander's advisors desire to remain in favor, Craterus instructs them on the consequences of failing to support his cause against Philotas. His cunning makes him an effective government official, but this is of course no impediment to Daniel's using him as a vehicle for a moralized interpretation of political behavior in great places—that is, how great men cloak private hate in faction, thereby setting an ambush for their rival's ruin (ll. 1110–47).

Daniel's management of those issues pertaining to Craterus' abuse of power shows much skill, even dramatic inspiration. As Alexander begins to fulminate against Philotas' ingratitude, his dangerous popularity, and his wish to capitalize upon Alexander's issuelessness (all themes that pertained to Essex), the poisonous effects of Craterus' counsel reveal themselves. Effective too is Alexander's ironic assertion to Craterus, "I haue both children, kindred, friends; / . . . And whil'st you liue I am not issulesse" (ll. 1301–03). The passage reveals how Alexander's acquired rhetoric triumphs over a rational assessment of the accession problem. Craterus' quiet presence throughout the scene testifies to the power he possesses but finds no need to flaunt. Daniel's visual use of the corpse of one Dymnus, a conspirator whose body remains onstage throughout Philotas' interrogation, adumbrates Philotas' fall. The sense of foreboding in the scene reaches its fullest intensity when Philotas demands to be confronted in law by the witnesses against him. At this moment, Craterus, pointing to the corpse, offers his exultant rebuttal—"Here, this dead traytor shewes you to be one" (l. 1441). Underlined in the margins beside this passage is a statement revealing Daniel's ideological republicanism: "Non testimoniis sed testibus" (beside ll. 1448–49). Although cast in Latin, this principle was (for Englishmen) confirmed by legal precedent.

The principle of inviolable law as the proper defense against tyranny is one that Parliament had begun to explore at the beginning of James's reign to strengthen its hand against monarchical encroachments. For Daniel, this theme becomes the focus of the last two acts. Alexander's desire to have the oracle proclaim him the son of Jove, and thus an absolute ruler, highlights the issue. Although he is no villain and knows his own frailty, Alexander endorses the pragmatic view that "maiesty / Needs all that admiration can lay on / To giue it grace" (ll. 474–76). By contrast, an increasingly idealized Philotas opposes Alexander's claim out of a love that has prompted him to take, as he puts it, "that dangerous liberty / Of speaking truth" (ll. 1581–82). Echoing this fear of despotism, the Chorus sententiously concludes, "Where Kings are so like gods, there subiects are not men" (l. 1815).

Having spoken eloquently in defense of civil liberty and his own personal honor, Philotas is hauled off to the rack. Daniel never allows him to appear again. This strategy permits the dramatist to treat Philotas' shameful, unexpected confession of guilt—as was Essex's—from a greater distance. One consequence is that the subsequent conversation between the courtiers Polidamas and Sostrates enlarged the political perspective. Through them we hear that Philotas' torture is being accompanied by a reign of terror—of searches and spyings, accusations and threats. Polidamas' own confession, that he was seized and coerced into incriminating Philotas' father, a man he loves, conveys a frightening sense of the spiritual devastation repressive regimes can bring about.

This nightmarish picture of the repressive state is central to Daniel's new conception of the tragedy. Polidamas' failure to withstand Craterus' assaults acts as prologue to the greater failure of Philotas. Throughout the last act, the Chorus, filled with trepidation, reflects on the differences between Eastern and Western forms of government. Conveniently comparing Greek and Persian governance, it finds little difference between Alexander's boldfaced absolutism and the highly touted descendants of Greek democracy. As the Persians observe, "Only herein they differ, That your Prince / Proceeds by forme of law t'effect his end" (ll. 1779–80).

Given his attack on subverted law in modern governments, Daniel was probably foolish to have Philotas performed at Blackfriars. The theme, with its allusion to issues in Essex's trial and its obvious parallels between Craterus and Cecil, should have made him tremble, but we now have a better idea of why he did it. The presentation of Philotas was a political act in keeping with the larger picture of dissident dramatic activity at the Blackfriars Theater in the early Jacobean period. The performance also conforms to a broad pattern of cultural activities undertaken at the time by estranged pro-Essex supporters.

Whatever peer support may have fortified him in staging Philotas, there is no doubt Daniel brought Cecil's wrath upon him. He paid with his reputation, and he was humbled. After 1605 Daniel's prospects quickly faded, substantially if not entirely, because of the disgrace Philotas brought upon him. Not until 1610 with the commission of his second court masque, "Tethys Festival," commissioned by the queen, did Daniel reestablish himself. By that time he had also made a show of penitence, for his 1609 edition of The Civil Wars is shorn of its previously published passages eulogizing the man he so admired, the first earl of Essex.[8]

Despite his own allegiance to Essex's name and ideals, Greville did not allow his Mustapha (rev. 1609; subsequently published in a pirated edition) to be dominated by so single a political cause. Greville's report of his desire to cast his Declination of Monarchy (generally known as The Treatise on Monarchy) in the form of tragedy reveals his keen awareness of the danger of "cast[ing] scandall upon the sacred foundations of Monarchy" and of "the fate of many Metaphysicall Phormio's before me, who had lost themselves in teaching Kings, and Princes, how to governe" (p. 153). Similarly, Greville's account of his interview with Cecil (when he sought access to Elizabeth's state papers) shows how uncomfortable he felt in setting down sensitive particulars of contemporary history, for in that interview Greville committed himself to the view that "an Historian was bound to tell nothing but the truth, but to tell all truths were both justly to wrong, and offend not only Princes, and States, but to blemish, and stir up against himselfe . . . the spirit of an Athenian Timon" (pp. 218–19).

But for Greville not all political writing required submission to Cecil's supervision. Once Greville was denied the opportunity to write documentary history, he turned back to political drama, to his closet *Mustapha*. By reworking this tragedy of state, he could partially satisfy his craving to write history on a broad scale, and more safely as well.[9] Thus, whereas Daniel composed political tragedy with personal application, Greville shaped the political materials of *Mustapha* into a haunting philosophic dramatization of man's benighted political life, which in turn reflects his benighted spiritual estate. Broader in scope and more general in application than *Philotas*, *Mustapha* is the more profound indictment of Jacobean political life.

The strange subject matter of *Mustapha*, which recreates the murder in 1553 of Prince Mustapha by his own father, Solyman the Magnificent, accounts in great measure for the play's obscurity. Other elements that have denied Greville a significant audience include *Mustapha*'s isolation from the popular dramatic tradition, its studiously abstract language, and its melodramatic rendering of situation and character. Despite these identifying marks, the revised *Mustapha* possesses remarkable poetic, even dramatic power, and like any important neglected work, its technique and spirit of composition must be recovered.[10] A comparison of the conversational narrative of the *Life* with the tough, concentrated thought of *Mustapha* readily reveals that Greville's verse works by more deliberate principles than his prose.

The clarity with which Greville conceived his own poetic is apparent in the *Life*, when he declares his own creeping genius to be unfit to produce what he calls the delicate "Images of Wit" created by Sidney in *The Arcadia* (p. 224). Rather, he has dedicated himself to "Images of Life," created "on that [true] Stage wherein himself is an Actor" (p. 224). How far Greville distances himself from the dominant poetic practices of his age may be easily gauged. He shows little desire to create either the lush, poetic descriptiveness of Spenserian romance, the imagistic fecundity of Shakespearean poetry, or the songlike clarity of Jonson's epigrammatic verse. He even lacks the metaphoric concreteness of most of the professional poets of his age. But in its sinewiness and difficulty, Greville's poetry bears a similarity to Donne's, whose work, we remember, Jonson prophesied would be forgotten for failure to be understood. This sad fate Greville has suffered in Donne's stead.

Greville, it must be admitted immediately, lacks the nimbleness of mind and disarming humor of Donne, but his poetry is full of that "recreation of thought into feeling" that Eliot praised in Chapman and Donne.[11] If good poetry must explore the nooks and crannies of everyday experience, Greville's *Mustapha* does little of it. To the contrary, in matter and technique *Mustapha* conveys an impression of comprehensiveness and vastness. This he achieves by the use of emblematic images of nature—sea, sun, sky, wind, storm, night, shadow, and valley. Reversing the usual poetic process, Greville strives to evoke the universal through the abstract, but to do so feelingly. The small stage of Solyman's tyrant fears is set against a cosmic array of

"Powers," "Thrones" and "Kingdoms" that has a lofty Miltonic ring. But if Milton is a poet of light, Greville is a poet of shadow and enveloping darkness. He is constantly driving the vast images of the macrocosm into the little world of man, who then mirrors the outer world's confusion.

Greville's imaginative landscape is not invoked for its intrinsic beauty or interest but rather for its serviceability in representing man's relationship to God. The sense of profundity and scale Greville's poetry imparts is owing to a complex convergence of features. These include his tightly organized metaphysical speculations, the juxtaposition of similar political events (both Christian and Persian) continents and millennia apart, and a texture of allusion to the Greek city-states as well as to biblical history.

Greville's mythic recollections of the Pillars of Samson, the Tower of Babel, and the Fall of Angels and of Man create a sense of momentousness, a cosmic stage where the theater of human passion appears sub specie aeternitatis. Greville attains this distant splendor by resonating the immediate action against the Aeschylean backdrop of his reflective choruses. In contrast to those of Daniel, Greville's choruses function not only as commentators but as institutional participants in the tragedy, fearfully implicated in the progress of Solyman's tyranny. Each of the choruses of Bashas or Caddies (i.e., councillors or judges), of Mohammedan Priests, Mohammedan Converts, and Tartars speaks in its own anguished voice, enlarging the tragedy's purview and confirming its anti-Jacobean political outlook. Through them the tragedy broods on the undermining effects of tyranny upon the institutions of modern government.

Although corrupted by its own vested interests, the Chorus of Bashas cannot forget its oath to counsel kings impartially and to administer justice so that its office is not bought or sold (1.Chorus.118). The power of this self-indictment is vivified by the Bashas' concrete description (which is drawn from Greville's observations of Jacobean government) of the oppressive burdens they heap upon the people:

> Thus Tyrants deale with vs of higher place,
> As drawne vp onely to disperse disgrace.
> *Ecchos* of Power, that pleasingly resound
> Those heavy Taxes, wherewith Princes wound.
> Exhausters of fraile Mankind by our place,
> To make them poore, and consequently base.
> With *Colonies* we eat the *Natiue* downe,
> And, to *increase* the Person, *waine* the Crowne.
> (1.Chorus.29–36)

Against their disheartened acknowledgment of complicity in the Persian tyranny, the Bashas' enlightened understanding of the way government ought to be administered dramatizes the tragic self-division at the heart of

Greville's understanding of the human situation. By the end of their speech, the Bashas have made their own situation into an exemplum of political bondages—"while Man striues to stand by Grace, / He offers Natures free-dome vp to Place" (1.Chorus.215–16).

The second-act Chorus of Mohammedan Priests treats the subject of religious factionalism topically, comparing religion's rule in Persia to that in Christian countries. Both churches have compromised themselves by corrupt practices, the Christians being merely more refined, their laws, doctrines, and discipline all purporting to uphold the "Man-built frame," but in reality supporting only the majestic scepter (2.Chorus.111–12). Government is thus "An Art by which Man seemes, but is not free; / Crownes keeping all their specious guiding reynes, / Fast in the hand of strong Authority" (2.Chorus.115–17).

Presenting a trenchant indictment of the onerous methods of taxation each kingdom employs, the Priests conclude that tyrants so abuse their power that the people's growing poverty eventually reduces the monarchs majesty and exhausts the state (2.Chorus.140–46). In a patent allusion to the state-dominated Church of England, Greville's Priests ruefully acknowledge religion's servile prostitution to such corrupted authority:

> The *Christians* take, and change Faith with their Kings,
> Which vnder Miters oft the Scepter brings.
> We make the Church our *Sultans* instrument:
> They with their Kings will make their Church content.
> They wrangle with themselues, and by dispute
> In questions, thinke to make the one side mute:
> If not, then sacrifice the weaker part.
>
> (2.Chorus.153–59)

For Greville, as for Daniel, republican ideals underlie the gloomy assessment of contemporary institutions. However, since the world is far gone in decay, such ideals have no potency; they exist only in memory to taunt the conscience.

This purview is magnified by Greville's invocation in the fourth-act Chorus of Converts of the archetypal patterns of corruption—the Fall from God of the Angelic Host, and then the Fall of Man. The sense of an imminent dissolution that reaches beyond the fictive stage of the play to envelop the Jacobean world is strong:

> So in that Noble worke of publike Gouernment,
> When Crownes, Church, Souldiers, of the Lawes, doe ouermuch dissent,
> That frame, wherein they liu'd, as fatally, dissolu'd.
> And each in gulfes of selfe-Conceipt, as fatally, inuolu'd.
> Thus reeles our present State, and her foundation waues.
>
> (4.Chorus.103–7)

At the center of this misgovernment stands Solyman. Like the others he is self-divided rather than evil; he sincerely strives to practice "The art of Monarchie" (1.2.233). But, unable to shrug off Rossa's pernicious counsel, Solyman becomes overwhelmed with fear of his son's rebellion and succumbs to the devilish phantasms of the mind: he who is king over other men cannot rule himself. With the sky above him obscured, Solyman resolves to act on his own purblind impulses, saying, "So haue all Tyrants done; and so must I" (4.1.43). Falsely fortified, he orders the assassination of his own son.

In this way self and world are dramatized as afflicted by nature's four warring humors. This condition of being Greville objectifies in the Chorus of Time and Eternity, whose nether realm man can never bridge by his own efforts. In this spirit, too, the Chorus Sacerdotum, placed in revision at play's end, meditates on the impossibility of trying to achieve a state of grace by living according to nature:

> Oh wearisome Condition of Humanity!
> Borne vnder one Law, to another bound:
> Vainely begot, and yet forbidden vanity,
> Created sicke, commanded to be sound:
> What meaneth Nature by these diuerse Lawes? (ll. 1–5)

Unable to feel the light of God and with no self-sustaining ability to fulfill God's law, mankind is left darkling. For Greville in *Mustapha* there is no answer to this personal and political blight. These too are part of man's inheritance and his tragedy.

Under such circumstances violent attempts to redress political injuries through rebellion are foolhardy; they cannot engender a better world. Cataclysmic change invites anarchy, a still further state of degeneration. Comprehending this truth, Mustapha resists the call of the priests to rebel against Solyman's tyranny. Rather than discard his filial obligations or his honor, the values on which family and civilization are based, he knowingly obeys the paternal command that issues in his death.

Thus, for fear of worse tyranny to come, *Mustapha* concludes in an exemplary act of obedience. A century or so later, a political analysis such as Greville's might well have led to agitation for reform, but as a seventeenth-century Calvinist who saw in the present age an irreversible pattern of corruption, Greville had no conception of effective political protest; it offended his metaphysics. Greville's Calvinism, however, was his life's guiding faith, and it gave to his political drama a philosophic, sometimes cosmic vision of man's benighted condition. By contrast, *Philotas* is at once more limited in scope and more animated by Daniel's pro-Essex, factional opposition to Cecil. Its sense of tragedy proceeds from the failed heroism of Essex and from what feels like a young man's awakening to the awesome power exercised by the machinery of modern government.

In their mutual tones of disillusionment and in their concerns with the poisoned relationship between sovereign and subject, the political closet tragedies of Greville and Daniel manifest strong links to the political tragedies of the learned professional dramatists, Jonson and Chapman. After all, three of the four playwrights composed for the Children of the Queen's Revels at Blackfriars, and the fourth, Greville, maintained links with dramatists and lutenists of that theater. Then too, Jonson, like Daniel, learned what it was like to be called to account by Cecil before the Privy Council for composing political tragedy that "paralleled the times." And Chapman, like Greville, was scouring contemporary histories—not of Persia but of France—to find appropriate matter to convey to *his* select indoor audiences an ideal of the immemorial liberty of subjects.

8

Tacitean Republicanism
in Jonson's *Sejanus*

As practitioners of tragedy, Jonson and Chapman display a number of elements in common with such academic dramatists as Samuel Daniel and Fulke Greville. These include a highly rhetorical, often forensic dramatic style, a predilection for gnomic or sententious statement, an inclination to place violence offstage, and even to flirt with inventive forms of choral statement. In *Bussy D'Ambois* (1604), for example, Chapman employed the stage balcony so that certain of his characters could step out of their roles on occasion and speak chorally. In "To the Readers" of *Sejanus* (late 1603), Jonson lamented his inability to discharge "the offices of a *Tragick* writer" by providing a chorus, but emphasized his retention of such revered elements as "dignity of Persons, grauity and height of Elocution, fulnesse and frequencie of Sentence" (ll. 5–24).[1] Both Chapman's and Jonson's tragedies also possess an operatic quality in their great set speeches, which is part of their rhetorical mission—to inspire and persuade.

These stylistic features in Jonson's and Chapman's tragedies are the formal signs of their ethical earnestness. Material evidence of this same high purpose is the concern of both for fit subject matter. For Jonson, Chapman, Greville, Daniel, and even Webster (although not Shakespeare), tragedy meant something like historical truth conveyed in weighty poetic meters. In "truth of argument," as Jonson called it, the lessons of history, which never grow old, appeared.[2] The behavior of illustrious men under the pressure of momentous events was always apt, always applicable, since human nature is at bottom always the same.

When Chapman departed from this accepted practice in *The Revenge of*

Bussy D'Ambois by creating a fictitious hero out of historical materials, he felt bound to summon his greatest eloquence in defending his innovations: "Poor envious souls they are that cavil at truth's want in these natural fictions: material instruction, elegant and sententious excitation to virtue, and deflection from her contrary, being the soul, limbs, and limits of authentical tragedy."[3]

Jonson's Roman tragedies and Chapman's French tragedies (along with his *Caesar and Pompey*) cannot, it is true, be labeled in any simple sense "allegories of Jacobean politics": they did not aim to disguise English characters in Roman togas or French uniforms.[4] "Truth of argument" did not generally work in such a reductive fashion. But in a more profound sense they addressed the momentous political issues of seventeenth-century English life. In short, they employed "truth of argument" to explore the relationship of past to present in the affairs of men of state. In so doing, they chanced the interference and sometimes the outright censorship of the civil authorities, just as Daniel and Greville had. They also fostered a dramatic tradition of guarded political dissent.

The Elizabethan phrase for this practice of composing histories with contemporary application was "paralleling the times." Since Jonson and Chapman (in his *Caesar and Pompey*) viewed Roman history from a decidedly republican perspective, their composition of historical drama was fraught with danger. That is, against the absolutism of Caesar (to whom contemporary princes such as James routinely compared themselves), each championed the heroes of the Roman Republic and of the Senate—notably, Brutus, Cassius, and especially Cato. Jonson's *Sejanus* explicitly announces this republican perspective through the presenter, Arruntius:

> Where is now the soule
> Of god-like CATO? he, that durst be good,
> When CAESAR durst be euill; and had power,
> As not to liue his slaue, to dye his master.
> Or where the constant BRVTVS, that (being proofe
> Against all charme of benefits) did strike
> So braue a blow into the monster's heart
> That sought vnkindly to captiue his countrie? (1.1.89–96)

The Appian way to this ideological perspective of Jonson's is through his prime source for *Sejanus*—Tacitus.[5] The sources a Renaissance writer employed in rendering Roman history usually reveal a great deal about his ideas of historiography. Livy and Sallust, for example, were admired for their impartiality, Plutarch for his probing analysis of character, and Tacitus for his detestation of absolutism and allegiance to Roman republicanism. Among disaffected aristocrats such as those in the Essex circle, Tacitus became a favorite for translation and interpretation.[6] Jonson, we know, professed intimacy with their work, for he told Drummond that the mysterious "A.B." who composed the 1591 Preface to Savile's translation of Tacitus was really Essex himself (*Conv.*, 368–69).

By tradition, Tacitean historians employed precise, analogic parallels that gave their work bite and pertinence. Along with Machiavelli, Tacitus was employed for "prognostic" or "politic" analysis, to determine the principles by which corrupt governments in fact worked.[7] For the historian the problem was to determine which of the reigns of the Roman emperors offered the best paradigm for analogy. In this spirit of prognostic analysis Fulke Greville composed *Mustapha,* and for this reason, presumably, Charles Lamb declared Greville to be "nine parts Machiavel and Tacitus, for one part Sophocles or Seneca."[8] After Tacitus, Jonson's main source is also Machiavelli.[9] These links ought not to be surprising, for Jonson and Greville were both dramatic historians charting the degenerative patterns of government.

Jonson's own testimony, as recorded in his *Conversations with Drummond,* shows his regard for Tacitus as a political model. "Tacitus," he declared, "wrott the secrets of the [Privy] Councill and Senate, as Suetonius did those of the Cabinet and the Courte" (ll. 146–47). Drummond's report of Jonson's boast that "in his Sejanus he hath translated a whole oration of Tacitus" (*Conv.*, l. 602) shows Jonson's interest in applying Tacitus. The boast, moreover, is true. The passage Jonson alludes to is the great speech of Cordus to the Senate on the need, in Tacitus' words, for "uncensored liberty to speak about those whom death has placed beyond hatred or partiality"— in short for freedom to interpret history without fear of reprisal.[10]

The pertinence of this issue in Jonson's age need hardly be emphasized. Greville's action in destroying his *Antony,* Daniel's interrogation for allegedly making treasonous parallels to Essex in *Philotas,* the bishops' burning of the prose satires in 1599, and Marston's repeated calls for freedom of written expression demonstrate the repressive milieu in which Jonson wrote. Elizabethan-Jacobean England was as familiar with the informer as Rome was.[11] *Sejanus* itself testifies to the timeliness of the Roman matter Jonson raises. The *Conversations* tell us that Jonson was brought before the Privy Council to answer charges for his tragedy. Of this event Drummond wrote, Jonson reported having been "called befor ye Councell for his *Sejanus* & accused both of popperie and treason" (ll. 325–27). Elsewhere, Jonson complains he was "accus'd to the Lords, to the *King;* and by great ones" who "urge[d] mine owne Writings against me; but by pieces" [i.e., out of context].[12] Herford and Simpson cite seven extracts from *Sejanus* "on which an informer could fasten."[13]

Not surprisingly, *Sejanus* survives in altered form. Even the 1605 quarto does not contain all of the original text since Jonson probably deleted much offending matter.[14] Jonson himself explains in his address "To the Readers," "this Booke, in all numbers, is not the same with that which was acted on the publike Stage, wherein a second Pen had good share" (ll. 43–45). The hand that held that second pen was almost surely that of Chapman, his scholar friend.

Not a successful play in performance, Sejanus was quickly adjudged a succès d'estime.[15] Evaluators have sometimes challenged even this judgment on the grounds that the villain-hero fails to excite tragic sympathy and that the focus shifts in the last two acts from Sejanus to his cunning opponent, Macro.[16] Such a perspective assumes that Sejanus ought to be a dramatized biography, but Jonson's conception does not answer to this expectation. The form of Sejanus is closer to the chronicle-history, but tighter. Not character but the evolving revelation of the tyrannical state under Tiberius governs Jonson's tragedy. From this perspective we bear witness to and in a sense participate in the dismemberment of an old civilization, the advent of a new, modern state.

Jonson's representation of this period of Roman history demonstrates the political consequences of the new Renaissance theory of government, the raison d'état. In so doing, he set himself against such state ministers and intellectuals as Francis Bacon. "On Ambition" (1597), for example, offers a pragmatic analysis of the means princes should employ to restrain aspiring individuals, thereby revealing Bacon's use of this newer theory of government with its rational exercise of power for its own sake.[17]

Jonson depicts Tiberius not only manipulating the institutions of power— the Senate, the army, the spy system—but also monopolizing the power to represent the state. From this vantage Sejanus dramatizes as a central part of its meaning the means by which the modern state controls the very power of seeing and conceiving. Indeed, the princely practice of overseeing and over-hearing everything becomes one of the tragedy's master metaphors. Vaguely described in the opening scenes as devious and subtle, Tiberius appears at first to belong to the tradition of the sleeping prince who nods while his kingdom grows ever more infected (see 4.215–18, .266–69).[18] In reality, however, he is Argus-eyed. His agents, as Agrippina complains, have "eares as long / As to my in-most closet" and "stuck with eyes, / And ev'ry wall, and hanging in my house" (2.450–54). This ominous imagery of nameless eyes and ears permeates the play, creating an aura of menace that accompanies Tiberius' campaign to control dissident discourse. When Jonson's commentator and choral spokesman, Arruntius, speaks, he must do so sotto voce, and even then is cautioned, "You are obseru'd, ARRVNTIVS" (1.258). Contrary to appearances, then, Tiberius is cat-eyed and sleepless; he gives new, sinister meaning to the medieval ideal of the wakened prince.

In contrast to this subtlety are the cruder machinations of Sejanus, Tiberius' haughty upstart. He's all "plotting" in the manner of the traditional villain-hero. Thus, to feed his political appetites, he schemes to seduce Livia, through her to poison Tiberius' heir Drusus, and by marrying his accomplice to make himself the new heir—all while soothing a seemingly indolent Tiberius.

Through Sejanus' conspiracy and Tiberius' timely counterstrokes, the play charts the relentless logic of self-interest, which illustrates how in the war of everyman against everyman no man is safe. Over such a godless struggle the goddess Fortuna presides.[19] Among the few who offer a principled but talky opposition to this new Rome are Sabinus, Silius, and Arruntius, the play's satiric commentators. These intellectuals have their own way of seeing, conceiving, and representing the Roman identity. The failure of Rome's leaders to constitute their political lives according to their ancient heritage presages, Silius laments, enslavement:

> We, that (within these fourescore yeeres) were borne
> Free, equall lords of the triumphed world,
> And knew no masters, but affections,
> To which betraying first our liberties,
> We since became the slaues to one mans lusts;
> And now to many. (1.59–64).

This point of view even Tiberius shares. Contemptuous himself of his servile supporters, he has been heard to cry out, "O race of men, / Prepar'd for seruitude" (1.52–53).

Those who divine in Tiberius something more sinister than his official image permits become the hunted objects of the emperor's machinery of state. This repressive hunt receives dramatic form in the kinds of dissident discourse that are successively suppressed. In the first instance, the dissident Silius is devoured by his fellow Senators. Slaves of Tiberius' whims, the Senate turns its back on its own traditions of free speech, accusing him of unspecified crimes against the state. The issues are larger than the man (he has been a minor character), but the man grows in stature to meet the event that engulfs him.

Standing up to his accusers, Silius calls attention to the abrogation of due process: "'I' [sic] am a *Romane*. What are my crimes? Proclaime them" (3.168). Tiberius' denial on narrow procedural grounds of Silius' request to have his case deferred (so he can prepare a defense) is just plausible enough to dramatize the legalistic forms in which tyranny loves to cloak itself. Against this king of power, Silius can only denounce the subversion of civil justice— "Why? shall he designe / My day of tryall? is he my accuser? / And must he be my iudge?" (3.199–201). But the gesture is futile. Utterly without recourse, Silius has only integrity of life (like Webster's Duchess of Malfi), and in a set speech of magnificent contempt for his accusers teaches the feckless Senate to mock Tiberius' tyranny by committing a Stoic suicide. The peroration is an excellent example of Jonson's ethical earnestness; it is Jonson's own invention.[20] More than this, the intrusion of this ahistorical matter into a serious historical study reveals Jonson's own commitment to a moralized truth that is more sacred than the mere facts some latter-day historians have revered as *their* standard of truth.[21]

Silius' passionate recollection of the service he has done the state evokes something of that tragic wonder at the disjunction between the lives such loyal men lead and the unjust ends they meet. But in the scheme of the play, personal tragedy is subsumed in a larger cultural tragedy. Immediately following Silius' suicide, Sejanus seizes the historian Cremutius Cordus. His crime, which has no precedent in Roman law, is that his history praises Brutus and Cassius to the detriment of Caesar and the state. Cordus' celebrated scholarly defense, over fifty lines in length, is the oration Jonson proudly translated from Tacitus (*Conv.*, ll. 602). In it Cordus invokes, first of all, the liberal practices in "divine" Augustus' time when there was toleration for political criticism. Second, Cordus observes that other respected Roman histories routinely praise Brutus' virtues. The enabling arguments here, we note, originate in an alternative memory of what the state ought to be, and was.

Cordus' third argument, in answer to the accusation that his book promotes treason because it recounts Brutus' rebellion, is that it is ludicrous to blame the historian for reporting what history and not the historian created. By this argument, Jonson, in effect, makes Tacitus' report of Cordus' case into a timely appeal to free history for what we used to think of as its calling—the recording of objective truth. In Jonson's time history often was the deliberate exercise of partisanship. As examples, the chronicles of Holinshed and Hall, to name only the most prominent, reveal as their ultimate aim the divine justification of the Tudor dynasty.[22] But Jonson's own position, we recognize, does not aim at what we might call impartiality in historiography. To the contrary, his boast to Drummond that he had imitated an oration from Tacitus should be interpreted as a declaration of his republican convictions in historiography. In *Sejanus,* reformist, homiletic history is *Jonson*'s truth.

Said to have "a BRVTVS brought in paralell," Cordus' books are burned, lest they "vpbraid the age" (3.396, 468). Sejanus singles out Sabinus for destruction for the same reason:

> [He] . . . doth taxe the present state,
> Censures the men, the actions, leaues no tricke,
> No practice vn-examin'd, paralels
> The times, the gouernments, a profest champion,
> For the old liberte. (2.308–12).

This charge, heavily underlined in *Sejanus,* is precisely the one that intellectuals in Tudor-Stuart England faced—"paralleling the times." For such parallel representations, the bishops in 1599 forbade the English history play, and other officials lodged the same accusation against Sir John Hayward for his *Life of Henry IV* (1599).[23] For what reason was this parallelism perceived to be so dangerous? Evidently, it offered second sight, that is, an alternative truth previous governments had embraced and by their precedent confirmed. Jonson's own *Sejanus* adeptly wields this weapon by dramatizing as tyrannous this "Roman" suppression of "parallelism." *Sejanus* thus both paralleled the times and ironically prophesied its own fate, for in its original form, it too was censored out of fear that Jonson had used Rome to "taxe the present state."

Having dramatized the suppression of free speech in the public forum of the Senate and then of published discourse reconceiving Rome's past, Jonson portrays the attempt to efface dissident patterns of speech in private houses—in effect all articulations of a possible alternative present. In a scene whose staging visualizes the issue, Sabinus is induced to express his disapproval of Caesar. As he speaks, two informers, presumably on the balcony above, lie ear to ground awaiting an incriminating disclosure.[24] No central figure himself, Sabinus, like Cordus and Silvius before him, is another of Rome's good men whose destruction is part of the disintegration of the eternal city.

With all outspoken opposition silenced, the action contracts to represent the Hobbesian struggle between the opportunists Sejanus and Macro. As Tiberius' instrument, Macro attains a prominence that betokens the wily emperor's quiet move to check Sejanus. In this way we see how the imperial power, effective as ever, rests not on loyalty or even on respect for law, but on the force of intellect and arms.

Argus-eyed Tiberius is this tragedy's Fortuna; his unfathomable motives govern the destinies of all who await his word. In dumb approbation, the Senate proves itself fit for servitude. Blind, it seeks to see with Tiberius' eyes. But Tiberius, as if scoffing, whips its members into a frenzy of apprehension with his equivocal letter. First lauding, then somberly criticizing Sejanus, then praising him again, Tiberius seems to evade the Senate's lurching efforts to embrace his ever-shifting point of view. Tiberius' final, unequivocal command that Sejanus be seized begets an unremarkable compliance. More notable is the Senatorial cry, "Liberty, liberty, liberty. Lead on, / And praise to MACRO, that hath saued *Rome*" (5.748–749)—the enabling "truth" that makes "just" Sejanus' dismemberment by a mob. For lack of enough principled resistance to Tiberius, Rome passes from civilization to controlled barbarism, its ancient institutions and heritage torn apart.[25] But Tiberius, it is clear, will bequeath his new principles of governance, which rest, if that is the word, on the rational exploitation of terror and the systematic suppression of all articulations of an alternative present or, for that matter, of an alternative Roman past.

Arruntius' final speech, obtrusively positioned in the sanctioned 1605 edition, throws the didactic emphasis, it is true, narrowly upon the erring aspirations of those who thirst for great estate, but Jonson's depiction throughout *Sejanus* of the suffocation of Rome's intellectual and spiritual life registers the greater truth. For Jonson's contemporaries with eyes to see and ears to hear, *The Tragedy of Sejanus* warned its readers to beware the possibility of a similar suffocation in England. To judge from the defense Jonson had to make before the Privy Council, the application of his critique to the Jacobean world was all too clearly made.

9

The Power of Princes and
the Integrity of Subjects in
Chapman's French Tragedies

Because Chapman staked out modern French history rather than ancient Roman as his domain, his tragic drama is not often seen, as it should be, in conjunction with Jonson's. In addition to his contribution to *Sejanus,* Chapman composed one independent Roman tragedy, *Caesar and Pompey* (1603–4), a work that links Jonson's Roman tragedies to the characteristic concerns of Chapman's French tragedies.[1] As a successful writer of political tragedy Chapman was, however, more willing to introduce topical satire into his tragedies, thereby creating past and present simultaneously. And whereas Jonson affirmed an ideal of public service, Chapman probed the ethics of a philosophic individualism that set itself above the laws of kings.[2]

The sole setting for Chapman's extant tragedies (*Caesar and Pompey* excepted) is the modern French court. This setting, unlike those of the unstable, petty dukedoms of Italy, permitted Chapman to dramatize the relations between monarch and subject in a settled national state. Modern France had the unique advantage that it was a country much like England but not England, with an established civil law, judicial structure, and heritage (if not of common law) of natural law and rights. Particularly analogous to England was France's feudal aristocracy, which upheld the rights of subjects against the claims of positive law. For a dramatist concerned with fundamental questions of personal integrity and right as against loyalty to one's sovereign, the historical accounts Chapman found of French courts offered vast, unexplored territory for dramatic treatment. Moreover, by drawing his history for the D'Ambois tragedies from a court in living memory and, in the

Byron tragedies, from the current one, Chapman made his French tragedies studies of the corrupted society of modern courts.[3]

Chapman, in fact, went still further. Since the scrupulous representation of another court for its own sake would have amounted to antiquarianism, Chapman, working in the tradition of Renaissance humanism, made his tragedies for use. And *use* in Renaissance parlance meant, not topicality necessarily, but application in the broad sense of timely lesson or theme. This end Chapman achieved deftly, just as he had in *The Widow's Tears*. Without insisting on the point in *Bussy D'Ambois*, he linked Henry III's court (in one early scene only) to that of James by having the French courtiers defame Bussy as "some Knight of the new edition," "out of the Knights' ward" (i.e., from London's Counter prison), and as "some new-denizened Lord" (1.2.111, 116, 154).[4] These remarks only make sense, of course, as allusions to James's "cheap" carpet knights of 1603 and his transplanted Scottish followers. In the Byron plays Chapman with numerous, more evenly distributed references, explicitly yoked Byron's career as Henry IV's favorite, and the lessons to be learned from it, to that of Elizabeth's Essex.

As a composer of tragedy Chapman was also able to depict as he never could in comedy a court world not only out of joint but evil, monstrous. Hence Bussy's opening soliloquy, which reveals the court as a pervasively pernicious influence in which "Reward goes backwards, Honour on his head," in which you "gain being forward, though you break for haste / All the Commandments ere you break your fast" (1.1.2, 99–100). Functioning in a similar, treacherous courtly environment, Byron falls victim to the seditious intrigues of malcontents even King Henry cannot control. Out of such debased courtly conditions, Chapman posed the dramatic question that preoccupied him throughout his career: Under what conditions can heroic individuals reform the court, or at least insulate themselves from its corrupting effects?

More unequivocally than the Byron tragedies, *Bussy D'Ambois* treats this challenge as a heroic enterprise. "I am for honest actions, not for great," Bussy declares in soliloquy, as he resolves to try to "bring up a new fashion, / And rise in Court with virtue" (1.1.124–26). Such a resolve to seek reward for merit at court *and* to present a model of virtuous behavior is an attempt, we realize, to achieve what Bussy's first words have declared to be an impossibility; yet Bussy's daring enterprise—or his attempt at least—merits approbation, for the alternative is to sleep in his green retreat (s.d.1.1.33) with the result that the world will remain as before.[5] The ironies that ensue from this decision are not lost on us as Bussy, claiming to be his own man, appears at court in Monsieur's expensive suit, thus *appearing* to be the kind of dandified courtier that Englishmen disdained (see 1.1.39–41). But Bussy is no inconsequential courtier. His ability to vanquish his tormentors on the dueling field demonstrates that he is no carpet knight, and *the* Nuntius' report of his valor elevates him to mythic status by identifying him by turns with the Titans and Achilles.

Chapman employs the duel as a vehicle for exploring an ideological crux that plays off the claims of personal honor and the authority of the state. By making Bussy's conflict with Henry result from this illegal, vengeful duel, from what Bacon in "On Revenge" called "a kind of wild justice,"[6] Chapman resurrects an issue of feudal rights, a ritual justice, that Jacobean aristocrats were fighting to preserve. The pertinence of the issue grows when we consider that James's administration was determined to eradicate this chivalric practice. James's exhortations on the subject culminated in two royal proclamations and in Bacon's treatise (as attorney general) against dueling (1614).[7]

Chapman, however, treats the issue as a transcendent one based on the superiority of natural rights to positive law rather than as a local issue of personal honor. This more restrictive kind of defense, which the historical Bussy is reported to have made, Chapman relegates to Monsieur.[8] But to Bussy, whose dueling is a capital crime, Chapman gives the argument that Henry should

> make good what God and Nature
> Have given me for my good: since I am free,
> (Offending no just law), let no law make
> By any wrong it does, my life her slave:
> When I am wrong'd and that law fails to right me,
> Let me be King myself (as man was made)
> And do a justice that exceeds the law. (2.1.193–99)

The cornerstone of the argument is that natural law is inalienable and superior to positive law because it is bestowed by God directly. The king's statutory laws, laws for ordinary people, enslave the virtuous man.

This tension between the power of princes and the fundamental rights of subjects was a recurring one in English thought. Parliament, for example, rooted its arguments of subjects' rights in immemorial common law; Chapman's Bussy, following a line of Stoic philosophy, in natural rights. Both positions ultimately address the same problem. If subjects must obey the laws of princes, as most seventeenth-century thinkers agreed, the only constraint upon such powers must come from a set of prior principles that transcend the laws of princes.[9] For this reason the Commons appealed to the "unwritten constitution," before kings held sway, when men, they posited, enjoyed their original liberties unfettered.[10] Chapman's Bussy appeals to natural law, which, all Englishmen understood, no king could rightfully abrogate. As both Bussy and Cato (in *Caesar and Pompey*) present the case, this larger latitude is open not just to anybody but to nature's aristocrats, who preserve untainted nature's highest gift of liberty. Indeed, Chapman's protagonists proclaim a more radical doctrine than Parliament did because they hold that rational men are a law unto themselves, preserving a higher degree of virtue than law can legislate. Bussy's position, individualistic as it is, carries no sense of inherent conflict with kings. Kings ought in fact to welcome the liberty that virtuous individuals preserve intact from the state of nature. Hence the dictum "Who to himself is law, no law doth need, / Offends no King, and is a King indeed" (2.1.203–4). The possibility of the state's safeguarding these original liberties was by no means new to English intellectuals. Edward Coke, for example, expressed such a view when he declared, "It was a Wonder for him to hear that the Liberty of the Subject should be thought incompatible with the Regality of the King."[11]

In Chapman's tragedy Henry *does* endorse this ideal relationship between king and subject. Proclaiming Bussy to be "Man in his native noblesse, from whose fall / All our dissensions rise," he further asserts,

> Kings had never borne
> Such boundless eminence over other men,
> Had all maintain'd the spirit and state of D'Ambois;
> Nor had the full impartial hand of Nature
> That all things gave in her original,
> Without these definite terms of Mine and Thine,
> Been turn'd unjustly to the hand of Fortune—
> Had all preserv'd her in her prime, like D'Ambois.
> (3.2.91–102)

The informing model behind Henry's peroration is not, strictly speaking, that of the Edenic man of Christian myth[12] but early man whose social condition the Stoics, among others, associated with the Golden Age. The position of Cicero and Seneca, authors Chapman knew well, helps to clarify the meaning of Henry's encomium. Before the age of kings, men, "fresh from the gods," possessed greater valor and natural prowess than their latter-day descendants, whom custom subsequently corrupted.[13] Early man also required an act of will to make his original virtue truly complete. Using statuary metaphors (see those in Bussy's opening and closing speeches), Cicero writes, "She [Wisdom] did not create man herself, but took him over in the rough from Nature; her business is to finish the statue that Nature began, keeping her eyes on Nature meanwhile."[14] Man, according to Cicero and Seneca, is the one creature in nature whose virtuous powers must be developed by his own conscious art. Underlying this ideal of human perfectibility is the conviction that man must free himself from the corrupting sophistications of civilized life—in Bussy's world it is the court—before he can realize his limitless potential. Thus, Bussy casts off his Christian fatalism of the first scene and the veneer of the smooth-tongued courtier in the second to live like man new-made by his own inner code.

The king's appointment of Bussy as his "eagle" to reform abuses is proof that Henry believes both that Bussy represents this preferred, original condition of virtue and valor and that this pattern of virtue can be employed in a settled kingdom to effect its reform. This extraordinary alliance between the king and his royal subject, who is independent on principle, is, however, quite short-lived. The alliance fosters one great speech, in which Bussy vows to hawk at the clergyman, the lawyer, and the "Great Man" who "Bombasts his private roofs, with public riches" (3.2.25, 27) until each confesses all and is hanged.[15] But one speech is all we hear. So quickly is Bussy's position undermined by the envious Monsieur that his program is never enacted or even tested.

Although this eventuality may suggest a signal weakness in the play's design, it results rather from Chapman's critical reappraisal of the humanistic doctrine enunciated by Pico della Mirandola, that human beings may determine their own natures by a process of self-fashioning.[16] The humanists' idealist philosophy also implied that by the application of reason and will man could marvelously reform his institutions. Chapman, himself a humanist, but a latter-day one, explores, to the contrary, the extent to which corrupted modern courts exert an ineluctable, pernicious influence over even the most independent of minds. The play's anticourt perspective thus proceeds from the double demonstration that Henry III's faction-ridden, effete French court is not amenable to reform and that Bussy, despite his radical self-fashioning and attempts to rise at court by his own "essais" and vision of the right, is not immune to the court's corruption.[17] Even after being made Henry's eagle, Bussy is rebuked for flying in the royal face and, similarly, Bussy's decision to resort to the conjuring of devils to protect his mistress differs only in motive from Monsieur's conscienceless scheming.

This interpretation of *Bussy D'Ambois* as a humanist's tragedy may be brought into sharper focus by recourse to the remarks of Thomas Greene, who observes that "once the Humanist mind discovered—or thought it discovered—the receptivity of the mind to fashioning, it was very difficult to determine where the upper limits of the fashioning process intervened. It was difficult to know when the ideal of individual development approached the superhuman, the impossible, the divine. Once one begins to dream of ever more noble forms to imprint on the wax of consciousness, one begins to forget the limitations of that wax."[18] Chapman makes these limitations central to his tragedy, for the work implicitly dashes the humanistic dreams of limitless self-fashioning and the reformation of court.

This disconsolate point of view appears to underlie Bussy's belated recognition of the "frail condition of strength, valour, and virtue" and his retreat at the end of the play to an anticourt, *Christian* homiletic: "Let my death / Define nothing but a Courtier's breath" (5.3.188, 131–32). The most that may be claimed is that the prospect of a state reformed by Bussy's herculean opposition to entrenched interests and invigorated by Henry's attempt to unite the modern state to the supernal laws of man in his original estate remains an unrealized vision.[19] The reason for this issue of events may be ascribed to the tragedy's view of nature, as well as courts, as degenerate—a view borne out by Monsieur's prophecy that if Bussy should perish "like a common spirit, / Nature's a Courtier and regards no merit" (4.1.101–2).

Chapman's enchantment with the doctrine of the superior individual as exempt from ordinary positive law found one last expression in his two-part *Conspiracy and Tragedy of Charles Duke of Byron* (1608). But in these Byron tragedies the attack upon the contaminated court world turns more sharply back upon the protagonist himself.[20] Hence, Byron's claim—"neither is it lawful / That he should stoop to any other law . . . / That to himself is a law rational" (*Consp.*, 3.3.142–45)[21]—is undercut with heavy irony. Self-infatuated, duped by flatterers, and filled to bursting with self-conceit (like Dr. Faustus), Byron is anything but a law rational.

But the blame is not entirely his. The execution for treason of Byron, Henry's great warrior favorite, followed by less than a year Elizabeth's execution for the same crime of *her* military hero, the earl of Essex in 1601, a parallel on which contemporaries such as Greville drew and on which the Byron plays also rely.[22] Extraordinarily popular figures, Essex and Byron had fought side by side in the Dieppe and Rouen campaigns and had returned to their respective courts in glory.[23] The subsequent treasons these men committed seemed incomprehensible to those who admired them. People had difficulty grasping what it was that brought these men, each the right arm of his country, to rebellion.

Chapman's Byron plays show that he understood a good many of the underlying issues. In 1604 James had Ralegh condemned for treason, and in the same year the conspiracy of Count D'Auvergne and Lord D'Entragues had been uncovered in France, the perpetrators convicted, and the count sent to the Bastille.[24] These events, along with the Essex and Byron conspiracies, marked the end of the last baronial threats to monarchy in France and England and the successful consolidation of royal power in a new era of peace. To men such as Chapman this new era of peace, which is accurately described as Byron's nemesis, signaled the end of a dream—that these charismatic military heroes might bring back a heroic age.[25]

Chapman's repeated association of Essex with Byron, as when the latter declares, "The matchless Earl" makes "a parallel with me in life and fortune" (*Trag.*, 4.1.133, 135), insured that his two-part tragedy would be powerfully felt in England, even in 1608. This end Chapman achieved too well. The most celebrated scene of *The Conspiracy*, in which Queen Elizabeth, point-ing to Essex's mouldering head at Tyburn, is supposed to have warned Byron during his embassy to London in 1601 to beware ambition, was completely excised by George Buc.[26] Chapman's angry protestation and his disheart-ened description of his plays as "these poor dismember'd poems" (Dedica-tion, ll. 23–24) tell the rest of the story.[27]

Despite this loss, Chapman's conception of the two tragedies remains in focus. Chapman made his *Conspiracy of Byron* the tragedy of a military hero who becomes the dupe of subtle courtiers. In an environment in which blandishments conceal men's true intentions, Byron's qualities of courage and magnanimity are useless to him. Moreover, the displacement such mili-tary men suffered in the idle life at court stimulated discontent and made them prey to such malcontents as La Fin, who cunningly draws Byron toward treason with the taunt "Peace must not make men cowards" (*Consp.*, 1.1.130).

Under Chapman's handling, then, Byron's treason is attributed to a com-plex set of circumstances. On the one hand, Byron's thirst for greater recogni-tion makes him a target for treason. His debilitated spiritual condition, Chapman makes clear, originates, ironically, in Byron's considerable achieve-ments on the battlefield. *The Conspiracy*, on the other hand, stresses the carefully prepared seduction of Byron by the scheming agents Albert, arch-duke of Austria, and the duke of Savoy, and by the déclassé courtier La Fin. An effective but embattled king, Henry cannot prevent his court from becom-ing a snake pit of dangerous intrigue. Byron can win Henry's wars for him, but he cannot win the peace. In this second battlefield La Fin wields the superior weapons and the fruit of his peacetime victory is, ironically, Byron's treason.

Chapman's tragic perspective thus encompasses a great deal more than Byron's megalomania. There is a pronounced anticourt perspective, charac-teristic of Chapman's work, here as well. Chapman's Byron is a genuinely mixed figure endowed with surpassing virtues and gaping flaws and brought down by his glaring weaknesses of character and by the treacherous environ-ment of the court. A heroic aspirer created in the mold of Achilles, Byron provokes wonder at the state of man, both in his seemingly limitless capacity for self-realization and, in a debased courtly environment, his equally limit-less capacity for self-negation.

From 1608 Chapman wrote no more of heroes who claimed to be exempt from positive law. But he never relinquished his desire to dramatize the plight of virtuous men striving to insulate themselves from the corrupting effects of courts, by their self-fashioning to become still a law unto themselves. In his last Stoic tragedies, Chapman created a new kind of tragedy based on the tension between the laws of princes, which good men ought to obey, and the laws of conscience, which are the highest laws for those who are truly free.

Both in *The Revenge of Bussy D'Ambois* (1610–11) and *Chabot Admiral of France* (ca. 1612) Chapman explored the conditions under which a loyal subject could lawfully exercise absolute control over his own life, despite the power of princes. But, unlike his earlier French tragedies, *The Revenge of Bussy D'Ambois* and *Chabot* portray a court in which the scope for heroism is sharply restricted by the king's extraordinary powers.[28] In such circumstances the tragic conflict is more cerebral than in the earlier tragedies. What emerges is a kind of passive resistance to the absolute authority of kings, particularly when it is not balanced by a recognition of the sacred rights of subjects.

Clermont D'Ambois and Chabot are not so much pure Stoics as they are humanist idealists, as was Chapman himself.[29] Furthermore, it is pointless to view Chapman's later tragic protagonists as possessing a tragic flaw; they have none, unless it is an excess of virtue. The tragic flaw, if we must look for one, lies, as K. M. Burton has perceived, "within the social order."[30] And although neither Clermont nor Chabot can reverse the trend toward an arbitrary exercise of absolutism or toward the decadence of modern society, both win converts to their standard by their steady devotion to virtue, and both by the example of their lives achieve a substantial victory over their courtly environments, although it is purchased at the cost of their lives. Theirs is an inward heroism for courtiers in an age of kings.

Although both *The Revenge of Bussy D'Ambois* and *Chabot* could easily be treated at length, the better-known *Revenge* will serve as illustration of Chapman's delicately poised anticourt position in his late tragedies. The problem Clermont is made to face in *The Revenge* is starkly put: How is he to fulfill the sacred call of conscience to revenge his brother (about whose death King Henry III has done nothing) without betraying the king's law, on whose authority civilized life is founded? "Never private cause," declares Clermont, "should take on it the part of public laws" (3.2.115–16).[31] This consideration, negligible in previous revenge plays because the regnant duke or petty king is the very source of lawlessness, assumes critical significance in *The Revenge,* for Chapman's Henry III is lawfully enthroned *and* rules as an unlimited monarch—a sovereign.[32] The ethics of obedience are, however, made difficult to follow for two reasons. The first is that Henry presides, as James did, over a land where "servile trains, and sumptuous houses" abound, while the virtue of poor ones goes uncommended (1.1.157); the second, more telling reason is that King Henry sanctions perfidy.

Henry's highly placed confidant and informer Baligny articulates the position: "Treachery for kings is truest loyalty" (2.1.32); and again, "The King's command / Is need and right enough: and that he serves / (As all true subjects should) without disputing" (3.1.14–16). Biligny's tortuous discourse on this subject, quite different from the Machiavellian shibboleths Marston puts into the mouths of his farcical villains, constitutes a practicable political philosophy. "All acts that seem / Ill in particular respects," Baligny contends, "are good / As they respect your universal rule" (2.1.34–36). This under-standing that the state is the highest political good, subordinate to no extra-political considerations, constitutes Chapman's cognitive political realism.

Chapman conjoins this doctrine of the *raison d'état* to the claims of absolute sovereignty then being asserted on behalf of the French king.[33] These latter claims dovetail with the Divine Right doctrine James had set forth in his parliamentary address of 1610 when he declared, "So is it sedition in Subiects, to dispute what a King may do in the height of his power: But iust Kings wil euer be willing to declare what they wil do, if they wil not incurre the curse of God."[34] It may be observed that the Henry of Chapman's *Revenge* hears Baligny justify royal authority by the same appeal to "the King of kings" and to "th' universal right of your [i.e., Henry's] estate" (2.1.46, 51). By bringing together the doctrines of political expedi-ency and Divine Right in the person of Henry III, Chapman forces his audience to confront the political implications of each.

The ethical issues between Henry, the sovereign king, and Clermont, the absolute subject in whom conscience is king, are explicated by recourse to classical paradigms. For example, Baligny identifies Clermont with "the best of th' ancient Romans"; in him "Rome's Brutus is reviv'd" (2.1.259, 103). Inviting treason, Baligny further insinuates that Brutus "would be the gods' just instrument" to curb Caesar's tyranny and that "sweet Antigone" taught Creon that "though his laws were a king's, they were not God's" (2.1.113–17). Ironically, Clermont deserves the praise Baligny only feigns. However, Clermont's potential to play Antigone's part against Creon or, in conspiracy, Brutus' against Caesar is never explicitly acted out; rather, it remains a possibility that teasingly hovers over this ideological tragedy.

In addition to Chapman's presenting the tragic conflict of his play in terms of political prototypes, he expounds the ideological issue theatrically. Thus, Chapman brings the two value systems into collision when Clermont is drawn into an ambush on the pretext of reviewing the king's troops. Mail-lard's defense of his betrayal, like Baligny's, also provides the occasion for a debate on how one can embrace a philosophy of governance that renders vice indistinguishable from virtue. Unlike earlier popularized renderings of Ma-chiavellian doctrine, Chapman allows that the conflict of his tragedy is between two conceptions of the public good. Maillard's position and Henry's is that the state's good is wholly separable from notions of private virtue; Clermont's, by contrast, champions the older notion that only virtuous personal conduct can serve the public good. Clermont's ideal underlies his tragedy: because he lives by a gentleman's code of honor, he chooses to accept the perjured word of honor of his host Maillard and therefore knowingly enters the trap that deprives him of his liberty.

With the abduction of Clermont, Renaissance individualism finds itself ambushed by that other major Renaissance development, the supramoral state. Thus ensnared, Clermont can only make clear to his opponents that the price of total commitment to one's sovereign is the loss of one's precious autonomy, the abdication of sovereignty over self. As tools of state, Baligny and Maillard become, to use Aristotle's term, "slaves," because they exist to serve the well-being of another.[35] The upright Clermont, on the other hand, is presented as philosophically consistent in fighting valiantly against his captors once the trap is sprung, since at that point he knows that the ideal of honorable personal relations among gentlemen has been breached.

The position is a delicate one. Henry himself is made to understand that Clermont, who is committed to the king's positive law, is no conspirator. Hence, the sententious position Clermont evolves: "Who breaks no law is subject to no king" (4.5.25). But this doctrine brings Clermont face to face with the basic dilemma the play poses—how Clermont is in an unredressed private cause to avenge his brother's assassination without violating public law. When the umbra of Bussy rises to urge Clermont to action, an implied solution appears: "What corrupted law / Leaves unperform'd in kings, do thou supply" (5.1.97–98).

Here the trial by duel, officially condemned in England but not yet discredited, provides Clermont with the means of accomplishing his revenge without committing murder. Peter Bement observes that this resolution, affirmed by supernatural mandate, brings about the restitution of natural law in a lawless state.[36] Clermont's subsequent duel with Montsurry, in which he compels his opponent to recover his long-rusted honor on the sharp edge of a sword, demonstrates the need to revive a decaying nobility by reinvigorating its chivalric code.

In this way the constitutional problems raised in *The Revenge* are not so much resolved as harmonized. Nonetheless, a review of the progress of the play's philosophical argument shows that the duel, employed as a supplement to inadequate positive law, avoids by a kind of fortunate technicality an irresolvable conflict between personal honor and the dictates of the *raison d'état*. Similarly, Henry's decision to free Clermont from prison appears to untie the tragedy's ideological knot without working out the problem.

But it is not Chapman's habit to avoid, in the manner of Beaumont and Fletcher, an ideological stance. Having dramatized the prospect of a well-ordered state in which all the claims of subject, king, and society are reconciled, Chapman allows the implications of Clermont's position to reach their tragic conclusion in the fate of the Guise. If Clermont is freed by Henry, the Guise, Clermont's other self, is suddenly seized, then slain. The king shows himself to "justify" this deed (5.4.42) on the grounds of the public good. In this way the lawlessness of Bussy's assassination is reenacted with the explicit sanction of the sovereign. Clermont, hearing of the Guise's instant death, is left to face the collapse of his vision of political harmony. His mistress, he learns, has lost her eyes weeping for his release. What is Clermont to do? "There's no disputing with the act of kings, / Revenge is impious on their sacred persons," he acknowledges (5.5.151–52). Yet reconciliation of king and subject has become impossible. Clermont has been exposed to the arrogance of power, "To all the horrors of the vicious time, . . . / None favouring goodness" (5.5.186–88). Rather than be a slave to corrupted authority, Clermont commits a rational suicide, again proving that he "who breaks no law is subject to no king."

By turning his sword to his own body, Clermont darkly affirms the inviolability of that narrow space a man may call his own. Chabot, who has suffered the torture of a wounded honor his king has impugned, makes a similar gesture when he dies brokenhearted, despite *his* king's command that he recover. But beneath Clermont's stroke of heroic self-sufficiency and Chabot's loyal independence there lies a humanist's sense of tragedy—the alienation of so much untarnished virtue from the life of state and the spectacle of public-spirited men driven to such melancholy ends.

If the comical satires at the indoor theaters gave English audiences the opportunity to see their king and court held up to ridicule, the tragedies of Chapman, and certainly Beaumont and Fletcher's *Philaster* and *The Maid's Tragedy,* offered far more respectful, even awe-inspiring representations of kingship. The doctrine of the king's two bodies, which distinguished between the fallible man and the divinely ordained office embodied in the king, provided a conceptual framework, acceptable to the government itself, in which the problems of allegiance to one's sovereign could be explored.[37] Theirs was a tragedy for gentlemen—that is, for persons of privilege whose status encouraged the development, which we see typified in the tragic protagonist, of a jealously safeguarded, self-consciously elaborated identity. Bussy, Clermont, and Chabot are not romantic individualists, however; the ambiguities created by their rank also make them conscience-filled servants or supporters of the king.

What, then, made Chapman's brand of tragedy, and that of Jonson, Daniel, and Greville as well, dangerous if not subversive? The form of royal tragedy appears large enough to articulate and yet safely contain, from an official point of view at least, the paradoxes, ambiguities, and tensions the system of personal monarchy engenders. Stephen Greenblatt observes that

the theatrical representation of royalty itself contains the power of subversion—"It is precisely because of the English form of absolutist theatricality
that Shakespeare's drama . . . [he is thinking of *1 Henry IV*] can be so
relentlessly subversive: the form itself, as a primary expression of Renaissance power, contains the radical doubts it continually produces."[38] In this
view *all* representations of authority implicitly contain an assessment of that
power and are therefore potentially dangerous.

Such a perspective in effect deconstructs *1 Henry IV* by eliciting from it
"the radical doubts" of Divine Right kingship even as it celebrates that
power. Subversive content in political drama becomes pervasive, inevitable—which well it may be—but the kind of ideological anticourt tragedy we
have examined here reveals its subversive content in more explicit ways.
Each of the foregoing tragedies treats with critical self-consciousness the
abusive power that royal authority can exert or breed, both in the polity (as
in *Sejanus*) and in gentlemen of honor (as in *The Revenge* and *Chabot*). More
important, each of these tragedies expresses an imagination of alienation,
each views king and court from the vantage of the courtier, the beleaguered
outsider inside, and each depicts his plight as a consequence of a suffocating
but legitimate royal authority. The protagonist-hero of these plays (which
should include Arruntius, as well as Silius and Cordus in *Sejanus*) stands on
the island of his own honor, as removed from the sustenance of the king's
court as a Beaumont and Fletcher setting is from an Elizabethan banqueting
house.

The suasive power of these plays lies, then, not merely in their hostile
depictions of a tyrannical practice of kingship—the palpable anticourt content—but in their painstaking fashioning of what we may call a peerless
noble identity that discovers itself to be distinct from—even if inextricably
entwined with—the authority of the king and of his inviolable law. The
dynamic force of such a conception may be measured against normative
patterns from early Tudor times, in which aristocrats (and by extension all
gentle classes) derived their status as retainers of the king and of his laws.
They, along with the bishops, uphold that cannon of universal law, including
positive law, which is of divine origin and which Hooker promulgated in his
Laws of Ecclesiastical Polity (1594).

Heterodoxy manifests itself as alternative orthodoxy. These take two
primary forms, philosophical and historical. Bussy D'Ambois articulates a
philosophy of natural law that makes him a king of himself. He may thus be
viewed, as Jonathan Goldberg does, as "a royal man, self-crowned and self-
contained," one who "identifies with the king . . . [and] re-presents him."[39]
But it is a mistake to identify him with the king's authority. Bussy is not a
royal absolutist but an absolutist from nature, appealing to a universal
natural law that is *prior* to the king's. Bussy's absolutism supersedes the

king's, and his radicalism (originating in Stoic philosophy) lies not in any synonymity with the kind of authority King James claimed, but in its invocation of an antecedent primal authority.[40] Bussy claims for himself the kind of radical independence from anointed political authority that radical Protestants claimed from anointed episcopal authority.

Sejanus, with its vivid recollections of ancient freedom in republican Rome, resurrects a historical pattern of governance that it opposes to the brute absolutism of imperial Rome. For Jonson, Roman republicanism offered a prior and—given his entopic view of civilization—a preferred model of governance. It takes only a minor shift in emphasis to recognize in this worldview the alienated perspective of Greville's *Mustapha,* a work that expresses the same dismal assessment of modern politics without Jonson's spirit of reform. One step further still and we see in Daniel's *Philotas,* with its treatment of Craterus as a figure analogous to Cecil, the most topically specific expression of Jacobean political alienation. Whether closet dramas or not, professional or private, these ideological tragedies address the social-political concerns of well-to-do audiences, are historically implicated in one another, and manifest an intellectual's alienation from the Jacobean political scene. Seen in conjunction, moreover, with the coextensive personal satires of the decade, with their mockery of James, his Scottish retainers, and his alleged insensitivity to English law and custom, these tragedies reveal a potent anticourt theater addressing ideological and topical concerns simultaneously.

Complementing these two kinds of elite anticourt drama was a sharply distinct form of anticourt drama performed in the outdoor theaters for London's predominantly citizen audiences. The focus of this other class-interested drama was not kings per se but courts, as the decadent embodiment of an unchristian, licentious, irresponsibly privileged way of life. By definition, this form of anticourt drama—Italianate tragedy—*never* chooses Whitehall for its setting. Rather, it seeks out the universal way of courts, and the attitudes it expresses, with its outsiders' field of vision, never appeared in the courtly masques at Whitehall except to be dismissed like a discordant antimasque. Italianate anticourt tragedy is in a sense the antimasque turned back upon the privileged life to uncover an endless, lawless nightmare.

III

ITALIANATE TRAGEDY

1606–1621

10

Popular Anticourt Attitudes

To maintain their dominance over the cities and fiefdoms they had brought within their circle of power, Renaissance courts had to become the radiant center of all. And they did. Kings and dukes, queens and duchesses offered the most liberal recompense for every human talent that could add luster to the pomp of state. Musicians, painters, dramatists, jewelers, tailors, poets, sculptors, architects, and engineers all helped to fashion the spectacle of courtly magnificence. The premium these courts set on conspicuous display often provoked envy and even condemnation from the surrounding cities and the conservative countryside. Yet throughout the sixteenth and seventeenth centuries, courts were the place to be.

To legitimize their authority and to make their courts alluring, Italian dukes, followed by French and English kings, patronized the philosophers and the literary lights of the age. The famous woodcut of the kneeling poet George Gascoigne presenting his book to Elizabeth typifies the pattern of royal and aristocratic patronage that the court encouraged.[1] If Plato's ideal of the philosopher-king could not be met, the Renaissance court offered the rich prospect of a king surrounded by humanist philosophers. For both groups the alliance was beneficial and, not surprisingly, the artist praised the society of the court to which he had gained admittance. Baldasarre Castiglione's *The Courtier* (*Il Cortegiano*) enunciated for the age the practical courtly ideals of refined manners, modesty, cultivation in the arts, personal virtue, chivalric service, and statesmanlike leadership. As a manifestation of humanistic ideals and as a manual of personal conduct, *The Courtier* enjoyed such a phenomenal success that it was translated into all the major European languages, appearing in some sixty editions between its original publication in 1528 and 1619.[2] With similar auspiciousness the English humanist Sir Thomas Elyot published his *Boke named the Gouernour* in 1531, a work that applies Castiglione's principles to the ideal English prince. Like *The Courtier,* it takes up the problem of educating the ministers who will assist the king in governing.[3] In 1561, Sir Thomas Hoby brought *Il Cortegiano* to England with his own brilliant translation, and in 1579 Spenser began to compose his medievalized romantic allegory of courtly service, *The Faerie Queene,* a work in which Elizabeth herself is the inspiring ideal.

But by the end of the century exemplary depictions gave way to real-life observations of courtiers, and that meant satire on their obsequiousness, ambition, insincerity, apishness, effeminate dress, and general uselessness. Jonson's "On Court Worme," Shakespeare's Osric, Chapman's Monsieur D'Olive, and the Frenchified Sir Petronel of *Eastward Ho* testify to the decline of the courtier in early seventeenth-century English drama. So too, popular chronicles and the novella, loosely based on fact, revealed the sensational, seamy side of courtly life. Rosset's *Histoires Tragiques,* Painter's *Palace of Pleasure,* and Belleforest's *Histoires Tragiques,* sources upon which Jacobean dramatists freely drew, are notable examples. Dukes' minions, courtly ladies, and courtly mistresses all had their dressing down.

To many people who stood outside it but felt its power, the court became a frightening institution. Its presence, no less than its coercive example, had the capacity to transform the way people thought and felt. Having appropriated a goodly portion of the wealth of the medieval church, the Renaissance courts of England and Italy had not only weakened a rival institution but had made themselves a secular alternative to it, more luminous in their sphere than the church. Some, who admired this splendor, learned how suddenly the spotlight could turn from one courtier to another. Others, who wished for the courtly light to shine on them, found that it shone brightly on but a few. Among those who stood beyond the verge, such as the city merchants, the tradesmen, and the country gentry—groups that supported the court with taxes—the potential for large-scale alienation was surely present.

In England latent reactions to the court—both positive and negative—tended to center on the court masque. A kind of ritual event that took place during the holiday season, and often on other festive occasions as well, the masque became the great showpiece of the Jacobean court. Everybody with any status attended the court masque and everybody else, it seemed, tried to. Jacobean statesmen conducted diplomacy by deciding which foreign ministers would be invited to the event and where they would sit.[4] For them and for the Jacobean court in general, the masque was *the* ritual occasion where the prominence of one's seat and the costliness of one's attire heralded one's status.[5] For those outside the court, especially in the city of London, the desire to imitate the court vied with envy and disapproval of its excesses. And with good reason.

Between January 1, 1604, and January 6, 1605, five court masques were shown, and on the first of these dates James let it be known that he had paid £40,000 for the main jewel used in "The Masque of Indian and Chinese Knights."[6] With increasing cost these spectacles continued unabated throughout the Jacobean reign.[7] It is hard to believe that James's court, so hardpressed financially, could afford so many extravagant occasions, yet it managed to do so, and with little regard to the expense. In the first decade alone over twenty court masques were performed at a cost for each that ranged from a minimum of £1,000 upward toward £10,000, and on one occasion in Charles's reign over £20,000[8]—handsome figures in an age when day laborers made about £15 a year and parsons, scandalously paid even by the standards of the age, often made an annual living of £10.

The masque also provided an occasion for competitive displays of attire and jewelry. Chamberlain reports that when one lady beneath a baroness appeared at one of these festivities with jewelry worth "better then an hundred thousand pound," the greater nobility could only strive to outshine her.[9] At the nuptials of Princess Elizabeth and the Elector Palatine in 1613, Anne appeared at Campion's "The Lord's Masque" in a gown valued at £400,000 and James with jewelry said to value £600,000.[10] Chamberlain's repeated criticisms of such "excesse of bravery" during the masquing season may have appeared old-fashioned at court,[11] but when his attitudes are placed beside the more severe judgments that sometimes appear in the popular drama, it becomes clear that Chamberlain was touching a national nerve. The city of London was all too aware of such "bravery," as John Pory's account of Jonson's *Hymenaei* (Jan. 5, 1606) suggests: "I think they hired and borrowed all the principal jewels and sets of pearl both in court and city."[12] Moreover, the feminine courtly fashion of appearing with only sheer lace covering the breasts, or on masquing occasions, as Inigo Jones's sketches show, with one or even both breasts exposed, flaunted an aesthetic repugnant to many elements both in city and country.[13] Queen Henrietta Maria so appeared in Jones's masques and Queen Anne wore a gown transparent at the breasts.[14] The court's own disdain for the philistine values of the city further encouraged the development of these daring masquing fashions.

There were also some grounds to support the contention of anticourt moralists that the masque was an occasion for lust. Even in Elizabeth's reign some taint had attached itself to the masquing occasion. For example, in *Euphues* Philautus explains to an indignant Camilla that masquers cover their faces so that they may openly act upon their desires.[15] But in James's reign people reported actual cases of lustful behavior at such entertainments. As early as 1604 a masque was presented at court in which, it was reliably reported, "one woman among the rest lost her honesty, for which she was carried to the porters lodge, being surprised at her business on the top of the Taras [terrace]."[16] The most conspicuous example of the depths to which Jacobean court behavior could fall was reported on the occasion of a private masque performed before James I and Queen Anne's brother, Christian IV of Denmark. Sir John Harington's eyewitness account records with relish the unrehearsed ironies of the allegorical occasion:

After dinner, the representation of Solomon his Temple and the coming of the Queen of Sheba was made. . . . The lady who did play the Queens part, did carry most precious gifts to both their Majesties; but, forgetting the steppes arising to the canopy, overset her caskets into his Danish Majesties lap, and fell at his feet, tho I rather think it was in his face. Much was the hurry and confusion; cloths and napkins were at hand, to make all clean. His Majesty then got up and woud dance with the Queen of Sheba; but he fell down and humbled himself before her, and was carried to an inner chamber and laid on a bed of state; which was not a little defiled with the presents of the Queen which had been bestowed on his garments; such as wine, cream, jelly, beverage, cakes, spices, and other good matters. The entertainment and show went forward, and most of the presenters went backward, or fell down; wine did so occupy their upper chambers. Now did appear, in rich dress, Hope, Faith, and Charity: Hope did assay to speak, but wine rendered her endeavours so feeble that she withdrew, and hoped the King would excuse her brevity: Faith was then all alone, for I am certain she was not joyned with good works, and left the court in a staggering condition: Charity came to the King's feet, and seemed to cover the multitude of sins her sisters had committed; in some sorte she made obeysance and brought giftes, but said she would return home again, as there was no gift which heaven had not already given his Majesty. She then returnd to Hope and Faith, who were both sick and spewing in the lower hall.[17]

To be sure this account is extreme, unmatched by any other in the reign. Nonetheless, there are normative elements in it. The masque and accompanying banquet were staples of Jacobean court entertainment, and on such occasions the king imbibed steadily.[18]

The hard-to-come-by evidence of citizen reaction to the Jacobean and Caroline court masque reveals a noticeable strain of disapproval. In 1609 William Ffarington wrote that "the Comonalty do somewhat murmur at such vaine expenses [of the court masque] and thinke yt that money worth bestowed other waies might haue been conferred upon better use."[19] Other sources as well reflect this perspective. Sir Edward Peyton's *The Divine Catastrophe,* a work not published until the Interregnum but composed by a disaffected Jacobean, declares that in Charles's reign "sin was hatched from an egg to a dragon, to devour holiness of life; insomuch, that the masks and playes at Whitehal were used onely for incentives of lust: therefore the courtiers invited the citizens wives to those shews, on purpose to defile them."[20] Osborne, too, speaks of the Stuart masque with disdain, recalling the vastness of its expense and the gluttony that often followed the performance.[21] Although we may doubt whether Peyton's and Osborne's testimony records the prevailing behavior in James's court, these reports conform to a pattern of censure that attached itself to the Stuart masque as a symbol of excess and vanity, especially from citizen elements in London. The entry of such attitudes into the Jacobean drama provides one of the most accessible but least-opened doors to popular antipathy to the courtly way of life.

Ann Cook has recently brought forth an impressive array of largely external data in an attempt to demonstrate that the privileged playgoers (nobles, knights, gentlemen and gentle ladies, ecclesiastical persons, and professionals)—not the "plebeian" playgoers (which for Cook include laborers, apprentices, household servants, and undesirables of various sorts)—were the decisive clientele in pre–civil war England.[22] Nevertheless, the internal evidence provided by the repertories themselves is as pertinent as the other kind of data Cook adduces in revealing the sociological composition of the various audiences London's theaters supported. Such a sociological awareness of the plays themselves is crucial in my view to an understanding of the Italianate revenge play as it appeared in the first two decades of the Jacobean period because heretofore the form has been examined mainly in generic terms under the broad heading of "blood" or "Senecan" tragedy, rather than as a species of popular drama in which citizen values figure prominently in the unrelenting anticourt outlook these tragedies reveal.

In London's popular theaters, reaction to court culture and to the masque was, it is true, far from uniform. Beginning about 1608 masquelike plays, in imitation of the courtly ones, began to appear in Shakespeare's romantic comedies and in Fletcher's as well. Both dramatists apparently responded to the city's desire to witness a version of what had sent Whitehall audiences into raptures. But Shakespearean drama is not the gauge for all. Italianate tragedies provided an unrestricted outlet for the expression of anticourt attitudes. Webster's *White Devil* and *Duchess of Malfi*, Middleton's *Women Beware Women*, and Tourneur's (or Middleton's?) *Revenger's Tragedy* all display Italian court settings with intense anticourt attitudes and with at least some explicit reference to English conditions. Furthermore, the last two plays employ a masque to achieve an ironic denouement in which the court's sinful revels become the occasion for a poetic retribution. Similarly, *The White Devil* depicts the revenger Lodovico promising, sarcastically, a courtly entertainment—"We have brought you a Maske" (5.6.170)[23]—to achieve his revenge, while *The Duchess of Malfi* employs a fourth act masque explicitly to call attention to the madness of the Jacobean world. Conventional although such uses of masquing are, they all express the debased nature of the court world.

The dramatists named above knew much more about English court conditions than Italian ones, as their emphasis upon the masque (rather than the triumphal entry, intermezzo, or entertainment, which were the dominant forms in Italian court revelry) demonstrates.[24] Other details point in the same direction. *The Duchess of Malfi*, for example, refers to the masquing revels proceeding beyond decency into the early hours of the morning. Such observation, we know, reflects the Jacobean experience, for court masques generally began after supper and continued well into the night. "Tethys' Festival" (1610) was not over "until hard upon sunrise."[25] So too, the masque of crazed citizens in *The Duchess of Malfi* is filled with Jacobean satire and has no analogue in the Italian sources. Indeed, it is an antimasque that depends on the prior development of the antimasque in the Haddington Masque of 1608 and the Masque of Queens, 1609.[26] Unlike Jonson, who invented the antimasque and subsumed its disordering potential within the larger affirmations of the main masque, Webster introduced his antimasque in *The Duchess* as the charnel house image of a debased world from which the Duchess seeks release. The contrast between these two uses of the anti-masque is one measure of the distance that could prevail between citizen and courtly perspectives of the masque.

The citizen perspective, with its frequently moralized Christian homiletic, is, in fact, essential to the type. Webster, Middleton, and Tourneur composed their anticourt tragedies for London audiences in such public theaters as the Globe and the Red Bull. Despite the growing tastes for romantic tragicomedy, these dramatists continued, at least for a time, to address a wider spectrum of Jacobean society. At the same time all three lived lives profoundly touched by the court world west of the city gates. Tourneur, about whom we know little, appears to have spent much of his life in the employ of the Veres and Cecils.[27] The other two certainly came from the city. Webster was born to a family of wagonmakers that had helped to produce London's city pageants between 1591 and 1613.[28] He himself became a member of the Merchant Tailors' Company and composed for that guild the ambitious, sumptuous "Monuments of Honour."[29] Middleton, a bricklayer's son, frequently composed mayoral pageants from 1613 and was appointed city chronologer in 1620.[30] By virtue of their positions within the city, both actively celebrated London and its civic values. The moral stance of these dramatists, their civic allegiances, their London audiences, and their interest in matters of state all helped to fashion a drama in which popular anticourt attitudes found ample and, as it eventuated, permanent expression.

The form of Italianate tragedy also permitted dramatists to play up sensationalized aspects of what Englishmen had heard or read about Italian courts. The Italy of English imagination was thought to be the mother country of evil practice. Real anxiety lay behind these stories of imagination. The degenerate example of Italian life, it was believed, taught traveling

English aristocrats to become "Italianate Englishmen" and to bring their new-learned vices home with them.[31] For example, a contemporary jingle attacking Ralegh asserts that his "originall," which is "too base to tell," came from Italy and "to Italy from Hell."[32] Like the French courts, Italian courts were reputed to teach Englishmen (and ladies) courtly affectations, but were believed to be in a class by themselves for teaching vice. The maxim "An Englishman Italianate is a devil incarnate" attests to the pervasiveness of this contemporary fear.[33] The popular Thomas Nashe brings together all of these assumptions in his *Unfortunate Traveller* when he exclaims, "*Italy,* the Paradice of the earth and the Epicures heauen, how doth it forme our yong master? It makes him to kis his hand like an ape. . . . From thence he brings the art of atheisme, the art of epicurising, the art of whoring, the art of poysoning, the art of Sodomitre. . . . it maketh a man an excellent Courtier, a curious carpet knight: which is, by interpretation, a fine close leacher, a glorious hipocrite."[34] A habit developed, as illustrated by the English visitors to Venice in *Volpone,* of using the Italian experience as a warning to Englishmen. Similarly, the practice in Italianate tragedy of "applying" Italian materials to English circumstances is clearly demonstrated by the marginal notations that appear in the 1631 quarto of Marston and Barksted's *Insatiate Countess* (ca. 1610). Apparently seeking contemporary examples of Marston's lustful countess, at least two seventeenth-century readers inscribed the names of eight *English* countesses, including those of Shrewsbury, Roos, Bath, and Castlemaine.[35]

For the most part, however, Italian courts provided English dramatists not so much with material for topical application—that is not how they function primarily—but for general instruction in the corrupted courtly way of life. Jacobean Italianate tragedy is broadly anticourt, providing occasions for alienated, brilliantly observed portrayals of privilege, ambition, and envy. All of the tragedies discussed here may be viewed, furthermore, as reactions to the humanistic enterprise of the preceding two centuries in Europe, when such figures as Erasmus and Castiglione envisaged the prospect of a truly enlightened civilized court in which princes, surrounded by the arts and men of letters, might blend the life of virtue and statecraft. In England, similarly, More, Thomas Starkey, and Thomas Elyot had proferred the possibility of a virtuous state served by humanistically educated courtiers and princes. But in response to this noble, influential movement, the major composers of Italianate tragedy portrayed, to the contrary, the horrific "reality" that the glorification of human values had produced in practice in modern Italy's Renaissance courts. Far from bringing human beings closer to the Divine Reason, the courtly exaltation of wit and will is represented by Tourneur, Webster, and Middleton as cutting men off from God and leaving them spiritually blind.

11

Economic and Social Alienation in *The Revenger's Tragedy*

It may be true that *The Revenger's Tragedy* presents a fanciful "symbolic 'Italy'" of perverted sophistication and moral corruption, of atheistic depravity, political treachery, abandoned sensuality, violence and vendetta,"[1] but, then, it is equally true that the tragedy provides a searing economic and social satire on the privileged courtly life. No other Jacobean tragedy depicts from the perspective of the dispossessed the decadence of court luxury and the aristocratic exploitation of the legal system. And although the locale is imaginatively generic, "A duchy of Italy," *The Revenger's Tragedy* draws freely upon materials from Guicciardini's *Storia D'Italia* and other historical sources.[2] The allegorical mold in which the characters are cast suggests, furthermore, not fanciful invention but a desire in the spirit of medieval homiletic to vivify general moral truths and to write bold judgments on God's lapsed courtly creatures.

To be sure, the play exhibits a sardonic, almost giddy humor—a "subversive black camp" as one commentator calls it[3]—but even this parodic wit issues from a hostile, ironic vision of courts and from its Reformation spirit. Vindice's self-conscious parody of courtly mores ironically celebrates his understanding of the court world's depravity as well as the conventions by which such depravity begets its poetic requital in the theater. When Vindice exults, "'Tis state in music for a Duke to bleed," or, "When the bad bleeds, then is the tragedy good" (3.5.218, 199), he is being much more than campy or parodic; he is savagely commemorating a perfect poetic retribution on a living court that one expects to prevail only in art. Revenge in *The Revenger's Tragedy* is parodic, angry, and grotesquely just.

Given its trenchant social satire, *The Revenger's Tragedy* could perhaps be dubbed "radical," as Jonathan Dollimore claims,[4] but far from rejecting received social values, it draws its convictions from a righteous, native, antihumanistic, Christian conservatism. That is to say, its hostility to courts may be explained in terms of a perceived debasement, as the example of petty Italian courts showed in extreme measure, of the humanistic glorification of man's reason and its commendation of comfortable, even luxurious living. In reaction to what *The Revenger's Tragedy* portrays as a riot of the senses, it emphasizes the imminence of God, whose "eternal eye" sees all (1.3.66), and the ultimate end of human existence, death and judgment. And in answer to the glorification of man's reason, whose debased expressions are "the reason of state" and the politics of self-interest, it portrays the madness of reason that cuts man from the chain that ties him to God.

Vindice's opening words, "Duke! royal lecher!" sets the mordant tone for the revelation of the royal way of life. Addressed to the skull of his once-betrothed lady Gloriana, whom the Duke poisoned after she refused to submit to his lust, the soliloquy provides a sexual motive for Vindice's vengeance. Broad social and economic motives follow. Vindice invokes Vengeance as "murder's quit-rent," the rent paid to a landlord by a free-holder.[5] He then makes the allegorized Vengeance a "tenant to Tragedy" (1.1.39–40). The metaphor establishes a class relationship between Vindice, the tenant, and Tragedy, whom Vindice will repay by murdering the Duke, the most corrupted landlord of all. A "terror to fat folks," Vengeance will reduce the wealthy to a skull "as bare as this" (1.1.45–49). To Vindice, retribution is thus more than a duty; it is the instrument that rectifies the injustices of social status.

In this manner the melodramatic revenge motive for Gloriana's poisoning yields to social and economic grievances, personally experienced. The play in fact insists upon this purview. By entering the service of the Duke's son Lussurioso, Vindice undertakes a poetic retribution for his father, who died of "discontent, the nobleman's consumption" (1.1.127). The preferment for which the father languished opens to the son, an outsider on the inside, a disguised Vindice become a Piato, a hidden one. Once established inside the "accursed palace" (1.1.30), Vindice immediately finds a third revenge motive as Prince Lussurioso instructs him to procure his own sister Castiza.

In the allegory of the tragedy, the spiritual death that court life portends is brought immediately to bear on Vindice's own family members. Significantly, Lussurioso's instructions indicate in a premonitory way that the seduction of Castiza is to appeal to the economics of her condition. Vindice is to assault the "portion of her soul" and bring Castiza into "expense" "like a stock of money" (1.3.113–16). The entire scene emphasizes the economic motive. Recognizing the lure of a life of comfort for poor folk, Castiza replies, "Were not sin rich, there would be fewer sinners. / Why had not virtue a revenue?" (2.1.6–8). This rebuttal in turn prefigures Vindice's successful temptation of his mother. "Madam, I know y'are poor," he asserts bluntly, "And, 'lack the day, / There are too many poor ladies already" (2.1.76–78). Vindice's cynical advice is, in effect, that Gratiana raise her estate upon her daughter's fall,

> And call her eyes my tenants; I would count
> My yearly maintenance upon her cheeks,
> Take coach upon her lip and all her parts
> Should keep men after men, and I would ride
> In pleasure upon pleasure. (2.1.95–99)

Beneath the surface glamor of the noble life, beneath even Vindice's mimicry of courtly Petrarchan poetry, is the unmistakable moral vision that culminates in the ironic suggestion of orgasmic delight brought on by the provident decision to prostitute a daughter.

The sociology of Gratiana's situation quickly leads to the expression of grievances. Only the hard, joyless life that this tenant widow leads could make this "pleasured" life of a great lady so appealing. Economic exigency makes virtue hard. Castiza, Vindice points out, has no prospects outside the court. Without a portion, she can at best live upon friends, at worst "fall to thousands" (2.1.208–11, 186). But as a court drab, she falls only to one, and such a one as can make her "forehead / Dazzle the world with jewels" (2.1.187–88). Castiza's capitulation before this temptation, and her own prideful wish to make poor "petitionary people" like herself envy her upraised estate (2.1.188) is, of course, deplorable, even grotesque, since her son effects it, but there is a naturalistic pathos that accompanies her double unmothering. The homiletic point could not be more feelingly put: "When his tongue struck upon my poor estate," Gratiana acknowledges, he "made my virtues bare" (2.1.107–8).

The economic analysis of Gratiana's family is soon expanded to include the society at large, this time with a pronounced Jacobean emphasis. In summing up his satiric counsel, Vindice recollects a series of events shaped by specifically English circumstances: "It was the greatest blessing . . . / When farmers' sons agreed . . . / To wash their hands, and come up gentlemen" (2.1.214–16). Lands once measured by the surveyor's rod, in what Vindice calls "The commonwealth," are now measured by tailors "by the yard" and the trees, "those comely foretops of the field, / Are cut to maintain head-tires—much untold" (2.1.217–21). The deforestation of the English countryside, a continual development through the seventeenth century, was promoted by the sale of manorial estates and by the crown itself, which sold substantial portions of its permanent land holdings.[6] Computations of timber sales in Cecil's lifetime have been put at £34,580 and combined land and timber sales between 1606 and 1610 at £45,000.[7] As Vindice depicts it, a productive land is being depleted of one of its few natural resources, and once-productive farmers are being transformed into fops. In *The Revenger's Tragedy* the recurring picture of velvet-attired men and women riding in coaches bespeaks a country embarked on the high courtly road to ruin, all brought on by an alliance of convenience between new commercial and old courtly interests.

These evocations of economic blight yield in the middle acts to their opposite, the luxury and license of court life. Chief among these is the scene Vindice stages for the lecherous Duke, in which he dresses Gloriana's skull in the attire of a pretty whore. Although interpreted by an earlier generation as a manifestation of Tourneur's prurient obsessiveness,[8] the imaginative focus for the scene is fixed, first, on the privileged way of life, and, second, on the allegorical Christian theme, lust as damnation and death. Vindice's mock-gracious address to the newly attired skull reveals his contempt for the courtly breeding that beautifies what is still prostitution and refines what is still sin with discretion:

> Madame, his grace will not be absent long.—
> Secret? ne'er doubt us, madame. 'Twill be worth
> Three velvet gowns to your ladyship.—Known?
> Few ladies respect that disgrace: a poor thin shell!
>
> (3.5.43–46)

Vindice's mimicry of courtly boudoir dialogue exhibits a repellent attractiveness in rendering with such precision negotiations for the bartering of chastity. The exhilarated cynicism beneath the self-produced colloquy betrays the satirist's moral vision: however resplendent the wardrobe, the soul inside the body is bare. This, not sexual prurience, is the obsessive theme of *The Revenger's Tragedy*.

In fact, there are moments when the parodic laughter behind Vindice's ventriloquism is suddenly superseded by blunt indictment. In a hauntingly effective speech, Vindice asks,

> Does every proud and self-affecting dame
> Camphire her face for this? and grieve her Maker
> In sinful baths of milk, when many an infant starves,
> For her superfluous outside. (3.5.83–86)

Here, the ironic mask is dropped, replaced by a direct expression of anger and sympathy. So too, the indictment of privilege implied by previous images of economic oppression becomes explicit in what is really a simple juxtaposition of the contrasting life patterns of extreme poverty and luxury. But the simplicity carries its own subtleties. The implied imperviousness of the proud dame to the starving children produces a powerful effect as does the evocation of many starving infants. Thomas Bastard summarized the problem when he wrote succinctly that England had "So fewe rich, and so many poore."⁹

The evocations of want in *The Revenger's Tragedy* are part of its tragic purview; they prepare for Vindice's revenge upon the court world. Whenever Vindice gleefully reports that things at court go "In silk and silver, brother: never braver" (1.1.52) or that the palace is full of "stirring meats," "Banquets abroad," "musics, sports," and "Nine coaches waiting" (2.1.195–202), he is exulting because the court is living out that decadent life that merits his anticipated vengeance, indeed excites it. This desire for retribution inspires Vindice's poisoning of Gloriana's skull. The Duke, in wooing his shy country lady, literally acts out his spiritual damnation; he kisses death and with lust engenders. Vindice's religious purpose, as he asserts with self-evident awareness, is to "put a reveler / Out of his antic amble" both at "unclean brothels" and "forgetful feasts" (3.5.90–94). Through the counterspectacle of the horrific skull, Vindice would bring the rich to see God—or Satan. Vindice's appetite for vengeance is itself fed by the Duke and Lussurioso's lustful appetites. Imagistically these appetites are rendered in the tragedy's two predominant clusters, money and food. Their interrelationship is an intimate one since the money images bespeak venality or the buying of bodies, and the food images appear in contexts that suggest excess; both spell out varieties of exploitation or greed. The entire tragedy may be termed a courtly banquet of lust because only the court is improvident and daring enough to try to satisfy all human cravings.

Just as the satiric representation of lust culminates in the murder of the Duke as he kisses the bare bone of Gloriana's skull, the satire on political lust culminates in Vindice's second revenge upon Lussurioso and the Duke's politically ravenous whelps. The hyperbolic panache of these farcical subplot scenes aims to ridicule that process of Renaissance statecraft that elevated human cleverness, or wit, in matters of this world above all moral considerations. This process, which the humanist movement had inadvertently abetted by its emphasis on cultivating a self-conscious awareness of one's virtue and cleverness in this world, is exhibited preeminently in Lussurioso. His self-congratulatory political wit, which shows that he sets himself above his fellow man and in the process has separated himself from God, is apparent in all his machinations, and these in turn are underlined by his clever maxims of statecraft, which reduce human beings to instruments: "Slaves are but nails to drive out one another"; "discontent and want / Is the best clay to mold a villain of"; "He that knows great men's secrets, and proves slight, / That man ne'er lives to see his beard turn white" (4.1.70, 48–49, 67–68).

A very similar kind of self-glorifying political cleverness reveals itself among the Duke's stepsons in their attempts to reverse through "flattery and bribes" (2.1.90) the capital judgment on the Youngest Son for rape-murder: "'Judgment in this age is near kin to favor'" (1.4.55); "Judgment speak all in gold, and spare the blood" (1.4.61); "Faiths are bought and sold; / Oaths in these days are but the skin of gold." (3.1.6–7).[10] The emphasis here, as in Lussurioso's speeches, is on knowledge, in fact mastery of statecraft reduced to principles—the special province of the young generation. This is the new "orderliness" that the study of political science produces, the misshapen, novel end of humanist learning. Significantly, this *sapientia* celebrates its accomplishments with eloquence, that outward form of courtly virtue (*virtu*) also misbegot of the new learning.[11] And underlying these parodic commemorations in epigram of crooked achievement is an outraged sense of civic injustice, of the corruption of officials in their public capacity, and of social grievance—that justice belongs to the well-to-do since they can buy it.

The long-awaited, grand revenge upon this newly configured court occurs, appropriately, during the banqueting scene and masque. The banquet, the outward expression of Lussurioso's prodigality and of Renaissance luxury generally, and the masque, the symbol ne plus ultra of the glory of the Renaissance court, commemorate Lussurioso's installation and, by extension, the temporal glories of court culture. Against these images of courtly extravagance and spectacle, *The Revenger's Tragedy* introduces another spectacle, magnificent and inexorable—a heavenly thunder and "a blazing star"[12] (s.d.5.3.0.3.41.2)—which signify the imminence of divine retribution. The masque Lussurioso summons to confirm him begets instead the two conspiratorial antimasques, as it were, of Vindice and the stepsons. Like produces like. Courts that promote appetite and self-advancing policy eat themselves up. Hence, the parodic design of the ending, in which Lussurioso's half brothers slay him, each brother in turn successively proclaiming himself duke only to be knifed by the brother next in line. This is the farcical rendition of ambition's self-destroying course, the last irreverent running gag on the glorification of policy and selfhood in Renaissance courts. This self-conscious toying with denouements *is* campy, exceeding in splendid ludicrousness Mendoza's dim-witted machinations in *The Malcontent*, but it also carries with it the contemporary perception embodied in the English proverb "At Court everyone for himself," as well as Guicciardini's empirical attribution in *La Historia D'Italia* (1561; English trans., 1599) of Italy's political decline to reckless individualism.[13]

Against the two retributive actions that move toward the judgment and damnation, there is one redeeming countermovement. Significantly, it takes place outside the palace gates in Vindice's mother's house. Whereas the courtly world prizes the amorous senses and elevates courtly dalliance to a way of life, the native medieval tradition is pietistic and misogynistic. These last are the values of *The Revenger's Tragedy*. Inside Vindice's own house, the sons administer a redemptive scourging to their mother—"Who shall be sav'd when mothers have no grace?" (4.4.27)—until she weeps in penitence and regains her maternal place. But even in this action the homiletic retains its homespun, anticourt bias:

> *Vind.:* [To be] A drab of state, a cloth o'silver slut,
> To have her train borne up, and her soul trail i'th'dirt,
> Great—
> *Hip.:* To be miserably great, rich, to be
> Eternally wretched.
> *Hip.:*　　O common madness. (4.4.72–75)

The class-laden term *common* paradoxically proclaims the play's judgment of privilege—to be great is to be common, to fall prey to the temporal distractions of great place.[14] This notion of the common is one of Vindice's idées fixes. He boasts for example that Gloriana "Shall be reveng'd after no common action" (3.5.70). The term ironically points to the talionic justice that marks Vindice's desires from the outset, but it also deconstructs his abhorrence of the aristocratic life. Vindice's own revenge is to be inventive, "rare," exotic; he will be the aristocrat of revengers. The retribution he wreaks on the Duke and Lussurioso satirically celebrates and poetically inverts the court's own debased revels, a grotesque recreation of royal entertainment. It both mimics and unmasks the court masque. In this sense Vindice's revenge-masque is true antimask, and his witty revenge the triumph of the common (i.e., universal) truth of judgment over all sophisticated maskings, over all arrogant, man-made celebrations of status and privilege, as court masques are.

From Vindice's point of view his revenge of Gloriana is a kind of wild "Gloria," a providential confirmation, as it were, of the Eternal Eye, whose agent Vindice believes himself to be. Through his inventive staging, the courtly dance of lust is translated into its spiritual equivalent, perdition made gay. The court amble is the dance of death.[15] But as his self-congratulatory revenges reveal, Vindice is himself caught up in the prideful arrogance of the court, reflecting a mirror image of its horror. Thus, flushed with blood-lust after the murders of the Duke's ambitious brood, Vindice giddily reveals his witty murder of the old Duke. Seized by Antonio, Vindice becomes the play's last victim, its final object of satire.

This dehumanization and satiric exposure of the title figure has appeared to some to make for a deficient form of tragedy.[16] Such a response originates, I think, in the assumption that tragic waste, as A. C. Bradley developed the idea, makes for the best kind of tragedy.[17] But Tourneur's play does not aim at any Shakespearean glorification of man and his works; Vindice is not and ought not to be perceived as a diminished Hamlet. *The Revenger's Tragedy* is, furthermore, no humanistic celebration of the blending of courtly and Christian ideals; it is a satiric vision of modern court life presented with a Reformation zeal, and it employs all its moral art to expose the spiritual blindness that accompanies the glorification of man, especially in the courtly world, where the prideful arts and sinful luxury abound.

12

Spiritual Alienation and Anticourt Application in Webster's Tragedies

The daunting amount of criticism *The White Devil* (1610) and *The Duchess of Malfi* (1614) have attracted has effectively canonized these tragedies as "universal works of art."[1] But one consequence of this elevation has been a slighting of the relationship between artist and audience, the context in which meaning is communicated. Although my analysis of Webster's tragedies, with emphasis on *The White Devil*, makes no claim to be definitive, it does seek to draw attention to several overlooked dimensions of these tragedies. My aims are to assign these works a distinctive place within the evolving subgenre of Italianate anticourt tragedy, to demonstrate that these plays are framed by a citizen perspective (in *The White Devil* in particular, Webster shapes our experience of the court world through the alienated perspective of an impoverished family), and, last, to establish that the Italian locale of these tragedies blends with a Jacobean frame of reference. In this last respect, my intention is to argue not that these plays function as topical allegories but, on the contrary, that their tragic perspective originates in a worldview of courts that includes England's. The universal application of these tragedies need not be denied, but we must understand that their tragic vision derives from a disenchanted citizen's perspective that Webster communicates to his London audience. The homiletic intention behind these tragedies, the themes of courtly reward and punishment, and Webster's use of the "White Devil" motif to signify in its broadest application the corrupted world of courts are all integral to the anticourt, citizen perspective in these plays.

The White Devil and *The Duchess of Malfi* mark a notable departure from

Tourneur's and Marston's Italianate revenges in that they abandon the reformist bent that invigorates these earlier works. For example, in its revised 1604 version, *The Malcontent,* a prototype for Italianate revenge tragedy, concludes with the admonition,

> Yet thus much let the great ones still conceive:
> When they observe not heaven's impos'd conditions,
> They are no kings, but forfeit their commissions
> (5.6.142–44).[2]

Kings stand warned in this work to obey God's law or risk losing the allegiance of the subjects. Webster, however, displays no such reforming civic purpose in his Italianate tragedies; yet he retains Marston's and Tourneur's satiric approach, for it is dispirited insight, not reform, that Webster offers.

The virtual absence of the reformist impulse in Webster must not be construed as an abandonment of an ethical viewpoint, however.[3] On the contrary, *The White Devil* and *The Duchess of Malfi* bring to a culmination the satiric indictment of court life, a feature common to the major Italianate tragedies. As Bosola's premonitory rebuke to his princely benefactor illustrates—"I would have you curse your selfe now, that your bounty / (Which makes men truly noble) ere should make / Me a villaine" (Duch., 1.1.295–97)[4]—the stamp of judgment is affixed to this perfidious court world from the outset. The reasons for this state of affairs are twofold: the court, unmasked in its true operation, has no need for virtuous men; it only seeks, in fact prefers, courtiers who will behave as functionaries to serve their prince's pleasure and the business of state. Second, the injunction, derived from both the native Christian and the learned humanist traditions, that princely power justifies itself by a godly solicitude for the commonweal, is shown to be completely undermined by purely temporal considerations of power and will.

In *The Duchess* and *The White Devil* Bosola and Flamineo, each of middling birth and needy, become the parasitic observers of a complex, subtle, high-spirited world, vicious beyond reform. Their alienation provides the vantage point from which we, like Webster's public theater audiences, experience the corrupted courtly ways of great ones. In both tragedies, moreover, the point of view is that of the disenchanted, Paduan-educated outsider on the inside—the neglected scholar (as Flamineo is) and the scholar-soldier (as Bosola is), both with lost ideals, cynical wayfarers in modern courts.

Webster's tragedies are, of course, anatomies of court life, not merely by virtue of Bosola's and Flamineo's choric commentary, but by the structure of the plays. Beneath the dazzlingly intricate plotting of *The White Devil,* for example, the unremitting anticourt outlook communicates itself from several perspectives (in what becomes an organizing principle) through Webster's depiction of the fortunes of an impoverished family of the gentry trying to make its way at court. To be sure, Vittoria, the play's "white devil," and her cynical, clear-seeing brother Flamineo stand out more prominently than their virtuous sibling, Marcello, or their widowed mother, Cornelia, who speak for an inoperative ethical code, but the family emphasis is there; so is the class perspective.

Each of the characters in Cornelia's family reveals an aspect of the blight the court world engenders. The deceased father is accounted for as one who (like many English country gentry) "prov'd himselfe a Gentleman, / Sold al's land, and . . . / Died ere the money was spent" (1.2.310–12). The virtual necessity of Cornelia's children going to court, a place they all believe to be corrupt, proceeds from the family's subsequent impoverishment. Flamineo, to cut a path to what he calls "mine owne preferment" (3.1.37), admits bringing his sister to court and pandering her to Bracciano. Marcello, the only sibling still trying, like Chapman's Bussy, to rise at court (the Florentine court) with virtue, offers a sharp counterpoint by castigating his brother for lack of ethics, but Flamineo in his turn offers the unforgettably prophetic rejoinder that Marcello's virtue is insufficient even to keep fresh chamois on his back. The aura of despair underlying all their efforts is aptly captured in Cornelia's own choric remonstrations—"What? because we are poore, / Shall we be vitious?" (1.2.307–8). She speaks for the uncourtly, wholly inoperative value system learned in the family's precourt days.

The contrasting ethical behavior among the family members is basic to Webster's tragic conception, for in the scheme of *The White Devil* the Marcellos and the Flamineos, the virtuous and unvirtuous alike, their hopes shattered, come to the same inglorious end. Furthermore, there appears to be no possibility of rising at court with virtue. This state of affairs is not rendered with the free-lancing hyperbole of *Antonio's Revenge, The Malcontent,* and *The Revenger's Tragedy,* but with a kind of authenticity of detail that originates in the sources that Webster followed so closely.[5] For Jacobean audiences this care for verisimilitude must have produced the shock of déjà vu. Flamineo reports, for example, following at his tutor's heels in Padua for seven years. After finding no suitable employment, he says he entered Duke Bracciano's service, "visited the Court," and returned "More courteous more letcherous by farre, / But not a suite the richer" (1.2.319–20).

Flamineo's experience at Padua reproduces those of an entire class of Englishmen. In the first two decades of the seventeenth century, the number of educated Englishmen rose beyond the capacity of the society to absorb them.[6] The universities, as Mark Curtis has shown, "unwittingly worked against the peace and tranquility of the realm not because they instilled subversive doctrines but because they prepared too many men for too few places."[7] The result was that men like Flamineo were constrained to take on menial positions or, if they dared, to try their fortune at court. Since the court was already overcrowded with noninheriting sons and with impoverished offspring of spendthrift gentry like Flamineo, the opportunity for advancement was slight. At the same time, educated courtiers such as Flamineo learned firsthand about the abuses of the patronage system, a knowledge that made their life situation less tolerable than ever.[8] His problem, like Bosola's, thus becomes not simple neglect but disillusionment. Reared intellectually in the humanistic environment of the University of Padua—as many Englishmen had been—Flamineo imbibes, as his own account reveals, a desire for public service, but finds no fit place to exercise his talents, and the humanistic program to bring a standard of ethics to the intractable world of public service in princes' courts proves, as Marcello and Flamineo each discovers, a vain ambition.[9] Hence, Flamineo's cynicism.

For these reasons thousands of disenchanted and (to use the dramatic term) "melancholy" types from professional and merchant families and the lesser gentry added their own disillusionment to an already gloomy Jacobean society. Intellectuals such as Webster, who appears to have lacked a university education, or Chapman, who attended Oxford for a time, needed no book to tell them what it felt like to be a Flamineo or Bussy D'Ambois.[10] In a real sense, these people (like the hoard of unemployed academic professionals produced in the United States in the 1970s) constituted a new, truly underprivileged class.

Contributing to Flamineo's negative depiction of court life is Webster's depiction of the court itself. The opening scene, in which Count Lodovico explains his banishment in terms of "Courtly reward / And punishment" (1.1.3–4), announces the theme.[11] Not only do courts frequently reward *with* punishment, but they also reward the iniquity of others. A prime example is Vittoria. After suggesting to her lover, the Duke of Bracciano (under pretense of recounting a dream), that Bracciano's wife, Isabella, and her own husband, Camillo, be murdered, Vittoria is rewarded with a life at court in which she can indulge her tastes for extravagant living.

Vittoria, like Lodovico, learns this courtly way, both in her tastes and her vengeance. Her treacherous cunning and extravagant lifestyle both receive a courtly punishment from the hypocritical Medici. At her trial for adultery and murder, Cardinal Monticelso depicts the dazzling environment in which Vittoria lives, accusing her of "counterfet[ing] a Princes Court, / In musicke, banquets and most ryotous surfets" (3.2.78–79). "Her gates were choak'd with coaches, and her roomes / Out-brav'd the stars with severall kind of lights" (3.2.76–77). For Monticelso, Vittoria is sham royalty, and the implication is that she, like a deprived person, has become a glutton for courtly ways she never knew before. Vittoria's defiant rejoinder that her only sins are "beauty and gay clothes, a merry heart, / And a good stomacke to a feast" (3.2.216–17), carries forward Webster's detailed evocations of the rich courtly life, echoing Court Lodovico's account of his own ruined fortunes, in which he consumed his entire estate (as did numerous Jacobean courtiers) in three years' time with "damnable degrees / Of drinkings" and "prodigall feastes" (1.1.18–22). Both scenes suggest that the uninhibited courtly life encourages human beings to exalt themselves as if they are gods. In this we discern the attack of a disillusioned humanism as it directs its satire against the Italian Renaissance courts that had become centers of human indulgence, not of reason and balance.

The homiletic strain so prevalent in *The Revenger's Tragedy* is less prominent in *The White Devil;* by contrast the problems of contemporary court life are treated with greater complexity. Thus, Webster depicts Vittoria, like Flamineo, as one both lured to the court and corrupted by it. Partly for this reason, despite her complicity in murder and her obvious sensuality, he accords her a strong measure of sympathy. But not just sympathy. Vittoria also plays the court critic, but from a citizen rather than an Olympian viewpoint. Her persistent theme is how authority misuses its powers to render the weak helpless. Her sham trial and brilliant defense in which she turns upon her accusers with a prosecutorial show of her own, crying, "A rape, a rape! . . . Yes you have ravisht justice" (3.2.285–86), alerts us to the great web of social injustice in which her own crimes are contained. Enamored as she is of the courtly artifice, Vittoria identifies herself with ordinary people, not courtiers, caught in the vise-grip of great institutions. Even at her death, the taunt she flings at her muderers—" 'Twas a manly blow, / The next thou giv'st, murder some sucking Infant, / And then thou wilt be famous" (5.6.233–35)—invokes the processes of simple nature as against artful cunning and strength. Despite the tragedy's hard, scintillating surface, the underlying pathos of victimization is difficult to miss. Indeed the theme is hammered into the structure of the play and first appears explicitly in the closing sententiae of the first scene—"Great men sell sheep thus, to be cut in peeces, / When first they have shorne them bare and sold their fleeces" (1.1.61–62). The victimizers, we note, are those of aristocratic estate who use up and then butcher those beneath them as if they were a lesser class of being.

Webster's celebrated oxymoronic images of candied poison that rots the eater convey the idea at the verbal level.[12] Rendered homiletically, these image clusters suggest that the bravura of the court world belies its deadly spiritual effects or, yet again, that the improvidence of the court is exceeded only by its duplicity. In moments of melodrama these patterns are rendered as images-in-action, as when Isabella suffers death because she devotedly kisses Bracciano's poisoned picture and the Bible.

Very important in terms of the audience's experience of the tragedy is that no figure is fully able to comprehend the double-dealing intrigue of the court world. Even Lodovico, the play's archrevenger who believes he has mastered the mysteries of state hypocrisy, is himself the dupe of the subtler revenger Francisco, who manipulates Lodovico's own vengeful efforts. Similarly, there is the brilliant scene in which Flamineo fakes a mutual suicide pact with his sister and her maid Zanche, permitting the ladies to "shoot" him and to fleer over his prostrate body only so that he can arise to triumph over them for being such shallow plotters. This momentary victory, it may be observed, is itself contained within the larger patterns of Lodovico's revenge, which succeeds in dispatching these three in earnest, and of Francisco's revenge upon all four, including Lodovico. The denouement thus enacts one of the tragedy's pervasive motifs, the unfathomable treachery of courts.

Since each of these actions also surprises the audience, this experience of the beguiling court world becomes theirs as well. The experience is an initiation for them as for the choral commentators and for all of Cornelia's family: the whole experience of the tragedy, as I have emphasized, presupposes an audience not of the court but in it, like Webster's own audience at the Red Bull, one undergoing, as in the last-act death scenes, an elaborate, horrific, ritual induction into the way of the court world.

At a deeper level, the anticourt design of *The White Devil* communicates itself emblematically as a protest of the spirit. If the anticourt perspective truly lies at the spiritual center of the tragedy, there ought to be a powerful dramatic emblem embodying that truth. Such an emblem appears in the macabre spectacle of Bracciano's death. In this scene Bracciano puts on a helmet to protect himself in barriers exercise only to discover that Lodovico's accomplices, disguised as Capuchin friars, have poisoned it. The lingering madness the poison induces brings to a culmination the homiletic theme of courtly reward and punishment. Bracciano's febrile ravings, with Jacobean application, of "Battailes and Monopolies, / Levying of taxes" (5.8.70–72), suggest a torment of conscience that is his apposite courtly punishment. The note of complaint insinuates itself as well when Bracciano imagines that his steward "Bought and sold offices; [and] oppres'd the poore" (5.3.84).

In the midst of Bracciano's surreal ruminations, there emerges the emblematic phantasm of the courtier. Unlike his imagination of his poor subjects, this figure appears rich, bedecked with blue bonnet, breeches, and a great "codpeece . . . stucke full of pinnes / With pearles o'th head of them" (5.3.100–2). "Doe not you know him?" the Duke asks an amazed Flamineo. Hearing no response, Bracciano identifies this great courtier:

> Why 'tis the Devill.
> I know him by a great rose he weares on's shooe
> To hide his cloven foot. Ile dispute with him.
> Hee's a rare linguist. (5.3.103–6)

Bracciano's emblem recalls the play's title; the courtier generic is the White Devil of the tragedy. The emblem applies, of course, to the title figure, Vittoria, and to Francisco, who as the black Mulinassar represents himself as a neglected courtier seeking preferment, a seemingly omniprevalent situation. At play's end this Francisco-Mulinassar, this black devil, this prince of darkness, who is in reality a white devil, remains unapprehended, his machinations still unplumbed by the callow Giovanni, who accedes to Bracciano's title.

No one person is, finally, *the* White Devil of Webster's tragedy, but they are all contained in the infernal world of the court, in which a thousand cloven-footed courtiers lurk. In emblematic terms, the court world is the union of self-prostitution and deceit, of whore and devil decked out in overglorious show. "O mee!" cries Vittoria upon seeing her lover strangled, "this place is hell" (5.3.182). She is right, of course. In Webster's *The White Devil* and *The Duchess of Malfi* as well, the path to preferment is the path to ruin. This truth Marcello learns on the point of his brother's sword. His dying words occasion a sermon that reminds us of the tragedy's design as an anatomy of the court world. There are sins, he asserts, that heaven punishes in "a whole family. This it is to rise / By all dishonest meanes" (5.2.22–24). The homily is uttered for once without irony and, significantly, it also reasserts the family emphasis as well as the citizen morality which, I have argued, is integral to the tragic design of *The White Devil*.

With characteristic concentration, Webster gives to Vittoria the more intense, alienated, anticourt realization: "O happy they that never saw the Court, / Nor ever knew great Man but by report" (5.6.261–62). These, Vittoria's dying words, like Marcello's, are admonitory, but they express more keenly than her wound the anguish of her own personal experience and her unsparing outsider's critique of the court; having the advantage of being one not born to that world, she speaks to those like herself who might yet avoid it.

This universality of utterance to which *The White Devil* and *The Duchess of Malfi* aspire is in an interesting, complicated mode tied to a more specific Jacobean frame of reference. By minor poetic touches, the audience is constantly being reminded that the experience of *The White Devil* and *The Duchess of Malfi* includes them, includes England. "Let others live by begging," Flamineo contends, "Bee thou one of them practize the art of *Wolnor* in England to swallow all's given thee" (3.3.45–47). Or again, "You are happie in England, my Lord; here they sell justice with those weights they presse men to death with. O horrible salarie!" (3.3.26–28). An air of complaint blends with these singularly observed, contemporary allusions. At critical moments Webster frequently inserts Jacobean allusions to achieve powerful local effects, as when Flamineo at his death admonishes, "Let all that belong to Great men remember th'ould wives tradition, to be like the Lyons ith Tower on Candlemas day, to mourne if the Sunne shine, for feare of the pittifull remainder of winter to come" (5.6.265–68).[13] In this disconsolate view, ordinary people in the great world of state are owned by that omnipresent abstraction great men. In a similar strategy of linkage, Webster introduces the English Ambassador, whose presence as analyst and observer (particularly, at the conclusion of the tragedy) emphasizes the idea that England has something to learn from the operation of these petty Italian courts.

Such Jacobean matter does not function to insinuate a topically specific allegory of the English court. To turn to *The Duchess of Malfi* for illustration, J. W. Lever's argument that "the court of Amalfi presents in miniature the court of Whitehall, with its adventurers, its feverish pulling of strings for office and promotion, its heedless and heartless pursuit of privilege" goes too far toward this sort of reading.[14] John Russell Brown's view that the setting of *The Duchess,* with its small court and concentration upon current abuses, creates "a syndrome for contemporary issues" that directs the audience's attention to England moves with more salutary caution.[15] Webster's tragedies do direct our thoughts to England, but they do not function as do the personal satires of the indoor theaters; they do not shadow the English court in the same way.[16] Rather, the strongest impulse in these tragedies is to evoke, through sententiae and homilies, general, often universal truths about the corrupted nature of modern courts.

It is in this spirit of universal application that Flamineo can compare the process of preferment to "knaves . . . [rising] . . . as gallouses are raised i'th low countries, one upon another's shoulders" (2.1.316–18). Preferment is death, and the universality of the insight is confirmed by its gnomic expression. Bosola's choric commentary works in this same way:

> Princes pay flatterers,
> In their owne money: Flatterers dissemble their vices,
> And they dissemble their lies, that's Justice. (3.2.278–80)

> I would sooner swim the *Bermoothes* on
> Two Politisians' rotten bladders, tide
> Together with an Intelligencers hart-string
> Then depend on so changeable a Princes favour. (3.2.307–10).

Italy per se is not Bosola's subject; generalizations about courts, with their venal politicians, court spies, and flatterers, are. Such characteristic, universalizing forms suggest that overspecific applications anchoring Webster's intentions in a single English context limit the scope of his comprehensive anticourt perspective. What Webster's tragedies demand is a more subtle interpretation—that their horrific vision of Italian court life (the lurid accidents of plot notwithstanding) includes Jacobean England without being limited to either locale. The application also works in the obverse; the manifestly Jacobean character of the antimasque in *The Duchess* (at 4.2.) functions broadly to provide an induction to the madness of the modern world. For English audiences, this is what general application in tragedy meant.

But if application is general, it is necessary to ask what limits, if any, circumscribe Webster's anticourt perspective. A reading of *The White Devil* may tempt one to infer that the idea of courts is anathema. However, as *The Duchess of Malfi* more clearly shows, contemporary court practices, not the philosophy of courts in the abstract, are the objects of attack. *The Duchess of Malfi* does portray a virtuous prince and courtier, and it offers, at least by way of allusion, the positive example of the well-ordered French court, which enjoys a "juditious King" and a "most provident Councell"—that is, a house of representatives—"who dare freely / Informe him the corruption of the times" (1.1.4–18); cf. 20–23).[17] Antonio is that rare courtier who, though desirous of preferment, rejects ambition for its own sake as "a great mans madnes" (1.1.483) and the Duchess is that rare prince who, in Bosola's cynical idiom of incredulous praise, has goodness enough "to prefer / A man, meerely for worth" (3.2.319–20). That is to say, the Duchess is always "Duchesse of *Malfy* still" (4.2.139); she embodies an ideal of princeliness.[18] Such a rendering of character as this precludes the inference that Webster's tragedies show all courts—conceived with their respective princes as a system of government—to be perforce iniquitous.

At the same time, however, his tragedies reveal a profound understanding that courts do function as distinct social systems, and the rationale of their existence has momentous implications for individual human beings. They show that in practice contemporary courts too frequently function for their own amoral ends, irrespective of the welfare of their subjects, or the spiritual need people have to serve institutions whose goodness they believe in. *The Duchess of Malfi* works as a kind of empirical test case in which the question is not whether virtue can exist in the courts of Calabria or Amalfi; rather, invoking a criterion Renaissance humanists habitually employed to evaluate statecraft, the play asks whether virtue in great place can prove effectual.[19]

The tragedy also broaches broad ethical issues, pitting marriage and preferment on the basis of achievement or merit as against reward by birth or rank alone. Ferdinand, the "purist" aristocrat with latent incestuous desires for the Duchess and a hysterical fear of her marrying down, represents an extreme defense of rank by birth alone; the Duchess, associated with fecundity and great creating nature, defiantly offers in her turn (what ought to be) life-giving preferment on the basis of merit—but her actions bring no better world.[20] The Duchess can prefer Antonio for his "vertues" rather than his "pedegrees" (3.2.301), but he will not thrive. Bosola can praise the Duchess's marriage to Antonio—"rejoyce / That some preferment in the world can yet / Arise from merit" (3.2.327–29), but the jubilation registers ironically since Bosola's discovery insures Antonio's destruction. Nor can the Duchess thrive. The life of virtue, integrity, wedded love, and children must live fugitive. Delio's observation about Ferdinand's making the law into a dark prison (discussed below) adumbrates, in fact, the Duchess's own imprisonment and her strangulation. All of these suggest symbolically the confinement and the eventual suffocation Ferdinand brings about in rigidly enforcing rank over merit and functional obedience over freely given loyalty.

The conclusion one draws from this deadly condition of courts is not that virtuous courtiers cannot be found in Webster's world, but that they are doomed, as are the courts themselves that function by such death-sustaining principles.

But just how widely applicable are the conditions in Calabria and Amalfi intended to be? As it eventuates, much more widely than at first appears. As a political tragedy, much of the force of *The Duchess of Malfi* depends on an outlook that cannot be restricted to local conditions in corrupted Italian states. The play works hard to achieve breadth of application. It opens with a universalizing emblem, in which the well-ordered state is compared to a fountain: "if't chance / Some curs'd example poyson't neere the head, / Death, and diseases through the whole land spread" (1.1.14–16; cf. 3.2.300–6). The abstract of the fable, not necessarily its particular details, is what justifies the tragedy as art. It need hardly be added that the spectacle of a disordered court, which is the matter of Webster's tragedies, was a subject more immediate in the seventeenth century than in ours. For Webster as for Tourneur, Marston, and Middleton, courts were a condition of life, a given; there was no other way. In the end the political conservatism of their Italianate tragedies only highlights the alienated perspective on courts.

General applications need not exclude more specific referentiality, of course. For example, in Ferdinand's bleak court, the Duke "speakes with others Tongues," "Doombes men to death, by information, / Rewards, by heare-say" (1.1.175–79). Furthermore, as Delio reports, Ferdinand uses the law like a foul cobweb, "He makes it his dwelling, and a prison / To entangle those shall feede him" (1.1.180–83). This precise delineation is not necessarily typical of English experience, but it is a Renaissance emblem, and it works powerfully because it reproduces recognizable features of England's political life.

Of all the anticourt features in Webster's tragedies, the most pervasive and generalizable is the sense that human beings have been set adrift by the institutions that should give positive direction to their lives. Castiglione and England's own Thomas Elyot, among other humanists, had envisaged courts as places where talented, virtuous people could realize their human potential while serving the state, thereby giving temporal meaning to their lives.[21] Webster's tragedies, whose materials as we have noted are drawn from history, show the reverse process of the decentering of man, alienated from the institutions of the church and the court, which no longer support or care about him as a spiritual being. Webster's characters are thus thrust upon their own devices. The Duchess's direct appeal to heaven to bless her "sacred Gordian" with Antonio—"We now are man, and wife, and 'tis the Church / That must but eccho this" (1.1.549, 563–64)—expresses alienation from institutional religious authority. Similarly, the Duchess's parable of the Dog-fish (that "eminent Courtier" who lords it over the poor salmon in this life, not realizing that only in the next world, "in the Fishers basket," a symbol of Jesus, will the salmon's true value be shown [3.5.150–62]) reveals the aliena-tion from the court world and, by extension, from all the vanities of this world. Estranged, virtuous individuals have only God to support them in their poor life's efforts.

Courts *are* the world in Webster's tragedies, and alienation from them is closely allied to spiritual isolation and disillusionment with life. These asso-ciations are epitomized in a remarkable way in the Duchess's death scene. About to acquiesce in her strangulation, the Duchess feels impelled to kneel, saying,

> Yet stay, heaven [*sic*] gates are not so highly arch'd
> As Princes pallaces—they that enter there
> Must go upon their knees. [*She kneels*] (4.2.239–41)

Her perception sets God's kingdom and that of princes utterly apart, show-ing with a deft touch of satire that princes, neglecting their own salvation, build castles to exceed their Maker's. Humility and faith in the next world's justice are the tragedy's only answer to the inauthentic vanities of this world, which the temporal ambitions of courtiers and princes exemplify. In such a "sencible Hell" (4.2.369) as this, escape rather than heroic confrontation is the wisest course; and so, Antonio's dying counsel makes its claim upon us: "And let my Sonne, flie the Courts of Princes" (5.4.84).

In the world of Webster's Italianate tragedies, the satiric impulse may be strong, but reform, the usual end of satire, is impossible. It took a dramatist who admired Webster[22] but who possessed a more robust sensibility, Thom-as Middleton, writing more than a decade later in a volatile climate of political controversy to introduce into Italianate anticourt tragedy the ex-pression of specifically Jacobean grievances.

13

The Anatomy of Court Culture and Jacobean Grievances in Middleton's *Women Beware Women*

Although in one sense *Women Beware Women* (ca. 1621) is easily identified as an Italianate, or blood, revenge tragedy, that designation is insufficient to establish its thematic purposes.[1] The presence of three overlooked themes demands a more specific generic identification of the play as an *anticourt* tragedy written from a citizen's perspective: the demystification of authority, the representation of the corruptive urbanity of court culture, and (partly as a consequence of the first two features) the depiction of contemporary grievances.

As the last major Italianate tragedy to express the anticourt outlook, *Women Beware Women* also reveals an evolution in the form. Whereas earlier Italianate tragedies had portrayed the court as luridly evil and had used choral presenters as principals to moralize upon the action, Middleton relegated such commentary to minor characters and elected to portray the fortunes of figures who found themselves successful aspirants to the courtly way of life. In addition, he turned the form toward the representation of notably Jacobean abuses. Anachronistic passages of transparently Jacobean grievances had frequently appeared in earlier Italianate tragedies,[2] but Middleton made such concerns essential to the tragic design of *Women Beware Women;* thus, he tied the main plot's broad anticourt perspective to the topical grievances in the subplot of enforced marriages and wardship.

Pervading the tragedy is what deserves to be called a reproving representation of authority. By depicting the Florentine court and the Duke cynically exploiting the images of royal representation, Middleton demystifies that authority. In this regard, the efficacy of the tragedy as homiletic depends in large measure on its status as a genuine, albeit loosely adapted, chronicle of sixteenth-century Italian court life.[3] That is to say, the tragedy embodies in a general way the ideal of "truth of argument," which Jonson and others who drew their materials from history exalted. The primary means by which the tragedy undercuts its otherwise orthodox representations of authority is its ironic, double-sighted rendering of major ceremonial court scenes (one is presented in each act).

The pattern is established upon the Duke's first appearance, when he is depicted solemnly entering his city of Florence, at the head of a stately procession. The expected, orthodox interpretation of the Duke's appearance is offered, almost chorally, by Leantio's trusting mother. She clearly perceives the intended public message of the entry. "The look he casts," she declares in submissive awe, "Is at his own intentions, and his object / Only the public good" (1.3.109–11). But these expressions of admiration and loyalty are, heavily undercut through Bianca, the Mother's unhappily cloistered daughter-in-law, who searches out immediately the Duke's appetitive private nature. When Bianca's attentive eyes meet the Duke's wandering gaze, a future sexual relationship is wordlessly intimated. Middleton's juxtaposition of the Mother's uncritical acceptance of the aura of princely authority and the reality of the Duke's lust offer us something more than the conventional distinction between the prince's fictional mystical body and his private self; it suggests the Duke's exploitation of his public incarnation to achieve his lowly sensual ends. This implicit judgment of the Duke's abuse of his authority blends with a decidedly critical representation of the sensual Bianca. The reason for the scene's double-edged irony, which is directed at both king and sensual lady, is aptly expounded by the Renaissance English proverb "Court to the town and whore to the window."[4] As we shall see, this kind of proverbial English folk wisdom frequently underlies the anticourt attitudes this citizen play expresses.

The climactic scene depicting the Duke's seduction of Bianca also unites the tragedy's anticourt purview with an object lesson in the desanctification of statecraft. In an ironic emblematizing gesture, the Duke reveals himself on the balcony "above," as "the sun" in his magnificent aspect (2.2.315s.d.; 319). Subsequently, he offers Bianca the prospect of wealth and honor. Only once does he suggest the brutal force that lies at his disposal should she refuse, and he touches lightly on the subject: "I can command, / Think upon that" (2.2.362–63), the point being that the Duke's power is so overwhelming that he hardly need invoke it. In this way, Middleton deglamorizes the gentility of the royal seduction.

A broader manifestation of Middleton's interest in reinterpreting received images of royal authority can be gauged by his painstaking attention to the staging of court ceremonies. For example, the Duke's successful endeavor in the third act to win Bianca over completely is achieved by ushering her in to "a banquet prepared" with "cornets" and entertaining her with "music" and "a dance . . . making honours to the Duke and curtsy to themselves" (s.d.3.3.0.1, 20.1,133, 200.1). As in the triumphal entry, Middleton begins by dramatizing the splendor of court life and then presents the wooing of Bianca in terms of a rhetoric of virtue. Constantly referring to his own courtesy, the Duke woos eloquently in the manner of the courtly lover, praising his mistress as "Of purpose sent into the world to show / Perfection once in woman" and commending the "music [that] bids the soul of man to a feast" as "a noble entertainment / Worthy Bianca's self" (3.3.23–24, 128– 30). The Duke's exaltation of music's transporting (i.e., sensual) effects, which he depicts as nobility of soul, echoes profanely the harmonic, spiritual authority of music in Plato's "Symposium" and in its courtly reinterpretation in Castiglione's *The Courtier.*[5]

This undercutting of courtly elegance is not allowed to stand unex-pounded. The Duke's taffeta phrases, silken terms precise, cover over what is still adultery, and his attempt to sanctify his lust in marriage offers a still greater misappropriation of the mystical ceremony, here of Mother Church. Hence, Middleton portrays the veneer of holiness, showing the Duke and Bianca entering "solemnly" "in great state . . . richly attired" to the sound of "hoboys," and then shatters the illusion by having the Cardinal "enter . . . in a rage, seeming to break off the ceremony" (s.d.4.3.0.1), subsequently expos-ing the inner meaning of the occasion as "religious honours done to sin" (4.3.1). The event, like the others, reveals Middleton's tragedy as decon-structing one kind of conventional symbolic discourse in favor of another.

The lack of correspondence between the outer and inner truth of court ceremonials also prompts a reinterpretation of the meaning of the superiority of urbane court culture over citizen culture. Middleton underscores the elegance of the scheme that removes Bianca's parental and psychological guard when Livia, feigning loneliness, draws the Mother to her home, bid-ding her bring her "lonely" daughter-in-law. In accord with a proverb of the time expressing distrust of court ways, Livia is "full of Courtesy full of craft" (C732). This assessment is brilliantly corroborated in the chess game, by which Livia distracts the Mother while Guardiano prepares Bianca for the Duke's pleasure. The Mother's casual observation of Livia's play, "Y'are cunning at the game" (2.2.295), introduces a popular anticourt theme. Clearly, chess, that courtly pastime Castiglione treats, is for a class of human-ity who have the leisure to cultivate strategies, to make elegant moves.[6] The scene also establishes allegorically, from a citizen's perspective, the hopeless inequality of the battle between virtue and vice, between trusting simplicity and callous premeditation. So much wit, so much energy, is arrayed against such unsuspecting victims. Emblematic of the whole scene is Livia's announcement that the "saintish" white king has been given the "blind mate" (2.2.392).[7]

As shapers of sophisticated tastes, the Duke's retainers are shown to appreciate other fine arts as well. Parallel to the Mother's defeat at chess is the cunning of Bianca's seduction, which is achieved by recourse to "pagan" paintings. Guardiano, leaving nothing to chance, recalls how he prepared Bianca's stomach for "Cupid's feast, because I saw 'twas queasy" and "showed her naked pictures by the way" (2.2.402–3). The imagery of the chess game and the naked pictures suits well the refinement of this courtly seduction. Ordinary people could not concoct such a plan; they could not bring their appetites, however debauched, to such a genteel plane.

Guardiano's speech unites the play's anticourt and Puritan perspectives. Considering that many members of Middleton's audience had Puritan sympathies,[8] Guardiano's account of his temptation of Bianca must have aroused hostility toward the decadent aestheticism associated with Renaissance courts, particularly in the visual arts—the masque, portrait painting, and sculpture. The pagan subject matter of such Flemish artists as Daniel Mytens and Rubens, the latter of whom Charles I commissioned in 1637 to decorate the ceiling at Whitehall, suggested a courtly preoccupation with the body and carnal pleasures.[9] The hallways of many an English country house also exhibited these advanced tastes.[10] The message underlying Guardiano's report of Bianca's seduction is that courtly sophistication and moral turpitude are akin. The hoodwinking of Bianca and her simple mother-in-law is of a piece with this aestheticism; it possesses an ugly beauty.

Middleton's ironic representation of court culture includes an analysis of the insidious effects of this genteel environment upon those who move up to it. Chief among these are Leantio and Bianca. Bianca, like Shakespeare's Cressida, allows herself to be bought by the person who can show her materially how much he prizes her. As Bianca herself admits, she is one who "likes the treason well, but hates the traitor" (2.2.443). The political metaphor resonates, recalling Leantio's lecture to his wife, beginning, "As fitting is a government in love / As in a kingdom; where 'tis all mere lust" (1.3.43–44). Although Leantio is, ironically, driven by lust himself and hardly one to lecture others, his invocation of the symbology of good governance calls attention to the Renaissance dictum that the true lord is above personal appetite; he is "like a good king that keeps all in peace" (1.3.48). But one driven by his appetites as the Duke of Florence is, creates an "insurrection in the people"; he begets Bianca's lust, her "treason[ous]" adultery (1.3.44–46).

Stated somewhat differently, the most dangerous thing about the royal way is that it fosters in others its own corrupted sophistication. The result in Middleton's rendering is that Bianca is both made and unmade by her elevation as the Duke's paramour. Leantio too finds himself entrapped by royal rewards. He who celebrated his elopement with Bianca as "the best piece of theft" (1.1.43) learns firsthand what bold theft is. Thus, when the Duke, fearless of reprisal, offers Leantio the sop of a captainship, the cuckhold has no choice but to accept. The same calm but firm demonstration of power that subdues Bianca subjugates Leantio. In some measure their ill-defined urgings lead to the lurid embrace that enthralls them, but neither could have dreamed that the smooth hands of a calculating court could reshape them so.

What we see, then, in Bianca and Leantio is Renaissance self-fashioning with a difference. Both are the products of their circumstances, but in the end they assent to their courtly fortunes. Middleton's rendering of this complex psychological process that brings people from innocence to corruption, from poverty to overrefinement, is nowhere better dramatized than in the fourth-act interview between Bianca and Leantio, after each has established a position at court. Richly dressed because he has accepted Livia's invitation to be her gigolo, Leantio recalls how he eloped with Bianca from no such carved window as she now stands before; Bianca muses on "How strangely woman's fortune comes about" (4.1.23). The courtier asks to see Bianca's "cloth-of-silver slippers" (4.1.55) and Bianca, at a scornful remove, inquires whether his cloak is quite lined enough. An eerie vacuum separates these two who were once married and legally still are. The interview is strained, the dialogue clipped. In the stifling, rich atmosphere, surface observations convey unspoken feelings of envy and contempt. Something overwhelming has happened to them and they cannot quite grasp what it is. Instead, they point to their altered attire, which dimly signifies to them some inward transformation. Eventually the two fall to recrimination, perfectly cold to each other's needs. At the end of his interview Leantio stumbles on a metaphor that captures their mutual experience. He speaks of blind folk being led to see the monuments, an image that recalls Bianca's seduction and one that offers us a second sight beyond appearances, that discloses the unseen workings of the court world, to which ordinary citizens are blind.[11]

This anatomy of court culture moves in the subplot scenes to specific Jacobean issues of wardship and enforced marriage. Both express the tragedy's moralistic citizen perspective and, particularly, a revulsion for the abuses of noblesse oblige, or, in Middleton's terms, "guardianship." Simply by mentioning his interest in the young Bianca, the Duke prompts the self-appointed ministers of his desire, Guardiano and Livia, to procure her. Instead of executing his office in fitting compliance with his name, Guardiano behaves in accordance with the cynical maxim "He that will in Court dwell must needs curry favel [favor]."[12] Similarly, the betrayal of the sensitive Isabella, first by Fabritio, who barters her in marriage, and then by her aunt

Livia, who misinforms Isabella about her birth so as to encourage an incestuous liaison with Livia's brother, reveals that the subplot pursues in its
own way the same theme as the main plot—the misuse of positions of trust to
exploit those whom the court should protect.

The major difference between the two actions is one of technique since the
subplot relies heavily on farce. By making the vulgar Ward the mismatched
husband of the sensitively depicted Isabella, Middleton underlines the cruelty
of enforced marriage. Isabella's bitter observation, "Men buy their slaves,
but women buy their masters" (1.2.178), announces the feminist perspective.
But to recognize Middleton's emphasis of the subject that George Wilkins
dramatized in *The Miseries of Enforced Marriage* (1606) without also recognizing his treatment of the great grievance of wardship, eventually a revolutionary issue, is to miss the double-barreled political topicality of his subplot.[13]

Even in James's Parliament of 1604, wardship, an institution administered
by the crown, was denounced as a scandal of the first order.[14] It was also a
national symbol of the corruption of the patronage system, particularly of
unjust privilege and of the legalized right to dissipate estates. So important
was this grievance that it became the basis of negotiation between the crown
and Parliament for the Great Contract of 1610. However, since the Great
Contract was never enacted, the result was that the detestable system continued. It took the English Civil War to abolish the Court of Wards and
wardship by parliamentary order in 1646 and again by act of Parliament in
1656.[15] As Christopher Hill pointedly reminds us, "Confirmation of this
legislation was the first business the House of Commons turned to in 1660
after hearing the Declaration of Breda, so great was the significance attached
to it."[16]

As the system operated in Jacobean-Caroline England, the king sold wardships in reward for service to gentlemen and nobles for a handsome fee. The
appointed guardian delighted in this political plum because he could bilk the
ward's estate during the ward's minority and could also marry his charge off
to the highest bidder. Wallace Notestein summarizes the functioning of the
system: "The acquisition of wardships was recognized as one of the ways of
getting on. . . . The guardian was likely to prove overthrifty about the up-
keep and education of the ward. He was likely, also, to draw all the immediate profit he could from the ward's lands."[17] At the time Middleton's tragedy
was composed, crown revenues from the sale of wardships were rising
steeply, and the abuses such sales brought were ever more visible.[18]

In *Women Beware Women* the functionally named Ward is so simple, so
uncivilized and crass, that there is reason to doubt whether a sincere attempt
to educate him would have done any good. All he seems to have learned from
Sordido is how to play Trap-stick and behave grossly. This aspect of Mid-

dleton's depiction dovetails with the contemporary stereotype, for the master of the Court of Wards also sold guardianships for idiots, lunatics, and simpletons.[19] This composite portrait of the Ward complements that of Guardiano, who in the spirit of the time makes a mockery of his name and title. The marriage he arranges with Fabritio between Isabella and the Ward sounds a shrill note of grievance that echoes back to Elizabeth's time when Henry Brinklow wrote, "'Oh merciful God, what innumerable inconveniences come by selling of wards for marriage, for lucre of goods and lands.'"[20] In this spirit of opportunistic salesmanship, Guardiano, cynical and aloof, commends his marriageable charge as "a great ward, wealthy, but simple; / His parts consist in acres" (3.3.113–14). The corresponding expression in the main plot of this cynical self-promotion is Guardiano's betrayal of Bianca. Since Guardiano's behavior parallels that of the other guardians who abuse their trust (Livia and the Duke are the others), his purely functional name ironically underlines his perfidious paternalism, as well as that of the Florentine court. Pertinent as the observation is that the masque is a conventional feature of revenge tragedy,[21] such a view can obscure our recognition that the concluding marriage masque in *Women Beware Women* offers a radical reinterpretation of the symbolic court ceremonies that Middleton relentlessly deconstructs. By tradition, the wedding masque is supposed to signify the reward that comes from the acceptance of the bonds of love, of mutual obligation and regard, which portends peace. In *Women Beware Women,* however, the festering abuses of enforced marriage and betrayed guardianship prompt Middleton to represent the royal wedding masque in terms of the superior symbolism of divine retribution.

Middleton's pervasively ironic dramaturgy proceeds, I have suggested, from a citizen's perspective on court culture. In this regard the court masque in general must be seen as a reaffirmation in art of the philosophical assumptions of Renaissance court culture. Giovanni Pico had declared in his "Oration on the Dignity of Man" that man has the freedom to determine his own nature.[22] This humanistic legacy, which Renaissance courts inherited, might be summed up in the phrase "ye shall be as Gods on earth."[23] This ideology found its most spectacular expression in the court masque, a form whose mythological synthesis of Christian sacramentalism and pagan allegory makes men and women into gods and goddesses and pagan deities into representatives of divine will. So too, as Middleton initially presents it, the urbanity of the celebratory masque functions as a paean to court culture and Renaissance self-fashioning, upraising preferred humanity to godhead. Hence, the crowning symbol of the nuptials masque is Livia, who plays the role of Juno, the patron and protector of women in marriage, descending, goddesslike, from above and presiding over the scene.

But the nuptials masque in Middleton's tragedy is not about the glories of courtly culture and self-fashioning; instead, it represents the overarching theme of the courtesies done to others in subplot and main plot. And as in all the previous ceremonial scenes, surface allegory is reconstituted as symbolic irony. Thus, as John Potter shows, the burning treasure of gold that Livia drops ironically recreates Zeus's mortally burning appearance before his human lover Danaë, the parting gift of the goddess to her suppliant niece.[24] The ironic poetic justice that redounds upon Livia, who is poisoned by the fumes of suppliants' incense, epitomizes the prime reason for her damnation—her spiritual poisoning of the charges placed in her care. In place of the charade of love, Middleton's masque, as it is actually performed, enacts a killing truth that uncovers, unmasks, the richly attired principals in a grotesquely providential antimasque, as it were. All of them then face a poetic justice, Christian, and, in a spiritual sense, self-inflicted.

Primarily because of Middleton's interest in the behavior of individuals within received institutions, the characters of *Women Beware Women* have been described as "victims of society, automatons crushed and deprived of humanity by the corruption of the social system under which they must exist"; yet these characters have also been described as responsible individuals whose fate results from their erring willfulness.[25] These views represent two poles of a tension in Middleton's tragedy, the interplay between the environment (preeminently the court) and the willing self. The characters in *Women Beware Women* are not wholly the product of their circumstances, but their circumstances condition their choices and propel them toward their destiny. Middleton's tragedy is thus not about victimization pure and simple, even for Bianca and Isabella. It is about the process whereby the appetitive and the subservient adapt to their circumstances, seize opportunity, and make alliances as best they can, thereby becoming participants in the process that corrupts them.

Stated in terms of tragic conception, *Women Beware Women* is not about the flawed greatness of human life, and it lacks altogether the kind of elegiac affirmation that we hear in *Hamlet*. To the contrary, Middleton's is a tragedy of judgment. This is the ineluctable perspective of the medieval cycle plays and the moralities, from which Middleton drew,[26] as well as of *The Revenger's Tragedy* with its premonitory thunder of judgment. Thus, as the Cardinal's homily in *Women Beware Women* explicitly reminds us (4.1.190 ff.), the Duke is held personally responsible both for himself and for the moral character of his realm. Robert Herrick gracefully epitomized this proverbial theme in the couplet "Examples lead us, and wee likely see, / Such as the Prince is, will his People be."[27] The complexities of this theology—everyone responsible, the prince (and other guardians) more responsible than others—has both public and private application. However much the characters of *Women Beware Women* are victimized by the arrogance of the court and by the abuses of wardship and constrained marriage, they also become complicit agents in the working out of their separate destinies. For this reason the tinge of satire, which always intimates reckoning, pervades the play. The sensational denouement brings this potentiality to fulfillment through its satiric allegory, which demythologizes the courtly, man-made allegory of the masque.

All of the tragedies considered in this part enjoy considerable reputations as works of art. But, these reputations rest principally on formalist interpretation, with the result that their political and moral content—their full impact as literature—has been diluted. The universality of these works, if there can be such a thing, emerges out of distinctive popular seventeenth-century preoccupations with the nature of courts in contemporary life. These preoccupations help to define the nature of the genre. Whereas the ideological tragedies of Jonson and Chapman probe courtly, aristocratic questions of fealty to one's sovereign, the liberties belonging to subjects, and the right of patrician leaders to criticize court policy, the Italianate tragedies of Tourneur, Webster, and Middleton treat the more palpable moral issues of court culture. The perspective of these popular Italianate tragedies is, as one might expect, that of outsiders moving up and looking in; as a consequence, the court world is treated censoriously as other.

The themes of Italianate tragedy are as few as they are repetitive and harsh, a telltale sign of their felt importance. In fact, the themes of the type may be reduced to three: first, the license of courts, portrayed variously in terms of sexual looseness, material extravagance, and lack of piety; second (and inconsistently), the economic and social complaint elicited by a class system in which the few privileged are so prominent among the many less fortunate; and, third, the poignant sense of courts as betraying their public trust by failing to provide the exemplary patterns of conduct and statecraft that make for an ordered, flourishing society. An important subset of this last theme, it may be added, is the political depravity of courts which, in forsaking Christian patterns of ethics, use up their servants, ignoring their sacramental nature, treating them self-interestedly as tools of state. The persistence of these themes with respect to sixteenth-century courts may be interpreted, as I have suggested, as latter-day reactions to the humanist enterprise gone awry, in particular, to its prizing of pragmatic reason, worldly sophistication, and self-fashioning, whose institutional manifestation is the Renaissance court itself.

In an age of courts that repeatedly celebrated its culture as a "golden age restored,"[28] London's popular Italianate tragedies alert us to a powerful but equally legitimized countercurrent. Perhaps this countercurrent may be called radical in the sense expounded by Jonathan Dollimore: it reveals humans beings to be the "decentered" products of institutions—here the court—rather than autonomous individuals forging their own destiny.[29] However, these tragedies do not parody the providential viewpoint or posit an existentialist materialism. Rather, their radicalism originates in their religious conservatism. Their Christian perspective, whether traditionalist or more radically Protestant, makes possible their relentless interrogation of modern court life. In the name of a transcendental spiritual authority, the temporal authority of secular courts is called into question.[30]

Such orthodoxy legitimizes the dramatic representation of damnable Italian court life and at the same time creates an unexceptionably edifying social theme. Furthermore, by the processes of application and the use of proverbial and other conventional topoi, as well as emblems and gnomic utterances, these dramatists took a universalizing anticourt stance, while attacking no living court in particular, thereby risking much less than the comical satirists who burlesqued James and his court. But instead of trivializing the significance of these formalized expressions of alienation, protest, and doubt (which frequently happens when the notion of conventionality is introduced), we owe it to ourselves to recognize that these forms provided the accepted civilized means by which this society permitted the drama to undertake its sweeping criticism of the age and of its most dominant institution.

The more topically specific criticisms of the late Jacobean court appear in a sustained way only in the relatively late *Women Beware Women,* with its topical critique of enforced marriage and wardship. However, its treatment of political issues from an ill-concealed reformist perspective is characteristic of the explosive, issue-oriented dramas of the Buckingham era, 1619–28. In some ways this later political drama was the most extraordinary of the early Stuart period, for it was restricted to no subgenre and limited to no single kind of playhouse. It was, furthermore, the most programmatically coherent, the most explicitly political, and potentially the most threatening to the government of any that had preceded. As such, these later anticourt plays, with their riveting focus on Whitehall and its policies, deserve to be called opposition drama.

IV

EARLY OPPOSITION DRAMA

1621–1628

14

Crisis of Confidence

The Buckingham Era

The most striking characteristic of the politics of the 1620s is that it was a decade of Parliaments.[1] Parliaments were summoned in 1621, 1624, and, under Charles I, 1625, 1626, and 1628, with an attendant session early in 1629. As in the first Stuart decade, these sittings focused national attention on long-standing issues of domestic grievances, including monopolies, the sale of honors, and the engrossing of offices by the king's favorite. In addition, Parliament debated with growing frenzy, as did the nation at large, the precarious posture of England's foreign policy.

James's troubles in foreign affairs proceeded from the rash decision in 1618 of his son-in-law Frederick, the elector-palatine, to accept the crown of Bohemia from an army of Protestant rebels that had overthrown its Catholic king, Ferdinand. Although James did support the cause of Protestantism in Europe, he did not approve of the violent overthrow of an anointed sovereign. Frederick's acceptance of the Bohemian crown was also fraught with danger, for it hazarded the intervention of Spain on the side of Ferdinand and increased the prospect of a widening war England could not afford to enter. Once Frederick made his decision, James pursued more vigorously a policy of peace with Spain, the centerpiece of which was a proposed match between Prince Charles and the infanta. Through Spain's cunning ambassador to England, Don Diego Sarmiento de Acuna, later Count Gondomar, Spain temporized, keeping negotiations alive as it secretly prepared for war. In 1620, to James's astonishment and fury, Spain invaded Frederick's own kingdom of the Palatinate with a formidable army under the famous Spanish general Spinola. By the end of the year Ferdinand's armies had delivered the

Protestant rebels a stunning defeat at White Hill in Bohemia while Spinola's troops drove Frederick's army out of every major town but two in the Palatinate. The elector's position became desperate; instead of being the exalted leader of two kingdoms, he was about to lose the one throne he legitimately held.

To Frederick's pleas for aid his English compatriots could hardly be deaf. Irresistibly, pressure for English intervention against Spain in the Palatinate mounted. James stubbornly maintained his unpopular pro-Spanish policy, for it was based on a realistic assessment of England's capabilities. An adept Gondomar had given him hope that although Spain could not permit the overthrow of the Bohemian king, a general peace accompanied by restoration of the Palatinate was still possible if Frederick would renounce his Bohemian claims. A union, then, between Charles and the infanta would bring England a much-coveted dowry. With enhanced prestige from the match, James could indeed be the *Rex Pacificus* of Europe. But James could not be certain that he possessed the influence to bring off the match. Without it, he needed to make ostentatious preparation for war, which most of his people would welcome, but stop short of waging it.

Early in 1621, and with some trepidation, the king summoned Parliament. James was right to be apprehensive. To Parliament and the general public, the evidence showed irrefutably that Catholic Europe, led by imperial Spain, had commenced a campaign to subdue the Protestant countries on the Continent and to convert England. The elector-palatine, the French Huguenots, and the Dutch Protestants under the prince of Orange were all victims, as they saw it, of Catholic oppression and were all on the defensive. On behalf of these beleaguered Protestants, the earl of Pembroke and his parliamentary allies prepared to undertake a military crusade. At such a time as this, the last thing they wanted to see was James preparing to make a papist match for Prince Charles with the Spanish. James, for his part, saw the virtues of pacifism. And if war was to come, he wanted to pinpoint conflict in the Palatinate, not an apocalyptic confrontation.[2] Even such a limited war, it was estimated, would cost an astounding £912,768 per year.[3]

These tensions between the hawkish, Protestant interventionalists in the Commons and the dovish, pro-Spanish faction at court intensified popular disenchantment with crown policy. Out of these tensions came confrontation. When the Commons petitioned the king to set up a Protestant match and to relieve pressure on the Palatinate by sending a diversionary expedition to aid Maurice's Dutch forces, the king rebuked them for debating publicly "matters far above their reach and capacity, tending to our high dishonour and breach of prerogative royal."[4] He then commanded the House "that none therein shall presume henceforth to meddle with anything concerning our government or deep matters of state."[5] Parliament's response, modeled in numerous details on the "Apology and Satisfaction" of 1604, took the form of a "Protestation of Right." In part the Protestation read: "That the Liberties, Franchises, Priviledges, and Jurisdictions of Parliament, are the ancient and undoubted Birth-right and Inheritance of the Subjects of England; And that the arduous and urgent affairs concerning the King, State and Defence of the Realm, and of the Church of England, and the maintenance and making of Laws, and redress of mischiefs and grievances which daily happen within this Realm, are proper Subjects and matters of Counsel and Debate in Parliament."[6] Peremptorily, the king (in an uncharacteristic gesture) prorogued the Parliament and tore the offending page from the House Journal.

Despite these ideological rifts, there was all along a practical desire on both sides for cooperation. Thus, in October 1621 the king, while unwilling to make war openly on Spain, allowed a "volunteer contingent" under Sir Horace Vere to fight in the Palatinate.[7] For their part, the Parliaments of 1621 and 1624 voted the king several subsidies as measures of good will.

In addition to the divisions over foreign policy, economic abuses clouded the domestic scene. These concerned, principally, the greed and opportunism of James's ministers and the crown's selling of monopolies. Frequently, the two issues joined inextricably. Monopolies were patents granted by the king to courtiers or businessmen of influence for the exclusive right to manufacture, trade, or sell a commodity. Often justified as means of encouraging economic development, monopolies were in practice sold simply to raise crown revenues. By the early seventeenth century they had become an abuse of the first order since even the most common household commodities from wines to butter to common thread had been sold as patents, creating exorbitant prices. Especially repugnant were the patents held by Buckingham's kinsman (by marriage) Sir Giles Mompesson, the principal figure whom Massinger satirized in *A New Way to Pay Old Debts*. Mompesson enforced his patents on the manufacture of gold and silver thread, which nearly everyone used, by resorting to illegal searches and seizures. He also held the patents for the licensing of inns and alehouses, but instead of regulating prices at these establishments, reducing drunkenness, and preventing prostitution, Mompesson renewed the licenses of notoriously disorderly taverns and of inns run by shysters in order to collect the licensing fees they brought.[8]

Ignoring the crown's efforts to muffle the scandal, the House investigated and demonstrated that Mompesson had used his patents for extortion. It demonstrated further that Mompesson's assistant, Sir Francis Michell, a corrupt justice, had used the alehouse patents to conduct a legalized shakedown operation. For his lack of care as overseer of the inns, Mompesson was ironically dubbed the "lord of hosts."[9] The vigilant Coke reported to the House that Mompesson had prosecuted 3,320 innkeepers (many of whom were rumored to lie rotting in jails) on obsolete and technical charges. Issues of Magna Carta were thereby raised. Coke then proceeded to produce evidence that in one county alone Mompesson had permitted the reopening of sixteen establishments previously closed as bawdyhouses. For his offenses Mompesson was sentenced by the House of Lords to be degraded from his order of knighthood (as was Michell), made a perpetual outlaw, deprived of his property, fined £10,000, and imprisoned for life.[10]

Important as it was in demonstrating the rank abuse of privilege, the Mompesson case became still more important because it led to bigger game, more difficult to cage. The Mompesson investigation opened up a trail leading to the clients and relatives of the king's favorite, the duke of Buckingham. Foremost among these were two of Buckingham's brothers: Kit Villiers, who was reaping lucrative rewards from the alehouse patents, and Sir Edward Villiers, who was deeply involved in the extortionate profits from the silver- and gold-thread patents. When Parliament questioned Buckingham about his relationship to Mompesson, he asserted that the patronage he conferred upon friends and relatives did not make him complicit in their doings.[11]

This testimony notwithstanding, Buckingham soon found himself accused directly. The key witness was Sir Henry Yelverton, an erstwhile Buckingham client, who after having fallen from favor was currently imprisoned. As a former attorney-general, Yelverton had issued the offending patents. His career a shambles, Yelverton had no wish to shield the agent of his ruination. Making the most of the forum granted him, he explained how his resistance to Mompesson's extortionate writs of arrest had prompted a vindictive Buckingham to cause the profits from Yelverton's office to be shut off, destroying Yelverton's private practice.[12]

Explosive as this testimony was, James shielded his favorite from injury. To assuage Parliament, the crown permitted Mompesson and Michell to be sacrificed, as it did the great Buckingham client Sir Francis Bacon, by this time lord chancellor.[13] Beyond them Parliament could not go. Further meddling would bring a prorogation. By this strategy Buckingham escaped impeachment.

Safe though he was, Buckingham had become a grievance in his own right. From his late teens until his assassination in 1628, he dominated the Stuart scene as no nobleman had ever done. This is why the decade of the 1620s is often called the Age of Buckingham. It comprehends both the crisis of confidence in James's reign in the early twenties and the first crisis of confidence of Charles's. In both periods Buckingham's diplomatic, military, and domestic activities played a pivotal role.

Because he became the center of the aging king's emotional (and probably sexual) life and shrewdly capitalized on this personal attachment, Buckingham vaulted himself over all rivals. Delicate in countenance, refined, graceful, and skilled in the dance, George Villiers reaped harvests without winters. In a single year he became chief justice in Eyre, master of the King's Bench office, joint commissioner for the office of earl marshal, lord lieutenant of the county of Buckingham, and high steward of Hampton Court. Raised to the peerage as Viscount Villiers in August, 1616, he became earl of Buckingham and a privy councillor not six months later. By 1618, he bore the titles marquess of Buckingham and high steward of Westminster, and in 1619 attained the great office of lord high admiral. After reaping still more offices and dignities between 1619 and 1622, Buckingham received, in Wotton's phrase, "the highest degree whereof an *English* Subject could be capable"—duke of Buckingham.[14]

And he kept rising. Nimbly negotiating the difficult transition to Charles's reign in 1625, Buckingham was quickly appointed gentleman of the bedchamber, chief commissioner of war, general of the fleet and the army, and lord high constable. As one of Buckingham's biographers puts it, "No other Englishmen ever accumulated so many honours or attained such enormous ascendancy. The sequence of his appointments and creations constitutes the record of a fortune absolutely unique in the annals of our nation."[15]

To gentry and nobility with a lineage, the parvenu Buckingham became a man despised. To dramatists and artists who looked for security and patronage to established houses of nobility, Buckingham's career aroused the deepest of anxieties, the specter of aristocratic degeneration. There were other reasons as well for the resistance to Buckingham. Unlike the earl of Salisbury, Cecil, who had earlier controlled the same channels of patronage, Buckingham carried the further stigma that he was the king's favorite. His role as government minister was thus joined incongruously to his role as self-seeking receiver of the royal bounty. Moreover, Buckingham was quick to spread the spoils of office to his large family. Every title, grant, patent, dignity, perquisite, and office conferred on Buckingham or his kin was one less that could be offered to deserving courtiers. Eventually, Buckingham himself became sole proprietor of the patronage system. That is why so many men of independent mind such as Edward Coke, Francis Bacon, and Lionel Cranfield became clients of Buckingham. There was no other way.

Given his influence over king and prince and his office as lord admiral, Buckingham also exerted an exceptional influence over foreign policy that was soon reflected in opposition dramas. In 1623 Buckingham sought a diplomatic coup by traveling incognito with Prince Charles to Spain to conclude the Spanish match, but the Spanish, unimpressed, had little intention of permitting the match or of resolving the Protestant debacle in the Palatinate. Infuriated by the neglect he and the Prince were experiencing, Buckingham suddenly renounced the match and joined the anticrown faction clamoring for war with Spain. For this deliverance the English populace gave the returning diplomats a tumultuous welcome, complete with feasts, bell ringings, and bonfires.

When Parliament met in 1624, seeking the war James could no longer forestall, Buckingham led the way. Zealously, he undid the very peers who had supported his former pro-Spanish policy and who had refused to reverse field with him. The earl of Bristol was made a scapegoat for the failure of the Spanish negotiations and, after being threatened with impeachment, accepted banishment to his country estates. James's fiscal reformer and loyal treasurer, Lionel Cranfield, the earl of Middlesex, fell when his reform program began to threaten Buckingham's own operation. When Cranfield continued to support the Spanish match (because he realized that the infanta's dowry might bring as much as £600,000 to an impoverished Treasury),[16] Buckingham engineered Middlesex's impeachment in April 1624, while a hand-wringing James looked on. By these maneuvers Buckingham destroyed the Spanish faction and put himself in sole control of foreign policy as well as of patronage.[17]

Having given relief to the nation by renouncing the Spanish match, Buckingham and Charles concluded the only other suitable match, with the Catholic Princess Henrietta-Maria of France November 1624—in the eyes of the people only slightly less evil. However, Buckingham's long-range plan of gaining the assistance of Catholic France in the Palatinate failed, for Richelieu renounced this vital part of the marriage treaty soon after Charles's marriage. Finding his diplomatic initiatives thwarted, Charles, through Buckingham, summoned his first Parliament in the spring of 1625 in order to prosecute the war against Spain. Parliament, however, had become infuriated with crown policy, for it learned that in signing the marriage treaty, England had agreed to send, and in fact had sent, its own navy to fight against the Huguenot enclave at Rochelle, England's Protestant brothers in Christ![18]

Buckingham's diplomacy inspired revulsion, and sentiment for his impeachment gathered momentum. Hard-pressed for supply as he was, Charles prorogued the Parliament to protect his favorite. For his part, Buckingham gambled everything on a spectacular attack on the Spanish at Cadiz in 1625. A smashing success would silence criticism of Charles, rehabilitate Buckingham as a hero, and open Parliament's purse strings. Ill-organized and poorly led, the expedition proved a fiasco.

The wheel of fortune turned a quarter circle. Charles, now desperate for supply, summoned a new Parliament, but it proved truculent. All the old domestic grievances against Buckingham were reinvoked with new determination to make them stick. Proofs of the favorite's military incompetence and maladministration were added to the list of particulars. With the support of key members of the House of Lords, the movement for impeachment went forward.[19]

On May 8, 1626, the House leadership formally charged Buckingham. The first three articles accused the duke of engrossing a multiplicity of offices and of having bought the lord admiralship. Subsequent articles accused him of delivering English ships to the French, of selling honors and places of judicature, of procuring honors for his kindred, all undeserving, of exhausting the king's Treasury, and, finally, of having administered (as rumor had it) unauthorized medicine to James on his deathbed. The fiery Sir John Eliot accused Buckingham of being a Sejanus, a rhetorical comparison that illustrates once again the habit educated Englishmen had of interpreting matters of state analogically, especially by applying Roman history to English conditions.[20] Whether Eliot had Jonson's *Sejanus* in mind when he addressed Parliament is not possible to say, but the tradition of such republican thought, both in the drama and in Parliament, is evident. Further evidence of this widespread historiographical tradition appeared in an English-language pamphlet from a Paris publisher entitled *The Powerfull Favorite, or, The Life of Aelius Sejanus,* which made its way to England in 1628.[21]

Charles, unwilling to permit the Lords to try the case against Buckingham on its merits, again summarily dissolved his Parliament and imprisoned Eliot in the Tower. Buckingham, still lord admiral in 1628, contrived yet again to vindicate himself with another naval expedition, this time to relieve the besieged Huguenots on the Île de Ré off Rochelle. The results were more disastrous than the first expedition, for the ill-coordinated assault brought disease, starvation, mutiny—and national disgrace. At home the atmosphere turned ugly. Cruel satires and ditties against the duke, the king, and the Laudian bishops (including two once attributed to the dramatist John Marston) sprang up everywhere.[22] In June of 1628 a London crowd caught Buckingham's physician and astrologer, one Dr. Lambe, and fatally mauled him.[23] In August, Buckingham was assassinated by an embittered survivor of the Rochelle fiasco. The king prayed; England rejoiced.

Most evaluations of Buckingham's career have been unstinting in their condemnation of his effect upon the English nation. Clarendon concludes, "He was guided more by the rules of appetite than of judgment"; Conrad Russell, that Buckingham was "one of the most corrupt ministers the Crown has ever had"; and David Willson that "Buckingham's ascendancy brought favouritism, corruption and debauchery, while his system of plunder poisoned the atmosphere and pointed the path for all who had business at Westminster."[24] In his definitive biography, Roger Lockyer emphasizes that Buckingham became an all-too-easy target for deeper problems that must be ascribed to fundamental deficiencies in the system of English government.[25] But he was without doubt a hated man. As Lockyer says, "They hated him not so much for what he was, as for what they feared he might become . . . and they succeeded in convincing not only themselves but subsequent generations that Buckingham was an enemy to everything that the name and history of England symbolised."[26]

By the reckoning of many historians, these first years of Charles's reign mark the beginning of an ideological opposition to crown policy. Although the case can be and has been overstated, the confrontations between Charles and his Parliaments did create large constitutional issues. His attempts to prevent the earl of Arundel from voting on Buckingham's impeachment by keeping him imprisoned for a minor offense and his imprisoning of MP's Eliot and Digges for libelous remarks raised fundamental issues of Magna Carta and habeas corpus.[27] Similarly, the king's levying of a "forced loan" without parliamentary consent raised constitutional questions concerning the limits of monarchical authority in a country endowed with a Parliament and an "ancient constitution." The refusal of several MP's to pay the levy for the loan prompted a constitutional test in 1627 of the king's right of imprisonment, in what has come to be known as the Five Knights case.[28]

These issues of arbitrary taxation and imprisonment and of parliamentary privilege combined with the national humiliation of the Île de Ré disaster to produce the famous Petition of Right in 1628. Far from being a revolutionary document in the sense of wresting power from the king, it was designed, as G. E. Alymer puts it, "to state what the existing law was, and to get the king's agreement that it should be observed."[29] However, inasmuch as the petition implies that Charles was not abiding by traditional English law, it may be interpreted as an expression of a conservative, nationalistic ideology that discovered in England's heritage of law the supreme expression of right rule.

Out of this turmoil of the 1620s there arose a spate of political plays as full of ideology as topical allusion and even personal satire. Along with surreptitious pamphlets, illegal sermons, and libelous ballads, these plays dramatized the views of vociferous critics of crown policy. In parallel developments, these plays appeared both in London's outdoor playhouses as well as in the elite indoor theaters, where similar sentiments were expressed with greater restraint and decorum. But whatever the auspices of production, the theaters aired the issues of the times; they became England's most public of forums.

Unlike the popular Italianate tragedies, these plays presented no sweeping attack on courtly life, its privileges or pleasures; their focus is more specific, more political, and in comparison with the satires of the Children of the Queen's Revels more policy oriented. As a group they dramatize something of the idealism of Jonson's and Chapman's tragedies but are more narrowly focused on current political affairs in England. In a word, these are plays whose anticourt character is revealed in their opposition not to courts in general (some are actually patrician in outlook) but to the conduct of James's and Charles's court in particular, to crown policies, and to prominent English ministers. Contumacious yet righteous, these plays of the 1620s, in both their popular and courtly expressions, merit the designation *opposition dramas*. I employ the term not as certain historians do, to indicate the advent of an unofficial party opposed on principle to the crown's policies, and not as Margot Heinemann does, to signify a concerted, largely Puritan movement to oppose government policy.[30] Rather, I wish to apply the term more restrictively to signify the work of playwrights (particularly those of the 1620s) who were frequently of widely varying social station and who were loyal to the idea of kingship as well as to the king but who opposed, often vehemently, one or more major tenets of the crown's foreign and domestic policy and, commonly, the architects of those policies, James's and Charles's closest advisors.

15

Censorship, Citizen Opposition Drama, and *A Game at Chess*

Beginning in the Buckingham era, the pulpits and the presses issued a multitude of political and religious commentary on England's problems in domestic and foreign affairs. To turn back this challenge to the crown's leadership, James issued two proclamations in late 1620, addressed to preachers and then to all subjects "against lavish and licentious speech in matters of state."[1] When these proved insufficient, out came a proclamation on July 26, 1621, to restrain "licentious and bold speaking or writing in matters of state,"[2] and when even this attempt failed to still the chorus of embittered voices, the king moved in September 1623 to suppress as seditious any publication not previously approved.[3] Unlike the censorship of the early Jacobean period, James's policy in the twenties amounted to a sustained policy to silence what he regarded as irresponsible, ignorant criticism of his policies.

The atmosphere of repression spared neither poet, prose writer, nor dramatist. In his elegy to George Sandys, Michael Drayton describes the apprehensions he experienced during these years:

> I feare, as I doe Stabbing; this word, State,
> I dare not speake of the *Palatinate,*
> Although some men make it their hourely theame,
> And talke what's done in *Austria,* and in *Beame,*
> I may not so; what *Spinola* intends,
> Nor with his *Dutch,* which way Prince *Maurice* bends.
> To other men, although these things be free,
> Yet (GEORGE) they must be misteries to mee.[4]

Drayton goes so far as to declare his fear of praising even a virtuous dead friend, "Lest for my lines he should be censured" (l. 18). Working behind the mask of "Democritus Junior," Robert Burton ironically depicts the "blessings" of living in England at this time where "the Gospel [is] truly preached, church discipline established, long peace and quietness, free from exactions, foreign fears, invasions, domestical seditions . . . [and where there rules] a wise, learned, religious king, another Numa, a second Augustus, a true Josiah, most worthy senators, a learned clergy, an obedient commonality, etc."[5] Burton's speaker goes on to lament the absence of "what liberty those old satirists have had," but then, fearing the censor's wrath, he self-consciously, humorously, and abjectly takes it all back.[6]

Massinger's courtly *The Roman Actor* (1626), a Blackfriars play, uses the setting of Domitian's Rome to represent the perilous situation theatrical companies faced in these times. Responding to an atmosphere of oppression precisely like that prevalent in London, where it is impossible to "Speake our thoughts freely of the Prince, and State, / And not feare the informer," the actors Paris and Lamia complain that the informer Aretinus plots to silence their company for having "galld [him] in our last Comedie" (1.1.68–69, 37).[7] This piece of information not only is pertinent to the issue Massinger was raising but also appears to be a specific allusion to circumstances involving either *A Game at Chess* or his own *A New Way to Pay Old Debts,* both performed the preceding season. This topical concern with dramatic censorship is fully aired when Paris is summoned by the Senate to give reason why his acting troupe should not be forbidden ever to perform again. There, the city's "Roman actor" scathingly rebukes the legislators for "descend[ing] / To the censure of a bitter word, or iest, / Drop'd from a Poet's pen!" (1.1.63–65).

"Jests" and "bitterness" are terms appropriate to satire, and in England as well as Rome, satires challenging official policy had become rife. Chief among the printed works James sought to suppress were the provocative *Vox Populi* pamphlets of the Puritan pamphleteer Thomas Scott. These lurid publications (from Holland where Scott had fled) were the very same that Thomas Middleton had employed as primary sources for *A Game At Chess.*[8] The full title of the second of these tracts, THE SECOND PART OF VOX POPVLI *or Gondomar appearing in the likenes of Matchiauell in a Spanish Parliament, wherein are discouered his treacherous & subtile Practises To the ruine as well of England, as the Netherlandes,* suggests something of the fear of Spanish intentions and, implicitly, the suspicion of James's complacency in meeting the threat.[9] Upon the appearance of the pamphlets and of *A Game at Chess,* James conveyed his apologies to Spain and sought to apprehend the respective authors.[10] The close relationship between the *Vox Populi* pamphlets and Middleton's satire shows that a powerful opposition literature did exist, that it enjoyed rather wide popular support, and that the drama of the period, unquestionably, and despite censorship, furthered the opposition ideology.

For these features alone *A Game at Chess* merits close attention, but there are others as well. The satire is unique in offering the most daringly detailed topical political allegory in the early Stuart period; it is also the most influential of all opposition plays. The nature of that influence upon both the drama and society at large has not been adequately treated and calls for further examination. There is, moreover, a continuing need for lucid explanations of the satire's content since its topical specificity continues to drive off modern readers, which is a pity since in its own day the content of this powerful drama was obvious to all.

A succès de scandal it was, running an unheard of nine consecutive days at the Globe before the government shut it down demanding that "the author and performers of the play are to be cited before Council, those most faulty imprisoned, the comedy examined . . . and measures taken for the severe punishment of the offenders."[11] Why did this play so threaten the Jacobean authorities? Clearly, it appropriated the representation of royalty, holding up James not to scorn but to critical examination. The scorn Middleton reserved for James's ministers and bishops and, finally, the Spanish diplomat in whom the king placed his trust, Count Gondomar. The power of representation, as Jonathan Goldberg has shown in another context, is a mighty one.[12] James could not allow a dramatist to take upon himself the mystery of things, to represent so publicly the issues and personalities on which the reputation of the court rested.

For the king and his court, the problem *A Game at Chess* presented was not the violation of the abstract principle (and law) that only princes have the authority to represent themselves; it was the satire's broad appeal, its charismatic authority. Although a popular melodrama, *A Game at Chess* was executed with an allegorical finesse worthy of the most elegant court masque; like *The Tempest,* it fashioned a world and its form was brilliantly adapted to its purpose. Whereas other dramatists had used foreign settings to make dangerous topical connections, Middleton overleaped such earthbound conventions, freely presenting within the world of the chess metaphor the Spanish and English courts of his day.

Over three thousand people a day, the Spanish ambassador lamented, packed the theater in "merriment, hubbub and applause,"[13] And every class of society, as Chamberlain observed, frequented it—"old and younge, rich and poore, masters and servants, papists and puritans, wise men, *et ct.,* churchmen and statesmen as Sir Henry Wotton, Sir Albert Morton [former Secretary of State], Sir Benjamin Ruddier, Sir Thomas Lake, and a world besides."[14] At a time when the Jacobean court was trying to close down the conduits of opinion on foreign affairs, *A Game at Chess* captured a wider audience than any government publication or court masque. Beneath this competition for access to the public mind lay Middleton's power to represent heterodoxly the present time as hawkish Protestants conceived it to be.

This conception was all the more powerful because the play and the title page of the unlicensed quartos represented the faces and figures of the English and Spanish courts with a "minute realism" no other Jacobean dramatist had ever attempted.[15] Making the duke of Buckingham the White Rook, or Duke, as it was then called, and Prince Charles, in accord with his chivalric virtues, the White Knight, Middleton reenacted their celebrated journey to Madrid in 1623 to conclude the elusive Spanish match. Around this primary action Middleton arrayed the most important political figures in the Spanish and English courts, assigning to each an apposite identity as a chess piece. As the title page of the first and second quartos shows, these figures—ten of them—are grouped around a chess table and clearly labeled. James, for example, is represented as the aging, bearded White King, in marked contrast to Philip IV, who as the Black King is boyish and unbearded. To perform the part of Count Gondomar, the leaping Black Knight, the players had gone so far as to dress their actor in Gondomar's cast suit and had secured the litter he used to ride in.[16] The letter of Secretary of State Conway, reporting that the play had "scandalous[ly]" "personified" "his Majesty, the King of Spain, Count Gondomar, and the Archbp. of Spalato," along with Chamberlain's shocked praise—"They counterfeited [Gondomar's] person to the life, with all his graces and faces"[17]—reveal how precisely rendered the real-life identities of the chess pieces were. Middleton and the Globe players had indeed purloined the jovian authority of representation, and this is one reason why government documents pertaining to it are legion.[18]

But Middleton and the players had done something more profound. They turned their power of representation into a power to conceive, into unforgettable categories of thought. Whereas the king endorsed a moderate view of Spanish intentions, Middleton equated the Spanish, who in his play are dressed in black—the color of the Jesuitical order and a favorite at the Spanish court—with darkness, evil, and, finally, perdition.[19] Subterfuge, connivance, and seduction are their attributes, whereas the English, in white, are full of trust, faith, innocence, and, in the case of the White Knight, chivalric heroism.[20]

Despite the conventional wisdom that such a polarized depiction of these two societies lacks historical perspective, *A Game at Chess* is clearly full of hindsight, as when the White Knight, alluding to the Spanish armada, recalls, "The Deuill has beene at worke since 88" (4.4.6). Sprinkled throughout the work are recollections of time past that include references to the Gunpowder

Plot and the alleged attempt of Dr. Lopez to poison Elizabeth at Spain's behest (2.1.243–44, 4.2.121–27). We may consider Middleton's satire an exercise in yellow journalism, but to many of his contemporaries his art represented political reality. Robert Zaller's account of Sir Edward Phelips's influential speech in 1621 records one respected statesman's view of Spanish intentions: "[Phelips] reduced all the complexities of power to a simple equation of good and evil. Catholics stood on one side, Protestants on the other. The aim of all Catholic states was the extinction of all Protestants. Spain was the greatest Catholic state, and therefore commander of the Catholic crusade."[21] Middleton's *Game at Chess* presents itself as a sensational rendering of topical events; in fact, its unique efficacy inheres in its holistic power of description. Description in *A Game at Chess* is potent interpretation, a complete worldview.

Within this Anglo-historical perspective, Middleton inventively depicted the reality of Spain's quest for world domination by framing his play with the induction figures of Error and Ignatius Loyola, founder of the Jesuitical order, whose historical mission was to convert the non-Catholic world. From Loyola, a stage Machiavel fashioned after Marlowe's Machiavel in *his* induction to *The Jew of Malta*, issues the master plan, evident among the Black chess pieces, to dominate the entire world. In accordance with this worldview and seventeenth-century practice, Black makes the opening move, Queen's Pawn to the fourth rank. After being met by White's Queen Pawn, Black moves its Queen Bishop Pawn to the fourth rank, offering the pawn to White and initiating the Queen's Gambit, appropriately named with reference to the proposed Spanish match. White's thematic second move of the Bishop pawn, declining the offer, initiates its counterplan, Queen's Gambit Declined, and precisely reenacts the disposition of political events after mid-1624. The entry at move three of the wily Black Knight, Gondomar, initiates the main action and signals Black's strategic attempt to implement Loyola's doctrine. The ensuing queenside struggle among the pawns over White's threatened Queen Pawn, rendered as a sexual assault upon the religion of ordinary English commoners, constitutes the play's subplot interest. "The Jesuit's desire to deflower the White Queen's Pawn" may also be taken, as Roussel Sargent points out, as "a metaphoric way of showing Spain's desire to take England by force."[22]

The Black Knight's Machiavellian leadership needs no special comment, but the political ideals for which he stands do. As the play's maker of evil, its Vice figure, he pledges allegiance to what he calls "the Vniuersall Monarchie," "the Hope Monarchall," or as another character puts it, "The hope of Absolute Monarchie" (1.1.264, 315, 2.1.142). The term *Vniuersall* signifies Spain's wish for world domination, and the phrase "Absolute Monarchie" appears intended to raise the specter of tyrannical oppression. In the parlance of Middleton's satire, Spain is tyrannical because she is absolute in her monarchy. Although England too might in a narrow sense be referred to as absolute since almost everyone agreed the King was "absolute in Parliament," Middleton was striving to draw a contrast between Spanish tyranny and what parliamentary leaders would have called English reverence for "fundamental law" and her system of representative government.[23] Middleton's polar depictions of England and Spain must thus be interpreted as signifying more than a political-religious struggle for survival; they signify the dramatist's commitment to an opposition ideology, which issues out of Middleton's appreciation of England's distinctive political heritage. The position, with its denigration of absolutism as tyranny, may sound anachronistic, but the evidence shows it is surely not.

If the foregoing analysis is correct, *A Game at Chess* not only undermines respect for authority but also, by its terminology, introduces unapproved categories of political thought. This penetration into the nature of things is, as I have indicated, subtler than the dissident depiction of political events. Indeed, Middleton's satire goes so far as to depict the treasonous spirit of some of the highest members of England's court and clergy. It is obvious that Middleton renders the international chess struggle of the middle game more freely—a modern might say *impressionistically*—than he does at the beginning and end. He departs from the strict moves of chess play, but gives us in return another formal pattern to apprehend the action.

At the time Middleton was composing *A Game at Chess*, the danger of subversion from crypto-Catholics, as they were called, seemed to be corroborated by experience, for Archbishop Spalatro had just renounced his appointment in England to embrace papism, and James's own treasurer, Lionel Cranfield (the earl of Middlesex), had been impeached by Parliament (April 1624) for supporting too enthusiastically the Spanish match.[24] Both of these events Middleton incorporated into the play as late additions. But the way he did so reveals a great deal about the power of conceiving as well as representing. Portrayed respectively as the Fat Bishop and the King Pawn, Spalatro and Treasurer Middlesex are revealed to be wearing Black's colors underneath their white uniforms (e.g., s.d. 3.1.297). The notion of defections among chess pieces appears to fit a John Le Carré novel better than the rules of chess, but in the global chess struggle Middleton is depicting chessmen as won or lost by the ideology that moves them. Middleton's literal rendition of "turning one's coat" is thus a species of psychomachia; it brilliantly reveals the psychological-spiritual terms in which his own drama represents political events. Events are but end products of ideas operating on the soul.

Beyond this, Middleton's depiction of Cranfield as a papist sympathizer does more than recollect the fact of his impeachment; it portrays Cranfield as being, body and soul, a crypto-papist. Such a rendering takes us beyond the mystery of things (as Lear describes it) of who's in and who's out; it takes us beyond events to a public labeling of the psychic essence of court figures.

Middleton does little less in holding the White King up to public scrutiny. Well-intentioned and wisdom-loving though he is, the White King is presented as unable to penetrate the Black Knight's cunning and flattery. The depiction represents James's long-standing tolerance of things Spanish and, particularly, his reliance upon Gondomar's advice in his own court.[25] The same conception of James is evident in the White King's obliviousness to the King Pawn's treachery, right under his nose as it were, and in his astonishment when the Fat Bishop, who enjoyed an all-too-rich living in England, defects to the Black side. So too, the White King stands incredulous when the White Queen Pawn cries rape and foolishly appoints the Black Knight to settle the case. The White King's failure of leadership and his inability to recognize or cope with the threats to the commonweal are tantamount to an indictment of James, although the king is spared the branding of a Middlesex.

Only the daring attack of the White Knight and Rook preserves the victory for the White side. In an imitation of Charles's and Buckingham's surprise Spanish "visit," the well-placed White Knight opens the unsuspecting Black King to a double check, revealing the White Rook behind it. By exposing Spain's stratagems to Parliament upon his return to England and by alerting all the English forces, Buckingham and Charles enable White to deliver "the Noblest Mate of all" (5.3.178). The Spanish gambit refuted, Middleton has Spain's Black pieces thrown into a great dark bag symbolizing hellmouth, a feature the Spanish ambassador duly noted in his dispatch to Duke Olivaras in Spain.[26] These sensational features of *A Game at Chess* contribute to the potency of the drama as a molder of English thought, for the work is at once an opposition and an unqualifiedly nationalistic play. The second makes the first the more powerful. In fact, in the conceptual set for England's political situation that is *A Game at Chess,* the reality proffered is, by default, the only possible one; there are no alternatives, ambiguities, or second considerations. By the time James, who certainly did hold another view, moved against the players and the playwright, the damage had been done; he had lost control of the situation.

Triumphant, then, as the white forces proved to be, *A Game at Chess* is an opposition drama. A sweeping view of the work impresses one with its chauvinism; closer examination reveals the layers of distrust, the suspicion, the division within England itself in a time of crisis. By play's end the satire succeeds not only in undercutting James's stewardship but even in undermining its own seemingly heroic treatment of Buckingham by making the White Knight accuse himself before the Black House of sins he was widely believed to have committed—gluttony and lechery, with an indiscrete nod toward his alleged homosexual behavior (5.3.63–64, 130–39).[27] Jubilant as its conclusion is, *A Game at Chess* attests to a peculiar English nationalism that cannot clearly identify the leaders who truly speak for England.

A *Game at Chess* is, however, finally more than an opposition play because it does more than oppose. Although contemporaries perceived it as a political satire *reflecting* the course of the times, *A Game at Chess* went far toward the making of policy. By its sensationally effective manner of dramatizing political relations inside the English court and, at the verbal level, its manner of conceiving the terms of England's struggle with "absolutist" Spain, *A Game at Chess* brought pressure on the crown to bring *its* manner of seeing the world into line with reality, in short, to change its policy. The wild popularity of *A Game at Chess* fostered, furthermore, a continuing condition of crisis. In the end, the powers for which *A Game at Chess* spoke proved the more potent. In June 1624 James issued his proclamation against Jesuits and committed himself at last to military confrontation with Spain on the Continent.[28]

Even after this shift in England's foreign policy, the influence of *A Game at Chess* persisted. A memorable passage in Jonson's *Staple of News,* composed in 1626, acknowledges what it calls the "Legacy" of the king's players in *A Game at Chess,*

> Both for their various shifting of their *Scene,*
> And dext'rous change o'their persons to all shapes,
> And all disguises: by the right reuerend
> *Archbishop* of *Spalato.* (3.2.201–5).[29]

The subsequent sad report that William Rowley, who played Spalatro, had died shows that at least one of the actors of *A Game at Chess* had become a celebrity after the fact. The play's political satire also continued to reverberate, as the request in *The Staple* for more "newes of *Gundomar*" (3.2.207) attests. Jonson's satire in fact satisfied that wish, pungently reporting that Gondomar was heard to have developed a second fistula, "For putting the poore *English-play,* was writ of him" to "sordid vse" as toilet paper (3.2.207–11).

The political stridency fostered by *A Game at Chess* was taken up by other dramatists opposed to Stuart policies or to the character of James's court, and they found ways of presenting issues with a similar kind of public recognition. For example, record survives of the revival in 1634 of a now lost topical play called *Doctor Lamb and the Witches* (1629?).[30] Dr. Lambe, the duke of

Buckingham's despised physician and astrologer and a dabbler in alchemy and magic, was mortally attacked in 1626 by a London mob which labeled him as "the Duke's devil."³¹ One popular ditty of the day ran, " 'Who rules the kingdom?' 'The King.' 'Who Rules The King?' 'The Duke,' 'Who rules the Duke?' 'The devil [i.e., Dr. Lambe].' "³² The hatred of Buckingham implied by the mob's attack upon his doctor is made explicit in a similar jingle: "Let Charles and George do what they can, / The duke shall die like Doctor Lambe."³³ What the precise content of the lost play on Lambe was we cannot know for certain, but almost surely it was satiric, seizing on Lambe's profane activities to further identify him and his spiritual progeny, the witches, with demonic divination and possession. Among the witches represented in this topical work was probably Dr. Lambe's "darling," Mrs. Anne Bodenham, who lived with him, wore a toad in a green bag around her neck, and later confessed to having learned the art of summoning demonic spirits from Lambe.³⁴ Mrs. Bodenham continued her conjurations, it was alleged, and was subsequently brought to trial, condemned, and hanged for witchcraft in 1653.

Buckingham's "devilish" association with Lambe was grounded, moreover, in a great deal more than hyperbole. As the *Briefe Description of the Notorious Life of Iohn Lambe* (1629) records, Lambe had been brought to trial in the fifth, sixth, and twenty-first years of James's reign for practicing "Diabolicall and execrable acts called Witchcrafts" upon his victim; he had been infamous for keeping many women about him and was, in addition, arraigned before the King's Bench and convicted of raping a young girl of eleven years named Joan Seager.³⁵ By thus dramatizing Lambe's perverted, diabolical activities, *Doctor Lamb and the Witches* and others plays not clearly in the opposition mold such as *The Staple of News* (see Intermean 1:50–53; 3:29–41), nevertheless had the same effect of fostering opposition sentiment.

More significant than the fact of a strident opposition drama in the Buckingham years is the way that it perpetuated opposition ideology. Whereas *A Game at Chess* had emphasized Spanish tyranny, praising England's republican institutions only indirectly, other city dramatists such as Robert Davenport in *John and Matilda* (ca. 1628) expressly invoked the principle of parliamentary authority to curb the excesses of *English* monarchy.³⁶ A Puritan, Davenport depicted King John's struggles with the papal envoy's demand for tribute in the years following the signing of Magna Carta. Although unhistorical in its treatment of John's lecherous passion for Matilda, the tragedy has a good deal of political bite. As a topical play the significant point is that the barons call on their king, as Parliament did Charles, not to sign the great charter (which John had already done), but to live up to it:

Perform but the seal'd Covenants you are fled from,
The Charter running thus, given by our hand
The seventeenth day of *June,* and in the year
1215 (the whole Realm being sworn to't).

(1.3.110–13)³⁷

The ceremonial invocation of the date commemorates Magna Carta as a sacred document for all posterity. And with similar momentousness, the Barons describe with anachronistic foresight the significance of the charter as a "Covenant" for the protection of "our Houses, Honours, / Our Fathers freedomes, the Lands ancient Liberties" (2.4.112–18).

The force of such ideas may be measured not merely by their expression in dissident plays but by their appearance in works such as *The Staple of News,* which records certain markers of intellectual change in the period. Thus, for example, on the question of how important Parliament and parliamentary ideals were (or had become) to contemporaries, we have the Puritan character Censure, whom Jonson devalues in favor of the more Cavalier Mirth, reporting apprehensively, "They talke, we shall haue no more Parliaments (God blesse vs)" (Intermean 3.50). And elsewhere, after a comical mad scene in which Pennyboy Senior falls to arraigning his dogs, the recovered man observes wryly that "learned *Counsell*" informs him that "by *Magna Charta* / They could not be committed, as close prisoners" (5.6.42–46). A very similar kind of commentary, equally trivialized, occurs in *The Magnetic Lady.*[38] Although they are only details, their very inconsequentiality reveals the increasing intrusion of parliamentary ideas into the English consciousness. And by giving voice to these notions, in whatever context, the public forum as the drama, we see their perpetuation.

Finally, I think the most telling testimony to the power of popular opposition drama lies in the record of its silences, its repressions, and reformations. These include, as we have seen, not only *A Game at Chess* and a flood of nondramatic opposition literature, but also such antipapist, anti-Episcopal plays as Thomas Drue's *The Duchess of Suffolk,* composed in the same year as *A Game at Chess,* 1624. This history, set in England during Bloody Mary's persecution of Protestant "heretics," Sir Henry Herbert declared to be "full of dangerous matter" and did not allow to be played until after it had been "much reformed by me."[39] Reformation for performance did not necessarily assure licensing for publication; and without that, more permanent silences could follow. *Barnavelt* (1619) and *Believe as You List* (1631), a play denounced (before it was reformed) as "contain[ing the] dangerous matter of the deposing of Sebastian king of Portugal," were both finally approved for performance but remained in manuscript until modern times, never having been printed, although the latter play was belatedly licensed for publication in 1653.[40] *The Spanish Viceroy* and *The Spanish Contract,* both composed in the same season as *A Game at Chess* and seizing on the same subject of foreign policy, were performed (*The Spanish Viceroy* without license) and *have* been lost to posterity, along with *Doctor Lamb and the Witches*.[41] The distinction of *A Game at Chess* in this regard lies in its brazenness, for by its spectacular successive performances and unauthorized publications in quarto, the government could only resort to punishing its author and the actors for having been heard so well. But it was not just in memory that *A Game at Chess* lived. As the work of succeeding dramatists, such as Mildmay Fane's *Time's Trick upon the Cards* (1642), was to demonstrate, Middleton's play made the chess metaphor a lasting emblem of the adversarial character of the political process;[42] it showed unforgettably that English kingship was not a matter of presiding over a prescribed world order but of contending, as an active participant, with the volatile religious-political forces of the world.

16

The Patrician Opposition
Drama of Philip Massinger

By no means did all opposition drama originate outside of court circles. There is no reason to believe that even such an illicit citizen drama as *A Game at Chess* found its way to performance through the tacit support or even approval of William Herbert, third earl of Pembroke, who was in 1624 the lord chamberlain, the highest government official responsible for overseeing the drama.[1] Within the court itself, William and his brother Philip (earl of Montgomery), renowned opposition leaders in the House of Lords, supported an opposition ideology in the arts. Their patronage is analogous to Greville's patronage of the musicians and dramatists who celebrated nostalgically the cause of the earl of Essex in the early 1600s,[2] but with this signal difference—the Herberts, throughout the 1620s, supported artists who gave eloquent voice to the parliamentary ideals they actively supported, particularly opposition to James's pacifist foreign policy and the undue influence of the favorite, Buckingham.

Chief among the opposition dramatists was Philip Massinger. The son of a retainer of the second earl of Herbert, Massinger imbibed the aristocratic values of the Herberts and sought their patronage in his maturity. It is certain that Philip Herbert did respond to Massinger's entreaties.[3] A clause in the dedication to him of Massinger's *The Bondman*—"your Lordship liberall suffrage taught others to allow it [the play] for currant, in hauing receaued the vndoubted stampe of your Lordships allowance" (ll. 20–22)—reveals both Philip Herbert's approval *and* recognition of the play's contemporary ("currant") application.[4]

The number of plays Massinger composed with an opposition orientation in the Buckingham era includes *The Tragedy of John Van Olden Barnavelt* (1619, written collaboratively with Fletcher), *The Maid of Honor* (1622), *The Bondman* (1623), *A New Way to Pay Old Debts* (1625), and *The Roman Actor* (1626). All of these, with the exception of the early *Barnavelt*, probably a Globe play, were first performed or (in the case of *The Maid of Honour*) revived in elite indoor theaters such as the Cockpit (built in 1617). More decorous and respectful of institutions than the era's opposition citizen drama, Massinger's patrician drama nevertheless reveals a sharp opposition ideology closely tied to parliamentary activities—in fact, the fullest dramatic expression of this ideology in the period.

Massinger's opposition plays are too numerous to be treated individually in detail; however, concentrating primarily upon *The Maid of Honour* and *A New Way to Pay Old Debts*, important representative plays on, respectively, Jacobean foreign and domestic policy, should make apparent the scope and character of Massinger's achievement as an opposition dramatist.

As the Globe presentation of *The Tragedy of Barnavelt* illustrates, Massinger's first success with a topical political drama was in the outdoor public theater. His experience with the tragedy also taught him straightaway the difficulties of speaking directly to the issues. Originally forbidden performance by the bishop of London,[5] *The Tragedy of Barnavelt* topically represented the war between Spain and the rebelling Netherlanders, who were trying to shake off the Spanish yoke. Written with little perspective or detailed accuracy, *The Tragedy of Barnavelt* was not so much history as news, and like other political plays of the era, a prejudicial rendering of a sensational event from a jingoistic English perspective. A gifted general, Barnavelt had staunchly opposed the Spanish occupation, but he was executed in May of 1619 following his conviction for encouraging an Arminian conspiracy against the Prince of Orange's more orthodox Protestantism.[6]

By idealizing Maurice's representative government and condemning both Barnavelt's revolt and the Spanish occupation, *Barnavelt* reveals its militant Protestantism. Through its depiction of Barnavelt's conspiracy, the tragedy also labors to distinguish Maurice's laudable quest for political liberty from ignominious treason. For King James, *Barnavelt* presented a dilemma. Although he supported Maurice's cause, he could not comfortably accept any serious treatment of the religious-political situation in the Netherlands so long as England still pursued détente with Spain.

The political content of *Barnavelt* was also too stridently republican. Following its initial prohibition, *Barnavelt* suffered heavy expurgation by George Buc, master of the revels, and was never licensed for publication; consequently, the tragedy was lost until A. H. Bullen recovered the original manuscript in the 1880s with Buc's notations and line crossings.[7] Among

Buc's heavy excisions is Barnavelt's oration at his trial, in which he warns
against the advent of tyranny:

> *Octavius,* when he did affect the Empire,
> and strove to tread vpon the neck of *Rome,*
> and all hir auncient freedoms, [tooke that course]
>   cutt of his opposites.
> [that now is practisd on you]: for the *Cato*'s
> and all free speritts slaine, or els proscribd
> that durst have stird against him, he then sceasd
> the absolute rule of all: [you can apply this]:
> And here I prophecie, I that haue lyvd
> and dye a free man, shall, when I am ashes
> be sensible of your groanes, and wishes for me;
> and when too late you see this Government
> changd [to a Monarchie] to another forme, you'll howle in vaine
> and wish you had a *Barnauelt* againe. (4.5.2434–46)[8]

The bracketed phrases, it may be noted, were marked for deletion before Buc
decided to excise the entire passage. Although whiggish readers have leaped
to interpret this speech romantically as a trumpet blast of accumulated
resentment against James's "absolutism,"[9] a more qualified assessment is
called for in view of Barnavelt's patent guilt and the self-serving nature of his
arguments. If Barnavelt's warning that Maurice's government will destroy
men's liberties by becoming an absolute monarchy is taken at face value,
Maurice becomes the villain. But throughout the play Maurice functions as
the model of a good prince. Massinger underlines this positive view of
Maurice by having English soldiers declare their loyalty to the prince and by
having the co-conspirator Modesbargen confess in open court the "too
pregnant prooffes against vs" (4.5.2385).

Even though Barnavelt's impassioned rhetoric turns back upon the speaker, the ideas he employs so theatrically are compelling. Very important are the
phrases that the government will be "changd to a Monarchie" and that
Caesar's tyranny threatens all Rome's "auncient freedoms." The latter term
demonstrates that the idea of a freedom vouchsafed by tradition was current
in the early Stuart period and that the drama amplified its significance. The
liberty of English citizens, as educated Englishmen well knew, was derived
from the Roman Republic. By tradition Roman law became England's legacy
in its common law.[10] Massinger clearly draws on this republican tradition of
historiography. Just as early Stuart parliamentary ideas of liberty display a
course of development from the 1604 Form of Apology through the 1621
Petition of Right, so does the literary expression of personal liberty and
"auncient freedoms."

The warning, moreover, of Dutch representative government being "changd to a Monarchie" simply appeared too prejudicial to England's monarchical government, even with its Parliament, for Buc to allow the idea to remain. Barnavelt's speech was rhetorically effective for English audiences because it played on the fear that representative institutions were under attack. Phelips put the issue succinctly in 1625 when he declared, "Wee [England] are the last monarchy in Christendome that retayne our originall rightes and constitutions."[11]

The topical significance of Barnavelt's speech is caught in a third phrase, also marked for excision, "you can apply this," by which the audience is exhorted to think of "auncient freedoms" and representative institutions in analogical terms. Despite the self-serving functions of Barnavelt's lecture, the parliamentary perspective it articulates is all too clearly marked, and for this reason Buc finally chose to cut the entire passage.[12] This notion of application, which is so important to Chapman's and Jonson's political tragedies, is essential to Massinger's courtly tragicomic drama, with its more freely imagined, Fletcherian use of remote settings. By resorting to such settings in his later plays, Massinger eschewed the debacle the historical *Barnavelt* created and yet was able to advocate with fervor military intervention on the Continent and, particularly, the urgent necessity of England's rehabilitating her navy.

In contrast to *Barnavelt*, which (remarkable as it is) stops short of rejecting James's moderate policy of peaceful negotiation with Spain, the subsequently composed *Maid of Honour* and *The Bondman* clearly cross the line into opposition theater. *The Bondman,* for example, opens in Syracuse, where all the city's ships lie "vnrig'd, / Rot[ting] in the harbour, no defence preparde" (1.3.205–6). The townspeople lament their inability to field a capable commander of their own, having to rely on general Timolean of Corinth, who informs them that Syracuse is weak because its house of representatives, its senate, has been debilitated by "ill gouernment," in which "the greatest, noblest, and most rich, / Stand in the first file guilty" (1.3.168–70). Syracuse's "Counsell" (like the Privy Council) has also been weakened by upstarts, who have bought their seats through "mercenary purchase" (1.3.193).

These conditions parallel precisely an oppositionist's perspective on England's political situation in the early 1620s. When Buckingham took over the administration of England's navy in 1619, its condition was said to be in a "desperate state."[13] James's decision to hire the German mercenary Mansfeld as the leader of England's (volunteer) contingent in the Palatinate was a disappointment to committed interventionists. So too, the composition of England's Parliament in 1621, like Syracuse's senate, was remarkable for the influx of parvenus, particularly tradesmen and arrivistes, whom aristocrats such as the Herberts disdained.[14]

Working on this same principle of application, Massinger set *The Maid of Honour* in Sicily, an island kingdom like England in which the dominant commercial product is wool, and its dominant domestic problem the doings of an avaricious, lustful favorite. An attack on a career recognizably like Buckingham's (as it appeared in 1621) develops quickly out of the sheep-shearing imagery. These "fortunate Islands" suffer because the favorite, Fulgentio, fleeces suitors, "shaving [them] to the quicke" (1.1.28–30). His "revenue lyes / In a narrow compasse, the Kings eare" (1.1.25–26) and as controller of patronage he imperiously demands a fee for the slightest entreaty. And just as Buckingham had become an influential appointer of Anglican bishops with Arminian leanings and a popish emphasis on ritual,[15] Fulgentio reportedly "makes more Bishops / In Sicilie, then the Pope himselfe" (1.1.35–36). So powerful is the favorite that "he can undoe / Or make a man" in the trussing of a point, and "Every houre [yields] a fruitfull harvest" (1.1.26–33).

Against this backdrop of domestic tension Massinger dramatized the looming international crisis of his time from the kind of hawkish vantage that Pembroke and Montgomery endorsed.[16] *The Maid of Honour* treats both the morality of interventionism (its oppositionist agenda) and the practical problems of launching a credible attack. *The Bondman*—which was performed by Lady Elizabeth's Men, named for James's immensely popular daughter, Elizabeth of Bohemia, wife of the elector-palatine, around whom the Thirty Years' Wars swirled—goes so far as to lampoon the rich and lordly who do not support their country's war effort. Driving home his point that many wealthy citizens are not shouldering their burden of responsibility, Massinger has the upright General Timolean replenish the city's empty coffers by decreeing that the untoward wealth of the avaricious "shall instantly be brought / To the publike Treasurie" (1.3.221–22). Massinger even allows a rebellion of Syracuse's bondmen to take place at home while the truly valorous are conducting an honorable military campaign. In this way Syracuse's indolent (the nouveau riche) are doubly punished, while the revenge of the bondmen (eventually put down by the returning army) allows Massinger to express his sympathy for the grievances (but not the rebellion) of the underclasses of English society.

The Maid of Honour displays its political-romantic materials by reproducing a situation in foreign affairs exactly parallel to England's in 1621–22. Ferdinand, the duke of Urbino, has invaded Siena because its duchess, Aurelia, has not responded to his amorous overtures. Siena has, however, turned Urbino's attack into imminent defeat by calling in a splendid general, Gonzaga, so that the original invader is about to experience an ignominious defeat. Desperate to save his honor, Ferdinand calls on his good friend Roberto, king of Sicily, to assist him militarily. This situation, as Gardiner first pointed out, recapitulates (the romance aside) James's situation when the elector-palatine begged assistance from England after his invasion of Bohemia had been thwarted by Ambrosio Spinola.[17]

Roberto's response, warning of "unjust invasions" and declaring he will "Let other Monarchs / Contend to be made glorious by proud warre" (1.1.158–63), reproduces James's own position as king of peace. Similarly, Roberto, responding to the entreaties of the chivalrous Bertoldo, falls into a foreign policy of equivocation that parallels James's own policy: Roberto will not openly support the cause of his erring friend but will, as James did, allow "voluntiers / (No way compell'd by us)" to try their "boasted valours" (1.1.255–57). The significance of this parallelism inheres in the opposition viewpoint that emerges from it, for the permission Bertoldo receives to lead troops to the besieged Ferdinand invites one of several purple passages that fan the enthusiasm for interventionism then rising from England's "war party":

> if examples
> May move you more then arguments, look on *England,*
> The Empresse of the European Isles,
> And unto whom alone ours yeelds precedence;
> When did she flourish so, as when she was
> The Mistress of the Ocean, her navies
> Putting a girdle round about the world (1.1.220–26)

The speech concludes with the exhortation "Let not our armour / Hung up, or our unrig'd *Armada* make us / Ridiculous" (1.1.229–31).

The pivotal term in the passage is *example,* the example of England, whereby it rather than Sicily becomes the subject of the encomium. The entire scene strains, in fact, to merge the two countries into one as Bertoldo emphasizes his country's lack of material resources and its singular fame as an island kingdom. From this identification emerges a paean to England's naval hegemony. An "unrig'd *Armada*" is shameful. But the uplifting "example" of England teaches that "Nature did / Designe us to be warriours, and to breake through / Our ring the sea, by which we are inviron'd" (1.1.202–4).[18] These last lines, which rework and echo John of Gaunt's chauvinistic eulogy in *Richard II* on England's place in the silver sea, jump out of the dramatic context to rouse its Jacobean audience to recapture an Elizabethan naval prowess. Indeed, despite views expressed to the contrary, *The Maid of Honour* is a piece of political persuasion, and in this respect it inaugurated a series of militantly Protestant plays, which ironically invoke the memory of Elizabeth's heroic masculine court to shame the pacifistic, effeminate, Spanish-leaning ones of James and, later, Charles.[19]

As far as Massinger's audience is concerned, we have certain knowledge that his most influential patron, Philip Herbert, did read political drama with a sharp eye to applying its matter to the contemporary issues of his own day. Herbert's extensively marked 1625 quarto of Chapman's Byron plays, filled with his analogical, anachronous commentary on the Palatinate, demonstrates this truth.[20] Massinger's manner of presentation seems particularly to foster such readings. *The Roman Actor, The Guardian,* and the several plays considered above all reveal that Massinger's tragicomedies routinely present their topical material in the opening act, but not very much in later acts. This technique, like the one Chapman uses in *Bussy D'Ambois* and *The Widow's Tears,* in which most of the patent Jacobean allusions occur in the first act, permits the dramatist to contextualize his intentions at the outset without insisting (as an allegory would) on precise parallelisms throughout. There is a deftness in this approach quite uncharacteristic of such citizen plays as *A Game at Chess.* It is as if the dramatist, having set up the contemporary resonances he needs, can then go about the business of developing his play, assured his larger hortatory meaning has been contextualized. Usually, near the play's conclusion, Massinger will again employ some contemporary anachronism or allusion as a parting reminder that the tragicomedy has truly fulfilled its bargain to mix the utile (a word whose moral meaning implies application) with the romantic dulce.

The Maid of Honour is in this regard unusual in extending its contemporary parallelisms and its applications well into the body of the work. Thus, the play portrays Bertoldo's ill-prepared force of "loose carpet knights" (2.5.20) shamefully defeated, Bertoldo captured, despite their high spirits. This situation, which calls for Bertoldo's ransom, affords Massinger an opportunity to moralize, through Camiola, on ethical priorities in government. When King Roberto at first refuses the request, Camiola admonishes, "He that can spare more / To his minion for a masque, cannot but ransome / Such a brother at a million" (3.3.119–21). In the 1620s the frequency of Jacobean court masques, at which Buckingham often entertained, had increased dramatically. By contrasting the king's spendthrift habits in pleasing his favorite with the national honor, Camiola brings the king and, presumably, the Jacobean audience to a higher sense of national purpose.

The play's expression of an aristocratic ethical imperative separable from the duty to obey one's king in all his commands is very strong. When Roberto, an erring sovereign twice over, commands that Camiola marry Roberto's lustful favorite,[21] the Maid of Honour shows that she is wed to the nation and not to personal affections. Endowed with this kind of authority, Camiola is thus able to instruct King Roberto on first principles: "Tyrants, not Kings, / By violence, from humble vassals force / The liberty of their [subjects'] soules" (4.5.63–65). She even limits the royal prerogative, asserting, "And to compell affection, as I take it, / Is not found in your prerogative" (4.5.66–67). Confounding an expected romantic conclusion, Camiola refuses to marry any of her suitors and instead ends the play with a behest that resoundingly reaffirms the principles the play has espoused from the beginning: "To reassume your order [of knighthood]; and in fighting / Bravely against the enemies of our faith / Redeeme your morgag'd honor" (5.2.287–89).

In this manner *The Maid of Honour* and *The Bondman* both wrap their oppositionist perspective in the English flag. Such a posture is easier to assume when the issues concern foreign policy and external threats, more difficult on internal issues when one's own court has fostered domestic grievances. Following the debacle at Cadiz in 1625, Massinger did turn successfully to England's domestic grievances in *A New Way to Pay Old Debts* and *The Roman Actor* because he assumed a voice that spoke effectively for all of England rather than for a cause.

Dedicated to another member of the Herbert family, the earl of Carnarvon, *A New Way to Pay Old Debts* depicts English grievances frontally within a Nottinghamshire setting. The play's opposition perspective displays itself in its villain protagonist, Sir Giles Overreach, whose Christian name is taken from Sir Giles Mompesson, the monopolist-extortioner, Buckingham protégé, and political enemy of the Herberts.[22] Overreach's accomplice, Justice Greedy, is also modeled in part on Sir Francis Michel, Mompesson's assistant and a justice of the peace who was degraded by Parliament in 1621 for his extortionary fining of innkeepers.[23]

Despite these topical associations, the formalist view that deprecates contemporary significance continues to prevail in the argument that Massinger, who was "writing four years after Mompesson's disgrace . . . probably had no thought of specific caricature [in 1625]" and used Overreach to dramatize "all the abuses permitted in James's reign."[24] Such a position dissipates the satire's significance and defangs its political bite. Topical and generic satire need not exclude each other. The notion, moreover, that Mompesson was a distant memory by 1625 is one that needs revision. Mompesson was still trying to work his obnoxious patents for alehouses as late as July 1623, and a decree dated February 8, 1624, commands that he leave the country forthwith.[25]

Certain of Mompesson's activities find their way into Massinger's satiric comedy. Prominent among these is the subplot dramatization of Tapwell's disorderly tavern. Operating under the control of Giles Overreach through Justice Greedy, the tavern is a haven for thieves, whores, and stolen goods (1.1.62, 4.2.12). Tapwell, along with the other inn- and tavern-keepers of the shire feels constrained (because of Overreach) to break the bonds of hospitality: "all / On forfeiture of their licences stand bound, / Neuer to remember who their best guests were" (1.1.81–83). Sir Giles Mompesson, we know, so abused his patents for the licensing of inns and taverns, collecting fees for their operation, even ones that had become notorious hangouts for thieves and rogues, that his monopoly became a national scandal. As a consequence, Mompesson was hauled before Parliament in 1621, which found him guilty of abusing his patents, and early in 1625 (the year *A New Way* was composed) it completed legislation reforming the licensing of inns and ale-houses.[26] Once Parliament convicted Mompesson of malfeasance (James and Buckingham having to acquiesce), Massinger became free to dramatize this national scandal.

Massinger's treatment of grievances is also powerfully rendered in the main plot. The connections between Overreach's activities as a land extortioner—the main action that renders him a villain—and those of Mompesson have not really been explored, but they are central to Massinger's reformist concerns. Massinger invests Sir Giles with a fearsome appetite for landed wealth. Along with his "heapes of ill got gold," Overreach has "so much land, / . . . as would tire / A Falcons winges in one day to fly ouer" (3.1.83–86). Furthermore, Overreach "frights men out of their Estates, / And breakes through all Law-netts, made to curbe ille men, / As they were cobwebbs. No man dares reproue him" (2.2.114–16).

The basis of this representation again seems to come from Mompesson's public activities. As S. R. Gardiner describes it, Mompesson also held "another patent for the discovery of Crown estates which had improperly found their way into the hands of private owners. . . . Before the last-named patent, it was said, no man's property would be safe. A century of quiet possession would not suffice, if the slightest flaw could be discovered in his title."[27] Mompesson's use of legal technicalities and of the judicial process (even when he had no substantive claim) to appropriate estates that had been safe for generations are fully developed points in the portrayal of Overreach. Overreach is neither an MP, nor a licensed patentee for discovering crown estates as was Mompesson, but the picture in its broad outlines fits.

The satire on Mompesson's business schemes is consistent with Massinger's support of the aristocratic values of the Herberts. The contrast between these two kinds of gentlemen, one made through extortionate deals, the Herberts by time and tradition, provides an example from life of the symbolic oppositions on which Massinger constructed *A New Way to Pay Old Debts*.[28] As Overreach confides to his lawyer-accomplice Marrall, there has ever been "a strange Antipathie / Betweene vs, and true Gentry" (2.1.88–89).

Justice Greedy Woodcock's rumbling stomach expresses viscerally the willful hunger that moves Overreach to covet and then engross the land of long-scioned aristocrats. Woodcock's "monarchy" (3.2.20) over the kitchen is a kind of tyranny that illuminates Overreach's grander appetites; it visceralizes the issues. Overreach's frenzied anger with one of his "rebellious cooke[s]" (3.2.86) projects in political terms the dangerous discord that obtains in the Overreach household. In this way Massinger's depiction of country-house life at the Overreach estate is made to symbolize the selfishness and predation that motivate Overreach and his confederates.

By contrast Massinger, following Jonson and the country-house poetic tradition Jonson inaugurated, highlights the hospitality of the Allworth estate.[29] Wellborn's scheme to regain his mortgaged lands from Overreach is, in fact, made possible by Lady Allworth's hospitality, as she makes a great fuss over him at the banquet table while the odious Marrall oversees all. Counterpointing this depiction is the artful banquet Overreach prepares in order to marry his daughter off to Lord Lovell. There, everything is built, to use the words of Jonson's "To Penshurst," on "enuious show" and on other "mans ruine," other "mans grone" (ll. 1, 46).[30] "Spare for no cost," Overreach cries, "And let no plate be seene, but what's pure gold" (3.2.1–4). Overreach's whole presentation has the touch of a tacky son of Midas. Symptomatic of the condition Massinger theatricalizes is Overreach's behavior at table. As Overreach frenetically starts up from his dinner, envisaging a windfall, Marrall interjects, "Sir the whole boord is troubled at your rising" (3.3.13). This reaction reverberates symbolically through the play, and beyond, to Massinger's audience.

The fraternity of convenience involving Overreach, Marrall, and Greedy—that is, among the extortionate landowner, the "term-driving" lawyer, and the corruptive JP—constitutes a grievous assault upon the conception of English justice and the tradition of country-house living. This is why Massinger's audience relished seeing the legalistic Overreach lose control over Wellborn's lands through the trick of the disappearing ink on the mortgage deed. Wellborn's resolve to join Lovell's regiment in fighting on the Continent provides a final reminder of Massinger's almost programmatic commitment to the opposition parliamentary ideology of the Herberts in foreign as well as domestic policy. *A New Way to Pay Old Debts* thus ends not in a posture of opposition but in confident celebration of the values of the Herberts. These values include aristocratic country-house culture, the reform of domestic grievances, and militant support for beleaguered Protestantism—all of which are made synonymous with England's welfare.

Despite the reputation of late Jacobean and Caroline drama for escapism and toadyism, Philip Massinger's courtly drama continued to promulgate a stalwart opposition ideology. These we may now epitomize in Massinger's support for military adventurism on the Continent, implicitly opposing James's Spanish policy, and, on the domestic scene, opposition, usually expressed in ridicule, to rule by favorites, specifically, Buckingham, whom Parliament tried to impeach in 1626. These positions are bolstered by ad-

vocacy of representative institutions as protections against absolutist tyranny and of the Tacitean ideal of "ancient freedoms." As *The Roman Actor*
illustrates, Massinger's use of Tacitus' *Histories* and *Agricola,* his recourse to
Juvenal's hostile account of Domitian in the *Saturae,* and his heavy reliance
upon Jonson's *Sejanus* for passages on tyrannical government and freedom
of expression place his tragedy firmly within England's Tacitean tradition of
republican drama.[31]

Massinger's drama exhorted and shaped opinion because the playwright
understood the theater's role in holding up to examination the cultural and
political values of his time. *The Roman Actor,* through its several plays
within-the-play and its reflexive character generally, demonstrates the ways
that the theater brings to consciousness Stuart political ideals and their
violation. Plays perform reconstructive or reformative functions, Massinger
understood, since the very act of representing human beings who function
within social-political structures opens those structures to examination and,
implicitly, reform. In so conceiving his dramatic art, Massinger became the
legitimate Caroline inheritor of Chapman's philosophic political drama; but,
more than Chapman, Massinger made his plays into instruments of social
change, even as they interrogated the ideological assumptions of the early
Stuart age.

By its eloquent defense of the stage against censorship and by its defense of
theatrical representation itself, *The Roman Actor* fulfills in obvious ways the
reformative functions characteristic of Massinger's art.[32] But then, as Martin
Butler has wisely observed, in *The Roman Actor* Massinger was "interested
less in [specific issues such as] the degeneracy of the corrupt court and the
Machiavellian stratagems that underpin rule than in the idea, we might
almost say the theory of absolutism itself."[33] By exploring in this and other
plays with faraway locales the nature of absolutism, Massinger offered to the
Caroline dramatists of the next decade—the last before the civil war—a
means of assessing the prerogative government of Charles I and the character
of his court.[34]

Associated though they were with greater aristocratic culture, Massinger's
plays from the Buckingham era thus reveal an unappreciated series of nexes
between the intellectual anticourt drama of the preceding generation and the
more radical, policy-oriented citizen drama of the succeeding one. The Globe
presentation of his collaborative *Tragedy of Barnavelt* illustrates the unusually broad appeal of policy-oriented opposition drama in this period, as
do the spectacular performances of *A Game at Chess.* Furthermore, the
patronage that the Pembrokes extended to Massinger and the assistance
William Herbert appears to have provided the players during the *Game at
Chess* debacle help to explain how a courtly and a popular city opposition
drama were sustained simultaneously.[35]

Taken in their entirety, the opposition plays of the Buckingham era are testaments to the apprehensions of the age. Fittingly, the two titanic villains this drama produced, Middleton's Black Knight and Massinger's Giles Overreach, were modeled on living figures and embodied, respectively, England's foreign and domestic fears. Sensationalized as they were, such representations clearly had the potential of galvanizing substantial segments of the population. When the superseding issue of England's foreign policy is included with all the others that cut across class lines—detestation for Buckingham's person and policies, the grievances of tavern and thread monopolies, government censorship, and an evident apprehension (at least in some quarters) that Charles might discard the English institution of Parliament—England's political destabilization presents itself as a real possibility.

We arrive then at a paradox. In comparison with the blanket condemnations of court life evident a decade earlier in England's Italianate tragedies, the opposition drama of the Buckingham era can be construed as anticourt only in a more restricted sense, for it was fervently nationalistic and offered no wholesale condemnations of modern courts. Yet it clearly posed a present danger because of its hypercritical focus on specific Stuart policies and administrators. Dramatization of policy issues at home meant much more than pervasive expressions of disillusionment with court life; it usurped the royal prerogative.

Nationalistic as these plays were—indeed, because of their chauvinism—the Stuart authorities found it difficult to neutralize their subversive force. Insidiously, the well-being of England and the policies of Stuart government suddenly appeared quite separable. Moreover, insofar as the great forums of the pulpit, the Parliament, and the playhouse opposed crown policy, they sustained a series of values that distinguished concern for England from loyalty to specific acts of crown policy. Authority was thus undermined. A little more than a decade later an English revolution did gather momentum.

Yet during the period of prerogative government, the major professional drama did not become, at least not self-evidently, more strident with the times. Strictly regulated, the court-centered, anticourt drama in the post-Buckingham era (1629–42) appeared to undergo a partial eclipse. Nevertheless, Caroline court dramatists (contrary to the received orthodoxy) found ways of expressing their anticourt, courtly concerns. Concurrently, a shadowy species of anticourt drama that we know only a little about began to thrive in London's old outdoor theaters. How the mainline court drama continued to endure through the closing of the theaters, despite scrupulous supervision, accompanied as it was by a genuine protest drama in the city of London—and the significance of these developments—are the two questions I wish to address in my final chapter.

V

LATER OPPOSITION DRAMA

1629–1642

17

The Dispersion of Opposition Conceptions of Governance

The still respectable view of the Caroline drama is that it is toadyish, priggish, and even decadent.[1] Certainly the Caroline masque and many court plays offered ever more embellished ways of celebrating the institution of monarchy during the period of prerogative government, but they hardly provide a complete account of the character of Caroline drama, whether from court or city. Martin Butler's recent investigation of this period has begun to right the balance by treating the survival of the popular tradition of dissent and exploring the often covert political matter in the plays produced by Queen Henrietta-Maria's circle.[2] Although my concern, as distinct from Butler's, is to reveal the continuity of the anticourt dramatic tradition, as well as the range of opposition attitudes that even Caroline courtly drama was able to sustain in the pre–civil war period, Butler's study provides what I take to be an incontrovertibly solid basis for the revaluation of Caroline drama as politically alive and frequently dissentient.

In carrying forward the process of reassessment, I intend to demonstrate three major propositions. First, the Caroline drama as a whole is more than a moribund survival; despite the continuing shift toward précieux plays with romantic premises and exotically remote settings, it maintains a bond of continuity with the anticourt tradition and, in fact, reiterates with special urgency major themes that Chapman, Jonson, Greville, and Middleton had previously dramatized. Second, although Caroline court drama lacks the raucous volubility of the chauvinistic plays of the Buckingham era, it displays a considerable range of opposition attitudes that were also spreading into other areas of English theater and society. Third, the Caroline political drama from court, city, and country reveals a powerful set of opposition concepts. The interlacing of these, in a process that might be traced with similar results in those other agents of dissemination, Parliament and Puritan publications, constitutes an emerging discursive formation.[13]

Despite the absence of Parliament between early 1629 and April 1640, it is worth illustrating that the theater was functioning in a volatile political environment in which conceptions of right kingship and grievances figured prominently. After Charles jailed the leaders in the Commons who had held the speaker down in 1629, preventing prorogation in order to drive through three final resolutions opposed by the crown, the king, assisted by his chief advisor, Thomas Wentworth, earl of Strafford, set about establishing an efficiently run government that had no further need of parliamentary subsidies.[4] Political issues then became enmeshed in economic ones. To free himself from Parliament's control of the purse strings, Charles embarked on his policy of "thorough," that is, carrying through long-neglected procedures for collecting fees and fines. In the widely watched "Ship Money Trial" of 1637, John Hampden challenged the crown's right to collect this form of unparliamentary taxation. The king's defense, that a national emergency existed, was in reality a pretext to collect the money, but it was legally sound and the courts upheld him. The result, however, was that although Charles continued to collect ship money, he did so by a legalism that taxpayers could only detest. And the distrust of Charles as a man of honor grew.

If Charles's economic initiatives alienated large segments of the countryside, his religious ones carried his court further from the majority of his people. Perceiving the instability that Puritanism was bringing to England, Charles and Archbishop Laud undertook to revivify Anglicanism by shifting the emphasis from divisive pulpit sermons to matters of ritual and ceremony. Usually referred to as "the Laudian reforms," this policy was intended to strengthen episcopacy in England, but it is easy to see how Laudianism was open to attack as popery in disguise. The situation appeared the more critical because Queen Henrietta-Maria, to whom Charles grew increasingly close, was a devout Catholic intent on converting the entire court. By the early 1630s, Charles's secretary of state, Francis Windebank; his lord treasurer, Richard Weston (earl of Portland); and his chancellor of the Exchequer, Baron Francis Cottington—all were Catholic, a situation unprecedented since Mary's reign.[5]

Aggravating the religious problem was Charles's decision to encourage the kind of intimate ties with Spain that his father had—and he went much further. Needy of cash, the king agreed in 1630 to mint Spanish silver and later acquiesced in its being used to pay Spanish armies then fighting the Dutch Protestants. In 1640 Charles, in hopes of securing a substantial loan, unsuccessfully undertook negotiations to allow safe passage for Spanish ships carrying soldiers due to fight in the Low Countries. Such diplomacy came perilously close to betraying the Protestant cause.

The combination of Charles's despised ecclesiastical and economic policies held explosive potential. By the policy of "thorough," the landowning classes, on whom England's social stability depended, were being thrown into the arms of England's religious malcontents, who in their turn were outraged by the enforcement of Laud's policies in local parishes. From this volatile situation there arose the prospect of an unusual alliance between England's peerage and the merchant and servant classes in opposition to the crown. If the flower of England's nobility closed ranks with the more radical elements of London, especially those bent on major ecclesiastical reforms, the country might truly face destabilizing conflict.

This potential for destabilization reveals itself in related but distinctive ways in the later plays of the Caroline period. The following discussion of courtly political drama and city and country drama shows the emergence of a network of opposition ideas that connects these several kinds of drama, despite their varied generic modes, auspices of production, and social perspectives. The discussion will also show that Caroline drama, including even Caroline court drama, contains in varying degrees of intensity a spectrum of anticourt and opposition thought. To illustrate this range of thought and sentiment, I will begin with "The Triumph of Peace" (1634), a royal masque, and then, moving continually outward from the center, I will consider examples of drama from the queen's side and from disaffected courtiers affiliated with "the country" and, frequently, with prominent opposition leaders.

An alternative interpretation of Caroline drama and culture stresses, not the continuity and widespread dispersion of opposition ideas, but the dichotomous development, as Christopher Hill emphasizes, of two separate, polarized cultures.[6] And there is a certain truth to this view. Major evidence for this polarization comes, strangely enough, from court plays where, far from eschewing timely social issues, vociferous criticism directed itself as from a great mountain at the blatant beasts, the city philistines outside Whitehall. Davenant's *The Cruel Brother* (1627), for example, attacked in the figure of "Castruccio" the Puritan satirist George Wither, just as Jonson had earlier in "Time Vindicated" (1623). Similarly, Shirley dedicated *The Bird in a Cage* (1633) with ironical point to "Master William Prynne," the Puritan lawyer whose *Histriomastix,* subtitled, *The Players Scourge, or Actors Tragedy* (1632), had indexed "Women-Actors" as "notorious whores" and the queen's favorite theatrical activity, "Dancing," as "a badge of lewde lascivious women & strumpets."[7]

Since Prynne's activism had already rendered him persona non grata among Caroline officials, the appearance of *Histriomastix* provided the attorney-general with a convenient opportunity to interpret Prynne's work as a personal affront to the queen, who had championed female performers after the French fashion, danced in court spectacles herself, and appeared with her bosom exposed in "Chloridia" (1631), an action many citizens would have considered fitting for the Whore of Babylon.[8] At the time Shirley was composing his comedy, the quarrelsome lawyer had already been taken into custody (January 31, 1633) and was, predictably, about to be sentenced to have his ears cropped, to stand in the pillory, to be fined 5,000 pounds, to be deprived of his livings, and to be imprisoned for life. In the mocking metaphor of Shirley's comedy, Prynne was indeed a bird in a cage.[9]

The king's own intervention in the artistic process was tantamount to a demand that composers support his policies and skewer his enemies. Charles's meticulous review of court plays, as revealed by the plot he provided Shirley for *The Gamester* (1633), later pronouncing it "the best play" in "seven years," and by the report of the theatrical censor, Henry Herbert, that Davenant's *The Wits* (1634) was "corrected by the kinge," who "is pleasd to take *faith, death, slight,* for asseverations, and no oaths," shows how closely supervised Caroline court plays were.[10] Then too, the king's own point of view had been emblazoned by Rubens on the ceiling of the Banqueting Hall in Whitehall, with its apotheosis of monarchy and allegorical encomium to James as King of Peace and Unifier of the British Isles. Furthermore, the king's "continental" view of kingship was being celebrated in the interiors of Charles's twenty-four royal residences by such renowned foreign artists as Van Dyck, Jan Van Bockhorst, Remi Van Leempit, and Peter Thys.[11]

In practice, however, even the king's inspection of court plays or masques did not necessarily preclude the expression of a dissident viewpoint. Soon after *Histriomastix* appeared, with its dedication to Prynne's fellow barristers at Lincoln's Inn, the king offered the lawyers of the four Inns of Court the opportunity to display their loyalty by presenting a court masque, whose form, we recognize, offered ample opportunity to celebrate the virtues of Caroline kingship.[12] This offer Prynne's fellow lawyers dared only accept, but the political statement they were able to make under these conditions is instructive.

Enlisting James Shirley to compose and Inigo Jones to design their masque, the lawyers entitled it, conciliatingly, "The Triumph of Peace" (1634). Its theme, by no means a slavish one, is the king's relationship to the law (i.e, *rex* to *lex*). Along with its lavish protestations of loyalty, "The Triumph of Peace" focuses attention on the abuse of the soap monopoly, recommending it be discontinued. In this way the spectacle enacts the principle of peace it articulates, of dialogue between sovereign and subjects. In the language of the masque, just governance requires a balance between the crown's rule and that of the law so that "The world shall give prerogative to neither" (l. 560).[13]

Tradition has it that Charles failed to get the message since he commended the performance,[14] but it is unlikely that the king, schooled in the symbolism of the masque, was so dull. At the cost of over £20,000,[15] the lawyers of the Inns of Court had professed their loyalty and sumptuously entertained the court. They had given the king everything he asked for short of complete capitulation, including a final speech of obeisance in which "the sons of Peace" with "humble knee" pay homage to "sacred majesty," "Acknowledging no triumph but in you" (ll. 819–23). The king had made his point, but the lawyers, working within the prescribed form of the masque, had found the means to make theirs as well. The city was still communicating with the court and with the king, still conveying its point of view.

One does not have to travel far from the royal dais before encountering the figure of Sir John Suckling. Swordsman, wit, poet, intriguer, and amateur dramatist, Suckling was the quintessential cavalier, closely identified with the king's faction due to his role in the "first Army plot" (1641) to overthrow Parliament and anathema to the Puritan cause due to his gaming, philandering, and impiety.[16] Yet Suckling enjoyed other affiliations that conditioned his flashily independent political outlook. In addition to enjoying the company of several courtiers on the queen's side, Suckling was attracted to the circle of statesmen and poets who gathered at Viscount Falkland's country estate at Great Tew, where John Selden, George Sandys, and the earl of Clarendon, among others, explored the principles as well as the practice of politics.[17]

One part of Suckling felt a disaffection for court life, and this side finds effective expression in *The Sad One* (ca. 1632), the unfinished play Suckling composed after he abandoned for a time his involvement in political affairs.[18]

> Those were the golden times of Innocence,
> There were no Kings then, nor no lustful Peers,
> No smooth-fac'd Favorites, nor no Cuckolds sure.
> Oh!—how happy is that man, whose humbler thoughts
> Kept him from Court, who never yet was taught
> The glorious way unto damnation. (4.4.4–8)[19]

The passage, it is true, expresses conventionalized anticourt attitudes similar to those in Spenser's "Mother Hubberds Tale" or Ralegh's "The Lie," but that is just the point—the anticourt tradition continues into the Caroline court drama. Moreover, the invocation in *The Sad One* of a golden age of innocence before kings held sway is part of a mythos of a preferred prior condition of natural liberty that is articulated in *Bussy D'Ambois* and developed by Caroline dramatists.

These general anticourt sentiments complement Suckling's astonishingly personalized portrayals of the complaints of great courtiers like himself. Repeatedly, Suckling's courtiers direct their anger at the sovereign himself, who never properly appreciates their noble virtues. Old Clarimont complains in *The Sad One* of the king's "black ingratitude" since he, Clarimont, "set the Crown upon his head, / And bid him live King of his Enemies" (1.1.5–7). Similarly, Brennoralt, the loyal but "discontented Colonel," who foreshadows Suckling himself after the First Bishops' War in 1639, acknowledges that "I am angry / With the King and State sometimes" and, by report, believes "the King hath us'd him ill (*Brennoralt* [1640], 3.2.38–39, 2.3.61). The prototypes for the noble soldier who becomes disaffected with the slavish courtly world are Chapman's Bussy and Byron; however, the kind of disaffection that recurringly fixes on the person of the king is a distinctive feature of later Caroline court plays, a fact that tells us something important about the ways that courtiers assessed King Charles's statecraft.

The distance Suckling establishes between the Polish king and his chief courtiers and advisors underscores the dark side of Suckling's royalist perspective, a darkness that envelops *Brennoralt* at its conclusion. The death-thrust Brennoralt delivers to the rebel Almerin intimates the mutual self-destruction civil war brings, since Brennoralt, although fighting in a worthy cause, is shown to act in pathetic ignorance of Almerin's noble motives. So too, the Polish king's belated attempt to reward Brennoralt becomes a futile gesture, and Brennoralt's last words rebuke him for conferring favors on "blasted blossomes"—"you should have giv'n me this / When't might have rais'd me in mens thoughts" (5.3.278–80). Still discontented, Brennoralt abandons the king's service, announcing, "Back to my private life I will returne" (5.3.283).

These complaints in *Brennoralt* against court and king combine potently with a judgment of Charles's trouble-freighted domestic and foreign policy.[20] When depicting the Polish king's predicament in attempting to prosecute the war against the rebellious (not Scots, but) Lithuanians, Suckling allows King Sigismund to be lectured on the prospect of prolonged civil war. A loyal retainer articulates Sigismund's problem (cf. Charles's)—"[how] To keep on foot the warre with all your wants" when the king can neither reward his friends nor buy off his enemies, "there's so little to be had" (3.2.141, 10). Significantly, this important council scene presents two advisors vigorously debating before an unassertive Sigismund, each urging from different perspectives the need for decisiveness.

More important still, Suckling's tragedy renders fundamental issues of governance in the same language employed several years earlier in "The Triumph of Peace." As Caroline government came to be identified with Charles's own person, dramatists reacted by representing absolutist government in terms of the "prerogative." Thus Suckling's cadre of Polish rebels complain that the king's lord

> judge[s] not right
> Of the Prerogative; For oft it stands
> With Pow'r and Law, as with; our Faith and Reason:
> It is not all against, that is above (my Lord) (3.2.4–7)

Although Suckling exposes the rebels as opportunists, he allows them to present potent current political ideals, as when they assert that the king's rights must be exercised in accordance with "Pow'r and *Law*." As contrasted with the terminology employed in "The Triumph of Peace," *Brennoralt* employs the term *prerogative* in a context that distinguishes power from legal authority. By the 1630s, it is clear, Charles's insistence on prerogative rule was becoming a dramatic focal point for depicting *one* conception of governance.

But not the only one. Prerogative rule, the drama clearly shows, connoted meanings that Charles did not initiate and could not efface. A notable example from the anonymous, probably open-air *Tragedy of Nero* (publ. 1624) illustrates that the idea was all too easily identified, even before Charles's accession, with despotism. The play portrays the Machiavellian favorite advising Nero, "Where right is scand, Authoritie is orethrowne, / We haue a high prerogative aboue it" (2.2.74–75).[21] As the citation indicates, claims of prerogative were popularly perceived as a despotic attempt to assert a power above what is right and beyond modification by rational debate.

Such conceptions of governance demonstrate that Cavalier playwrights, far from writing in splendid isolation, voiced sensitive issues of governance and clearly conceived of the Caroline state's sickness as an ideological rather than a limited political problem. This understanding enabled Suckling to sift the issues King Sigismund faces to two: "Religion / And Liberty" (3.2.74–75). The self-confessed hypocrisy of the rebels, who "Presse much religion . . . / And for our selves reserve th'advantages" (2.3.29–31), helps to explain the plays' disdain for them, but the council scenes nevertheless bring home the formidable ideology the king confronts. To fractious subjects, "Liberty," which though never defined is believed to decline as the king's unilateral powers increase, and "Religion" have become like "a young Mistris. . . . / For which each man will fight, and dye" (3.2.106–7). Whether he decides to make peace or hateful war, Sigismund must no longer temporize; an extended truce (such as that at Berwick) will only undermine the king's fragile position.

Royalist though it is, Suckling's tragedy becomes a vehicle for airing the oppositionist agenda:

> Nor are you Sir, assur'd of all behinde you:
> For though your Person in your Subjects hearts
> Stands highly honour'd, and belov'd, yet are
> There certaine Acts of State, which men call grievances
> Abroad [among "The Common People" (l. 100)]; and though
> they bare them in the times
> Of peace, yet will they now perchance, seeke to
> Be free, and throw them off. (3.2.93–99)

The condescension of the advisor's speech and the implication that Sigismund has never heard of his people's grievances are evident. Even if one does not *agree* with the substance of these grievances, the possibility arises of acceding to them for pragmatic reasons. As in art, so it was in life, for in a letter of 1641 Suckling advised Charles to "doe somethinge extraordinary," "by doing more, doing something of his owne" the people "expected not." He went on to urge the king to abandon his impugned ministers. There the pragmatism that informed Suckling's politics becomes explicit—"before the King hath power to preserve, hee must have power."[22]

This kind of association of grievances with the prerogative and other fundamental ideas of political rights attains eloquent voice in William Habington's *The Queen of Arragon* (1640). Devoutly Catholic and closely associated with the queen's circle, Habington, along with William Cartwright, was one of the exemplars of the Queen's précieux school of courtly love. Yet drama on the queen's side was far from being aseptically apolitical, and Habington himself maintained a complex network of allegiances outside it. Like Cartwright, he was, first of all, a classical scholar, trained to apply the wisdom of the past to the present. Second, he belonged to that notable circle associated with the opposition leader Philip Herbert, Habington's kinsman through his marriage to Lucy Herbert. Third, Habington possessed a "country" value system that was more fundamentally hypercritical of court culture than Suckling's.

Inspired by his wife, Habington composed his graceful, morally exemplary book of poems, *Castara* (3d ed., 1640), which, in addition to praising a chaste private ideal, betrays a pronounced anticourt strain. Thus Habington opposes Castara's name to those who "court loud fame" ("All Fortunes," p. 21), and with a lighter touch than that of Chapman, whom he admired, disdains the witchery of "Court applause" ("Against Opinion," p. 68).[23] He commends Lord *Windsor* in "Perdam Sapientiam Sapientum" for "fly[ing] /

The glorious troubles of the Court" (p. 120) and, echoing *Bussy D'Ambois*, mocks the swelling designs of the "Great Statist!" whose ambitions are contracted in a tomb ("Solum mihi superest sepulchrum," p. 124). Habington's country values emerge explicitly in *The Queen of Arragon* in the subplot representation of the philandering nobleman Sanmartino, who can domineer in his villa "O'ere th'humble country-gentleman, who stands / Aloof and bare" (p. 364).[24] Through Sanmartino, Habington offers an Overburian-like portrait of the "absolute cavalier" who pretends to "state-designs all day" while "At night; he'll play, he'll drink,—you guess the rest" (p. 363).

Striking as this anticourt satire is, it pales before Habington's critique in *The Queen of Arragon* of the practice of kingship and the presentation of grievances. The tragicomedy, it is true, employs lavish costumes and always works toward a balanced, nonpolemical conclusion, quite unlike the firebrandishing dramas of the 1620s, but for that very reason it could gain the royal ear. For all the play's temperance, moreover, the political issues cut deep; they also synthesize considerations of political ethics that other plays treat piecemeal. For these several reasons, one infers, Philip Herbert "caused" Habington's play to be performed at court and then promoted its publication.[25]

The most important issue raised in *The Queen of Arragon* is the monarch's problematic relationship to her people. Queen Cleodora admits, "My fame is 'mong the people yet unsettled, / And my capacity for government / Held much too feeble" (p. 371). This set of circumstances does more than adumbrate Charles's own situation; it airs profound concerns about his evident inability to secure the hearts of his countrymen. One aspect of this problem manifests itself in the Caroline habit of scrutinizing kingly bearing and character. This is true not only of Ford's *Perkin Warbeck* (1629–34) with its depiction of the noble-speaking, doomed pretender to Henry VII's throne, Warbeck, but also of Cartwright's *The Royal Slave* (1636), which depicts, along with its Persian sovereign Arsamnes, the mock king and slave Cratander, who after being invested with "All the Prerogatives of Majesty" is shown to "carry / All things with such a State, and yet so free / From an insulting Pride" (ll. 181, 284–86).[26] Compared to Persia's Arsamnes, Cratander offers a second, superior role model for kingship. The dramatic interest that begins with kingly character ends in Ford's, Cartwright's, and Habington's plays with the necessity of kings securing subjects' loyalty. As Arsamnes' queen warns, however warlike kings my be, their armies "have something / Left yet to Conquer; [subjects'] Breasts" (1331–32).

This fixation on the personal exercise of majesty joins with that other characteristically Caroline feature, the tendency to dramatize almost by replication the unstable political situation obtaining in England in 1639–40. In *The Queen of Arragon*, Cleodora's country is being menaced by invasion from Castile. The deft touch by which Habington makes the Aragonian ruler a queen highlights the political danger of Aragon's being delivered into bondage if Cleodora should become enamored of the enemy king. Symbolically, Charles had himself long been enamored of Spain with its sophisticated court culture and the powerful authority of its king. Then too, Charles's decision in 1630 to mint Spanish silver in England that would later be used to help finance Spain's war against the Dutch could well be interpreted as a deliberate turning away from basic English interests (cf. the huge loan Charles tried to negotiate with Spain in 1640 in return for protecting Spanish ships). Habington actualizes such threats as these when he has the king of Castile woo Aragon's Queen Cleodora himself.

These allegorized recollections recapitulate obsessive concerns about England's political instability and anticipate more specific, bold attempts to depict and thereby analyze the problem. Though Cleodora's general, Decastro, succeeds in putting down the initial invasion, the prospect of civil war continues because Decastro fears for his country's sovereignty. These fears have two foci—Cleodora's having fallen in love with the noble Castilian general Florentio and her subsequent disregard for her own people's fear. The issue is again the royal prerogative since royal marriage was a matter that Tudor and Stuart kings had long claimed to be beyond the debate of Parliament. On this score Habington portrays Decastro, the people's spokesman, as self-righteous and proud but irreproachably honest and fit to rule. His loyalty is symbolically expressed by his pressing a love-suit to the queen, although she spurns his cause. The root cause, however, of Cleodora's distaste for Decastro is that he exerts an irksome check on her autonomy. Cleodora cannot understand how her private preferences in love are just matter for Decastro's criticism; he ought only show her the obedience of a dutiful subject. This view of the royal prerogative Decastro answers eloquently:

> Then, great madam,
> I must acquaint you that the supreme law
> Of princes is the people's safety, which
> You have infring'd, and drawn thereby into
> The inward parts of this great state a most
> Contagious fever. (p. 349)

This invocation of a "supreme law" above princes operates in effect as a justification for rebellion. Issued from a highborn person whose integrity remains unblemished, it points to a coalescence of opposition notions impossible in the era of Beaumont and Fletcher, who in *Philaster* portray rebellion sympathetically but never approvingly. Decastro's rebuke goes so far as to adumbrate a balanced theory of government, one that redefines fealty as an obligation subjects owe in return for the people's safety. Although not explicitly affirmed, this view of the preferred relations between king and commonweal is endorsed by the issue of events. Once Cleodora begins to accept the military as well as the amorous advances of the Castilian invaders, Decastro leads a rebellion in the name of national liberty (a key term). These events bring a true knotting of opposing principles. Habington's play will not sanction Cleodora's insensitivity to popular demands, but neither will it approve the subjection, marital or political, that Cleodora would feel if constrained to wed Decastro. However, in a fine balancing act, Habington allows his queen to realize her personal desires, her prerogative, in wedding Florentio (not the king of Castile), and this personal end she achieves only after Decastro has secured the state from within.

The Queen of Arragon exhibits the tension between the absolute exercise of prerogative and subjects' privilege, or contract. These, we notice, constitute a continuity of concern from Jonson's and Chapman's ideological drama, but the terms of conflict have become more specific, focused, legalized, another characteristic of late Caroline political theater. Furthermore, the rhetorical quality of Caroline theater is itself expressive of a milieu in which political issues are being voiced with self-conscious urgency and awareness of their forensic power in the theater of life. This heightening explains the spectacular conclusion of *The Queen of Arragon,* in which Cleodora presents Decastro, the voice of her people, with a charter and tells him, "Write in that blank all your demands, and . . . I'll deny you nothing" (p. 406). This magnanimous gesture combines a recollection of Magna Carta with the need to address the long list of grievances the Parliament of 1640 was expected to put on the table,[27] and it echoes Suckling's notion about the advisability of Charles acceding to the popular demands. Decastro's equally sublime gesture of returning the blank unsigned suggests an ideal to which no royal audience would want to take exception, that the relations between sovereign and realm work best not by legalisms but by the mutual faith of the one estate in the other. The play's aristocratic hope is to redress grievances through the superior concord of hearts, not divisive demands. The hope as well as the doubt is gracefully implied in Habington's conceit: "if the queen / Would make a statesman, she might cure a lover" (p. 375). The queen of Aragon must prove a tactful statesman if she is to make her way in the politics of love and cure her country's woes.

To an even greater degree than Habington's compositions, those of Sir John Denham reveal this emerging matrix of opposition political ideas that conjoin ideology and myth with the grievances of 1640. Although Denham sided with the king when the civil war broke out, his work reveals him to be the most outspokenly critical of all the courtier dramatists we have considered. Like Habington, he maintained close ties with the parliamentary leader Philip Herbert, at whose home "at Wilton and London," Aubrey reports, he spent "a yeare" in 1652.²⁸ Denham was also the product of an opposition culture. His distinguished father, Sir George Croke, was the most outspoken of the judges who supported John Hampden's claim that the king's collection of ship money was an illegal form of taxation, subverting "fundamental law." Denham himself composed an extravagant elegy to Croke, beginning, "This was the Man! the Glory of the Gown / Just to Himself, his Country and the Crown!" (p. 156).²⁹

Remembered today for his famous neogeorgic poem "Coopers Hill" (1642), Denham there displayed his talent for blending the contemporary moment with specific historical settings that evoke an almost mythically sanctified past. In this spirit "Coopers Hill" recollects the signing of the Magna Carta at Runnymede, anachronistically introduces Charles as a royal hunter, and laments, "not long in force this Charter stood; / Wanting that seal, it must be seal'd in bloud" (ll. 335–36). The unequivocal double judgment that concludes the poem exonerates neither king nor populace:

> Thus Kings, by grasping more than they could hold,
> First made their Subjects by oppression bold:
> And popular sway, by forcing Kings to give
> More than was fit for Subjectes to receive. (ll. 343–46)

Denham's only play, *The Sophy* (1641), a King's company production, employs a similar method that links basic ideas of governance to a recognizably Caroline set of conditions. Denham's recourse to a Persian political setting for his melodramatic tragedy owes something to Caroline predilections for Eastern settings (e.g., Massinger's Turkish-set *The Emperor of the East* [1631]), but a great deal more to the kind of probing, intellectual political tragedy Greville's *Mustapha* provided almost two generations earlier. Like *Mustapha*, *The Sophy* employs its Persian setting to explore the paths of tyranny; likewise, it depicts a contemporary court history and attempts to deliver through charged, epigrammatic utterance a searing experience of the consequences of the corrupted practice of politics.

The Sophy is particularly deserving of examination for its structural and symbolic presentation of character. Representing the functions of state through a triumvirate, Denham portrays King Abbas as flanked by two principal advisors, his ecclesiastical minister, the Caliph, and his preeminent minister of state, Haly. A parallel between this trio and Charles, Laud, and Strafford is, however, of less moment than the fact that Denham constitutes the state in this three-pillared fashion, which embodies so well the situation in Caroline England during the prerogative period. Just as Habington depicted Decastro as the representative of the people, so Denham renders Prince Mirza symbolically as "the People's Idol" and the leader of a stirring, popular power (pp. 253, 259), which Abbas is taught to fear.

The self-aggrandizing, hypocritical advice that these two pillars provide their vulnerable, isolated king engenders his ruin. Ironically, the tragedy's pivotal epigrammatic truth—"Sir, where Subjects want the priviledge / To speak; there Kings may have the priviledge, / To live in ignorance" (2.1.143–45)—is delivered in deceitful flattery by Haly. A still deeper irony inheres in the fact that King Abbas's conscientiousness in trying to embrace the truth, which the "priviledge" of free speech brings, actually draws him further into Haly's spell. As Cleodora's ill-founded rebuke of Decastro for his "Ill-tutored priviledge" (p. 350) of speech shows in *The Queen of Arragon*, the idea was attaining growing currency in Caroline England. When early in 1642 Charles attempted to remove the five members from their seats in Parliament, the House members, outraged at the invasion of their sacrosanct chamber, shouted "Privilege! privilege!" The privilege of the chamber is, of course, closely related to the privilege of debating without outside interference. Tragically, the attempt of Denham's king to hear unflattering speech causes him to be ruined by his advisor's misconstruction of events. Pathetically dependent upon Haly to interpret political events, Abbas learns to fear a rebellion; and to forestall a usurpation that was never planned, he orders the terrible, symbolically devastating blinding of his own son Prince Mirza.

Denham's emphasis upon the perfidious favorite finds a structural complement in Denham's portrayal of the Caliph, who acts as ecclesiastical executor of the king's misbegotten policy. Belying his pious rhetoric, the Caliph willingly enacts Abbas's policy, although he knows it to be based on false intelligence, and he does so in a cynically effective way, proclaiming to his council that the Prince's "conspiracy" was revealed to him by "Great *Mahomet*" "in a Vision" (3.1.52, 54). By repeatedly protesting that he exercises only a limited "function," the pharisaical Caliph also attempts to evade moral responsibility for his behavior. But the undercutting political wisdom of the tragedy betokens in the manner of *Mustapha* a deeper truth of the state's deformity:

> [Princes] advance you to advance our purposes:
> Nay, even in all Religions,
> Their Learned'st, and seeming holiest men, but serve
> To work their Masters ends.
>
> (3.34–37)

Significantly, this timely Caroline rendering also echoes that offered in *The Queen of Arragon* when Decastro charges "the present state" flatters itself "And make[s] divinity serve human ends" (p. 396).

The Sophy enforces its repelling depiction of compromised ecclesiastical authority through a philosophical debate in which the Prince's loyal advisors find religion to be the overriding cause of discontent. Princes are "mis-led" by religious advisors; they "that should be / The curb . . . [are] made the spur to tyranny" (4.1.16, 21–22). Furthermore, "whatsoever change the State invades, / The pulpit either forces, or perswades" (4.1.63–64). The turmoil at the top begets a corresponding reaction among the populace. Religion "swells the torrent [of discontent] higher," sanctioning force, which "calls to mind the old prerogatives / Of free-born man" (4.1.43–44, 46–47). The fact that this consideration of "the old prerogatives" recollects passages from "The Triumph of Peace," *Brennoralt,* and *The Queen of Arragon* points to the coalescing power of an evolving political discourse. Here, Denham clearly demonstrates his understanding that popular complaints have become inextricably entwined with fundamental ideas of right. Prerogatives, it is being asserted, belong to subjects as well as kings. Denham's use of the adjective *old* before *prerogatives* recalls *ancient* prerogatives, and in a further crystallizing association recollects something of the mythos of immemorial subjects' rights dramatized in Chapman's *Bussy D'Ambois,* which was revived in 1634 and 1638. With slightly different emphasis the theme reappears in *The Royal Slave,* when Queen Atossa insists that her husband "shall grant that the Ephesians may / Still freely use their antient Customes, changing / Neither their Rites nor Lawes" (ll. 1424–26).

Not that Denham welcomes radical religious reform from below. To the contrary, it frightens him because it feeds sentiments for full-scale rebellion. This consideration mutes the radical potential in Denham's depiction of the Persian realm's distractions. Once authority and sacred laws fall into disregard, the nation is lost. The accession of the Sophy, the Prince's son and Abbas's grandson, reaffirms the importance of the continuity of the succession. Thus the play comes to rest in the symbolic affirmation of a continuous lineage that unites in *The Sophy* both king and (through Mirza) commonweal. However, the depictions of Haly and the Caliph underline the need for a new order of administration, and a much darker, Greville-like side to the tragedy hovers over its seemingly hopeful conclusion. A self-protective sensibility appropriate to civil war England is already evident in Prince Mirza's cocoonlike withdrawal from the state, affirming Clermont-like "A world within my self . . . [as] / My empire" (5.1.25–26). The tragedy ends, moreover, with a graphic representation of the torture that civil war brings to people and to states. Just as Chabot's emaciated servant Allegre reappears after having been put to the rack in the conclusion of *Chabot,* so too Denham reintroduces the once-gay courtier Solyman "as from the Rack," declaring with nervy wit that he, like "the Body Politick," needs "a good Bone setter" (s.d., 5.1.593.1; 606–8).

The contempt for ecclesiastical authority that courtier dramatists dispiritedly record was expressed with savage satire and mimicry in the less reputable public theaters of London among unknown citizen playmakers. These dramatic composers exhibit the reformation zealousness so much feared for its revolutionary potential by courtier dramatists, however oppositionist. They thus represent the most extreme opposition voices that the late Caroline drama contains. But again, it would be unproductive and misleading so to dichotomize the pre–civil war drama. Between the varied manifestations of opposition court drama and the extremist religious satires of London playwrights may be placed the more moderate opposition plays of Richard Brome, a London-based professional, and Lord Mildmay Fane, the earl of Westmorland, a country playwright. Our brief examination of these forms of opposition drama, which were composed far from the center, will serve to round out this demonstration of the plenitude and scope of anticourt drama in the late Caroline period.

Because many Puritan dramatists of London expressed an uncompromising hostility to Laud's religious policies, Henry Herbert had little interest, it appears, in the kind of accommodation he sought to achieve among courtier dramatists who promulgated opposition sentiments. Like *A Game at Chess,* these citizen plays draw inspiration from subversive Puritan pamphlets, and neither Herbert nor Charles appears to have demurred at suppressing them. The result is that few of these citizen plays survive, but precious records of their performances do. On February 16, 1634, the censor Herbert, although himself of mild Puritan sympathies, had a pawnbroker imprisoned in Marshalsea "for lending a church-robe with the name of JESUS upon it, to the players in Salisbury Court, to present a Flamen, a priest of the heathens."[30] On May 8, 1639, "the players of the Fortune were fined £1,000 for setting up an altar, a bason, and two candlesticks, and bowing down before it upon the stage, and although they allege it was an old play revived, and an altar to the heathen gods, yet it was apparent that this play was revived on purpose in contempt of the ceremonies of the Church."[31] *The Valiant Scot* ([ca.1626]; publ. 1637) by one J. W. was also conveniently revived in 1639 in London after Charles's unsuccessful attempt to force a new prayer book upon the Scots. According to one Puritan pamphleteer, *The Valiant Scot* "played five days with great applause, which vexed the Bishops."[32] So too, as the title of the suppressed lost play *The Whore New Vamped* (1639) suggests, the work appears to have capitalized on the same hostility to Laud's program for increased ceremony in the Anglican Church.[33]

A substantial stride to the right of these obscure citizen satires is the work of Richard Brome, whose status as a professional dramatist demanded accommodation to governmental authorities. However, Brome, apart from Massinger, was the most important professional dramatist of independent social conscience to continue to offer a spirited, dissident voice in the 1630s. Resolutely resisting the trends of sentimentality and platonic love, Brome made his drama a vehicle for the satiric expression and evaluation of public issues. Considered as a corpus, his plays display something of the broad national purpose to which Massinger and Middleton had directed their drama in the Buckingham era. Toward this end Brome, in his social satire on England's "mad," divided condition, implored his audience in *The Antipodes* (1636–37) "To keep the weakest branch o'th'stage alive."[34]

The opposition content of Brome's work might be discovered in many of his dozen plays; for our purposes it must suffice to examine his most important political comedy, *The Court Beggar* (1640). One pertinent interpretation of this satire is offered by Butler, who treats the play as the most "fully realized" example of the "subversive possibilities of the popular style."[35] For him *The Court Beggar* is an unabashedly radical work of major significance. This claim seems to me to be startling and to misrepresent through overgeneralization the social purposes of Brome's comedy. In my view the play is not so radical; its opposition content is hard-hitting but specific and well within the range expressed by other professionals and by Cavalier playwrights. The difference in our respective evaluations may seem minor, yet what is at stake is the social perspective we are to attribute to professional anticourt (to use my term) playwrights in the pre–civil war period.

The satirized title figure of *The Court Beggar,* Sir Andrew Mendicant, is a monopolist, or "projector," whose activities actually include the begging of wardships (i.e., "Lands / Are found of men that make away themselves, / And so of fooles and madmen" [p. 188]) as well as patents.[36] The play therefore attacks simultaneously two of the most persistent grievances in early Stuart England. By satirizing the abusive system of the court of wards, *The Court Beggar* brings to culmination three decades in the portrayal of the grievance that Middleton had treated in the 1620s in *Women Beware Women* and Massinger in the 1630s in *The Guardian.* So too, *The Court Beggar* revivifies half a century of protest against monopolies, from the wry Jacobean allusions in Chapman's and Marston's satiric comedies to the more pointed topical satire of the projector-monopolist in a *A New Way to Pay Old Debts* in the 1620s, to Shirley's rude Caroline burlesque of six very uncourtly patentees in "The Triumph of Peace," to Brome's *The Weeding of Covent Garden* (1632).

Brome's rather slight plot, in which Mendicant is foiled in his plan to marry his daughter Clarissa to the disreputable courtier Ferdinand, who is Mendicant's court conduit for obtaining his obnoxious patents, recapitulates a familiar pattern from Elizabeth's time in the depiction of usurers. From *The Jew of Malta* (ca. 1589) and *The Merchant of Venice* (1594?) through *A New Way to Pay Old Debts,* the usurer (or, simply, the land or money cheat) was repeatedly depicted as a widower with one grown daughter, whose secret marriage to one not of the father's choosing foils the father's avaricious schemes. Brome's application of this pattern to the patent-beggar emblematizes his assessment of this court sycophant as a threat to every decent human being and (in the context of Brome's play) the nation itself.

In addition, Brome satirizes his rival William Davenant as the affected dimwit "Court-Wit" and Davenant's courtier friend Sir John Suckling, who had just acquitted himself ignominiously in the First Bishops' War, as the mad, cowardly Ferdinand.[37] The personal animus and choice of targets in Brome's lampoon attenuate somewhat the national scope that Massinger's and Middleton's satires on Mompesson and Gondomar had offered a decade earlier, but Brome's brand of personal satire does explain why *The Court Beggar,* which had also been performed without license, was forbidden and its theater manager, William Beeston, imprisoned.[38] In combination with its satire on wardships and projectors, the attack on two such prominent courtiers as Davenant and Suckling illustrates the specific objects of Brome's anticourt barbs.

For Butler, the personal attack on Suckling is incidental to a much more comprehensive one on courtiers in general. Evidence for this reading is an observation that Ferdinand has proved to be "as mad / As you can thinke a Courtier must be / That is more mad then all the rest" (p. 189). Madness, Butler deduces, is endemic to courtiers, although the passage that immediately follows this, which derides courtly ambition, soldiering, poetizing, and gaming, fits Suckling precisely. So too the third act coup de theatre keeps the emphasis firmly on the personal satire of Suckling when Ferdinand, in patent imitation of Suckling's inglorious performance as a Cavalier officer in the war against the Scots, is brought on stage "bound and hooded," ranting, "Am I then taken prisoner in the North? / Wounded, disarm'd and bound?" (p. 218). Insofar as Suckling fits the impious mold of the Cavalier courtier, the satire is indeed generic, but Brome's comedy is not fundamentally hostile to all courtiers, It aims at the debased tendencies within the court, not at the idea of the court itself. In this regard it is also well to remember that the other face of Brome's satire is romance, and in this affirming spirit Brome depicts the proper, courtly, and altogether worthy Ferdinand, who distinguishes among kinds of courtiers (*Court Beggar,* p. 235) and whose own virtue wins him Clarissa.

Butler concludes that Brome's satire on Mendicant's various forms of monopoly-begging constitute "a condemnation of the whole system of preference" with its "hierarchy of parasitic courtiers" and, furthermore, that "the tremendous dominance of the court and its clients is dragging all wealth and power from the rest of the country to London, there to be frittered away."[39] If this conclusion is taken to mean that Brome opposes the *entire system* of patronage, it goes substantially beyond the warrantable evidence. Brome was not aiming to dismantle the patronage system wherein courtiers were rewarded with reversions and offices in return for service to the crown. An alternative to such a system of maintaining the bureaucratic network of governmental services was hardly conceivable, the modern system of salarying employees being unknown. Rather, this "son of Ben" was responding to economic abuses whose origin was not unlike what caused the imposition of the forced loan—the crown's dire need of revenue, particularly after Charles's unsuccessful attempt to force prayer-book conformity on Scotland. Brome was thus attacking another odious economic practice already under attack, the irresponsible conferring of rights of monopoly and estate supervision for a fee upon courtly entrepreneurs to the detriment of the commonwealth. Brome was not, however, spoiling for revolutionary change, and his anticourt perspective is not so sweeping as to encompass an alternative social organization. To the contrary, he was vigorously dramatizing specific grievances, flinging his barbed lampoon directly at the court, and seeking redress, just as his forebears had done.

The spectacle at the end of the play in which Mendicant finds his mercenary plans confounded, his own estate "beg'd" away from him (p. 264), and his daughter well-matched to her own liking, illustrates once again Brome's point of focus. Mendicant enters "attir'd all in Patents; A Windmill on his head," crying, "Roome here: a Hall for a Monopolist, / You, Commonwealths informers lead me on. / Bring me before the great Assembly" (p. 267). So emblematized as the monopolist generic, the embodiment of the court's rapacious troop of patentees, Mendicant becomes a figure of unequivocal national grievance, whom "the Great Assembly," Parliament, must brand and remove. In this fundamental respect the play is without compromise. But even as Brome probably began composing his satire in 1639, the king, under great pressure, had already canceled more than twenty offensive monopolies.[40] Brome was dramatizing a winning opposition issue that had already gained reluctant royal assent. Further reform of grievances there must be—through Parliament. The end will not be revolutionary change but wholesome reformation once "the Projects are all cancel'd, and the Projectors turnd out o' dores" (p. 268).

Brome was by no means alone in his eagerness for parliamentary intervention. Outside London, Mildmay Fane, the country lord whose seat was at Apthorpe, Northamptonshire, and who had served in Parliament throughout the 1620s, joined Brome's explicit call for Parliament to redress economic grievances.[41] When compromise became impossible, Fane sided with the royalist cause, but he conceived of effective government as meaning the king *and* Parliament. His play *Candy Restored* (1641), an allegorical, masquelike pastoral, ascribes the decayed condition of a formerly idyllic state to the banishment thirteen years before of "Dr. Psunodarke"—that is Parliament (ll. 287–97).[42] As in Brome's fanciful depiction of England's "madness" in

The Antipodes, the summoning of a doctor of physic is a sign both of Fane's reformist orientation and of dire contemporary assessments of the state's sickness. Since Candy's bounty has been consumed with heavy taxes— "stuffed with impositians Noueltie" (l. 353), Fane welcomes Dr. Psuno-darke's return. Through "Th' assembly both of people, and of states" the land will be "monopolye, and proiect free," and "a passing bell [will 'knole'], / For th' patent, and the Patentee" (ll. 1037, 1043–45). "Proiects" will "no more endure / Nor the freeborne become a slaue"; then, peace and plenty will "restore" Candy (ll. 1072–73, 1127).

Accompanying Fane's parliamentary bias, *Candy Restored* reveals the same evolving discursive formation discernible in the plays from the city and the court. The litany of economic grievances—here, impositions, patents, monopolies—is immediately associated with Parliament, the curative "assembly." Even more significantly, Parliament is conceived as bringing about a "restoration" of a prior arcadian condition; it is empowered by myth and an abiding principle of political right—"freeborne" life. This constellation of associated ideas in Fane's work (see also *The Change* [1642]), along with that of the Caroline playwrights of the city and court, weaves opposition ideology as well as myth and topical grievances into a seamless discourse such that any one element seems irresistibly to call up related ones.

To conclude this argument on the emergence of a distinctive, reformist, political discourse that sweeps across the late Caroline drama, I propose as a kind of coda to compare three dramatic representations of what was commonly regarded as the most flagrant abuse in the period of prerogative government, the forced loan, and to examine its treatment in the Cavalier tragedy *Brennoralt,* the courtly but opposition-oriented *The Sophy,* and *The King and the Subject* (1638), an opposition play by the professional playwright Philip Massinger. Considered together, they also help to refine our understanding of the regulation of Caroline political drama.

The fact that all three works treat the problem of supply, which is extraordinary in itself, illustrates how the means used by the king to alleviate his economic distress had taken possession of the late Caroline dramatic imagination as a basic issue in the ethics of governance. As we have seen in plays treating other issues such as prerogative or privilege, the crown's problem of supply draws to it a network of ideas that we properly associate with parliamentarian, civil war thought—the forced loan, grievances, subjects' hearts, liberty, Roman tyranny, original freedom, and the prerogatives of subjects as well as kings. These ideas constitute a discursive formation that implicitly calls into question the powers of the king and invests subjects and Parliament with fundamental rights and responsibilities.

Sympathetic to the crown as it is, *Brennoralt* unflinchingly spells out *its* king's dilemma of supply. He can neither confer rewards "Where there's so little to be had," nor "with all your wants" can he properly prosecute a war (3.2.10, 141). As the council scene shows, the king's efforts to relieve his gnawing insufficiency of supply are quickly associated with "certaine Acts of State, which men call grievances / Abroad" (3.2.96–97). These grievances have so stimulated thoughts of righteousness and "Liberty" that "All is now too late" to "disabuse" "The vulgar in Religion," and civil war is threatened (3.2.75, 82–83). The invocation of the shibboleth "Liberty" (although it is denigrated as a "specious" name) (3.2.75) and the association of supply with grievances reveal Suckling's own assimilation of the rhetoric of opposition thought. In a way, Suckling's contempt for the cantankerous opposition, to say nothing of the "Common People" (3.2.100), provides the most cogent demonstration of the power of opposition thought to shape the content of Cavalier discourse.

The Sophy is more daringly comprehensive in its reproduction of contemporary circumstances surrounding Charles's attempts to tax prerogatively. It is also more judgmental. Recalling, it seems, Charles's position in the aftermath of Scotland's occupation of the north country, *The Sophy* describes not only King Abbas's exhausted exchequer but the anguished weakness it enforces upon him. "Tell me what Province they demand for ransom" (1.2.67), Abbas demands. Out of these circumstances Denham reenacts Charles's presumptuous demands upon the city fathers in 1639: "Let twenty thousand men be raised, / Let fresh supplyes of victuals, and of money / Be sent with speed" (p. 238, 1642 edition). In fact, Abbas explicitly orders "the Bankers" to be sent for, even though they have become reluctant lenders (1.2.48–51), just as London's merchants had been made to submit to the crown's excessive, sometimes coercive, borrowing powers despite its inability to repay.[43] The 1642 edition adds:

> *King.* Talke not to me of Treasures, or Exchequers:
>   Send for five hundred of the wealthiest Burghers,
>   Their shops and ships are my exchequer.
> *Abd.* [*aside.*] 'Twere better you could say their hearts. (p. 238)

The passage is memorable for its linking in one felicitous line the grievances of "ship" money and merchants' "shop" money. In this poetic manner, country and city grievances become discrete expressions of a single arrogant economic policy. These economic abuses in turn suggest political abuse of the merchants' freedom to deny the loan. *The Sophy* virtually labels the crown's relationship to the city as exploitative, in effect justifying the city's unwillingness to grant the crown the loan. Loyalty, indeed, becomes the underlying issue. Abdall's aside functions as no benign advice to princes but as a condemnation whose implicit standard of proper governance is the love ("hearts") that princes earn. King Abbas is to be held responsible, Denham implies, for losing his subjects' loyalty. Economic grievances thus become associated with royal arbitrariness, and these perceptions in turn provoke the hostile counterassertion of the proper relationship of kings to subjects.

Still denser in the network of ideas it evokes is Massinger's lost *The King and the Subject,* in which, ironically, only the censored passage on the forced loan has been preserved:

> Monys? Wee'le rayse supplies what ways we please,
> And force you to subscribe to blanks, in which
> We'le mulct you as wee shall thinke fitt. The Caesars
> In Rome were wise, acknowledginge no lawes
> But what their swords did ratifye, the wives
> And daughters of the senators bowinge to
> Their will, as deities.[44]

There is a distinctive intensity to Massinger's portrayal. Massinger's king is not just peremptory in his exigency but insouciantly arbitrary, raising supplies "what ways we please." And whereas Denham's king presumes upon the bankers, Massinger's explicitly rejects any check on his authority to tax, asserting his right to "mulct." Furthermore, Massinger's king cites approvingly the Roman tradition wherein "the senators"—Rome's parliamentary body—bowed down to the emperor as if he were a god. The king's invocation of the Caesars, it may also be observed, reproduces in an ironic dramatic context the iconography of Charles's court, in which such analogies linking Charles to the Roman emperors were fondly employed.[45] All together, these details demonstrate that Massinger conceives of his king as a despot, as the play's alternative title, *The Tyrant,* denotes.[46]

It is particularly significant that Massinger's king wishes to justify his actions by appealing to precedent. In this respect the passage reflects the ideological intensity of the late Caroline period. With a deft topical touch, Massinger portrays his king as rationalizing his policy of forced subscriptions by appealing to the precedent of the Caesars and by claiming that the Roman citizenry applauded such decisiveness. Further justifying his absolute authority, the king appeals to a preferred Roman epoch when force, metaphorically rendered as "swords," "did ratifye" instead of "lawes." All the categories of this argument, including the mythical-historical justification, proceed from ideas essential to parliamentary thought, but with a reversed, perverse emphasis. This discursive mode becomes especially apparent in the king forcing his subjects' compliance through "blanks," which is to say through "blank charters," "carte blanche," precisely the same economic grievance underlying the critical depictions in *Richard II* (1594–95) and *Thomas of Woodstock* (1591–95) of the ill-fated rule of Richard II, who lost his throne over grievances such as this. And whereas Habington's *Queen of Arragon* offers her subjects a blank charter to redress grievances, thereby suggesting the rights of subjects in Magna Carta, Massinger's king claims a magna carta for himself to work his arbitrary ends.

Charles's own reading of these lines demonstrates that the argument contains its own refutation, for as Herbert's office book records, the king wrote angrily, "This is too insolent, and to bee changed."[47] This frequently cited action is usually adduced to demonstrate the Caroline period's programmatically ruthless brand of literary censorship. But of the three passages on the forced loan, only Massinger's was in fact censored. In this context of censorship, it has been customary to make suppressed plays and passages the basis for generalization, not those on the same subject that have escaped suppression. The fact that Suckling and Denham were able to portray the sensitive forced loan issue whereas Massinger could not suggests a more complicated picture of the way that Caroline censorship operated.

The key word in Charles's notation would appear to be the intensifier *too*. Charles's order suggests an attempt to curtail the overstepping of some ill-defined boundary. When Massinger represented not merely the issue of the forced loan but the player king from a disrespectful, even hostile, point of view, the dramatist had gone too far. Such an interpretation suggests the presence of an unwritten system of rules for interpretation between playwright and censor,[48] else why would Massinger have submitted his manuscript for approval in the first place? The Caroline drama found itself able enough, as we have seen, to communicate its dissident ideas, but the mode or tone of expression appears to have been crucial, and the price for crossing beyond the unwritten limits of acceptable discourse, for communicating a hostile intention, could sometimes be suppression. Yet even *The King and the Subject* was approved as reformed,[49] which is to say that Massinger was in the business of writing plays for production, and Herbert and Charles of regulating, not suppressing them.[50]

Such a revised view of Caroline censorship will enable us to account for the substantial body of opposition and anticourt plays the period produced. That record permits us to trace the continuous dispersion of opposition ideas across a spectrum that includes amateur Cavaliers, dissident courtly dramatists, professionals from city and court, as well as the country dramatist Mildmay Fane. Country, city, and court plays, each with its own ambience and style, cast a spotlight upon grievances, court corruption, misgovernance; they exhort, satirize, advise, and proffer their own ideals of governance. But they do not seek revolutionary change. For neither Fane, nor Brome, Denham, Habington, Suckling, or the lawyers of Lincoln's Inn was there an inevitable civil war, and for none was civil war an end to be sought. To the contrary, they all directed their anticourt sensibilities and their opposition convictions toward reform, toward making the established government work. To that end, despite the regulations of censorship—and perhaps even through them—England's anticourt and opposition plays performed their normative social functions through 1642, trying to hold a society together by bringing to heart and mind ways to achieve a balance again, to make things right.

Epilogue

Tradition perpetuates the half-truth that in their hostility to the arts Parliament's Puritans destroyed the dramatic tradition that produced Shakespeare by shutting down the theaters. But when in 1642 Parliament passed the ordinance proclaiming that "publike Stage-playes . . . being Spectacles of pleasure, too commonly expressing lasciuious Mirth and Levitie," do not agree with "the Seasons of Humiliation" or with "publike Calamities," it was not *mere* hostility to dramatic representation that lay behind the edict.[1] Many playwrights of Puritan sympathy, even of deep Puritan sympathy as Margot Heinemann has shown, could and did contribute to the discourse on the public stage.[2] Rather, the closing of London's theaters, an event never intended to be permanent, signified that the time for dialogue, for compromise, had passed. As London's sole effective government, Parliament's revolutionary forces moved effectively to suppress a kind of discourse it could not otherwise control. A more immediate incentive was, very likely, that Parliament wanted badly to prevent conspiratorial gatherings at public places where ideas as well as people met.[3] Both motives signaled the same radical truth, that Parliament had moved to appropriate to itself the language of power. In so doing it effectively curtailed a dramatic tradition in which a spectrum of dissident belief could try to exert its influence on England's social conscience as well as on unfolding events.

Yet despite its decree, Parliament could not obliterate the habit of culture that English political theater exerted. Shutting down the theaters meant silencing an opposition—a royalist opposition this time—that wanted to find again *its* public voice. The sub rosa political drama that England continued to produce after the ban illustrates the sound basis of parliamentary apprehensions. Composed almost exclusively by royalists, the political plays of the Commonwealth ere were, as their titles suggest, contemptuous burlesques of the Puritan cause—*The Levellers Levelled* (1647), *The Committee Man Curried* (1647), *Crafty Cromwell* (1648), *The Devil and the Parliament* (1648), *The Jovial Crew, or The Devil Turned Ranter* (1651), and *The Rump* (1660). Theirs is the record of an opposition drama no longer anticourt but anticommonwealth.

In looking back over the half century of Stuart anticourt plays to 1642, we may recognize three overarching features. First, far from being radical in intention, England's anticourt plays, in all their various forms, were fortified by profoundly conservative ideals. Second, in a society that before 1642 had no conception of a legitimate opposition to the idea of English monarchy, one unexceptionable effective means of protesting government policy or court culture was to appeal to the identity or ideals of the English nation-state itself. Third, by this same constraint, critics of courts and kings could dramatize their alienation by invoking the ideal of the good Christian life or, more specifically, of English Protestantism.

Despite their apparent benignity, such appeals to accepted norms and traditions became the means by which serious issues of court policy and conduct could be engaged. At the beginning of the Jacobean period, when the Children of the Queen's Revels lampooned king and court, the recurring points of attack were James's Scottish retinue (which is to say, from an English viewpoint, "foreigners") and James's wholesale preferments, which were interpreted to mean that he was diluting the quality of England's leadership. The scathing depiction of modern courts in popular Italianate tragedies appeals homiletically to received Christian standards of right living, and through their universalizing techniques of sententiae, emblem, and allegory, these plays catechize the luxury and sexual license of court life, as well as its cynical, dehumanizing practice of statecraft.

The frequent representation of sovereigns ruling, as the Tudors and Stuarts claimed to, by Divine Right raised ideological issues of fealty and aristocratic concerns about the rights belonging to subjects. A recurring response of dramatists was to portray, as Chapman did, the inviolability of personal honor or the tragic dilemma presented by the claims of conscience and of loyalty to one's sovereign. In themselves neither the social satires nor ideological tragedies of the first Jacobean decade need have signified more than abrasive points of friction, but the "un-Englishness," as many critics saw it, of the Stuart reign reappeared in new ways, perpetuating earlier impressions that might otherwise have dissipated. James's support of the Spanish match and his pursuit of peace on the Continent, despite the embattled state of Protestantism in that region, was from this perspective disastrous policy. *The*

Tragedy of Barnavelt, The Maid of Honor, and *A Game at Chess* all ringingly affirm an English national identity impelled to assert itself against Spanish imperialism and (in Middleton's satire especially) those internal elements in the English court that would, it appeared, compromise the country's security. Such plays did more than capitalize on topical political currents; presented as they were to cross-sections of Jacobean society, they fortified England's post-Reformation identity, an identity comprised of a militant Protestantism, a regard for English institutions, and the English conception of kingship. By virtue of their presentation on public stages, these plays helped to disseminate an opposition ideology and, in the period of prerogative rule, to foster the dispersion of a network of opposition ideas of governance. It is this incessant association of specific grievances with an enabling opposition ideology—a new language of right—that makes Caroline drama a culmination of earlier expressions of the anticourt dramatic tradition.

Caroline opposition drama thus did a good deal more than survive; it drew from the anticourt dramatic tradition and found new ways to distinguish between kingship and an ideal of kingship, between king and country, sovereign and people, sovereign and the entirety of government, prerogative rights of the sovereign and prerogative rights or liberties belonging to subjects. In a word, the symbols of office were made to confront the practice, the king's "two bodies" made to face each other.

The effect, then, of the tradition of anticourt drama in the early Stuart period was to stimulate a demystified conception of royalty as well as of courts and courtiers. Out of this tradition came a probing, dissentient drama, sometimes even subversive of orthodoxy, whose aim in both satire and tragedy, through ridicule, admonition, and example, was to bring England to a deeper, more constructive sense of purpose and destiny. From this conservative ideal there evolved during the civil war period an ideology splitting off Parliament from king, although the pre–civil war drama, which never sought this revolutionary end, only adumbrates it. Rather, through its powers of representation early Stuart drama, among its several other achievements, was able to articulate an enabling opposition ideology—a new language of right—that embraced the power of Parliament and the rights of subjects along with those of the king, and it is this particular achievement that makes Caroline drama a culmination of the anticourt dramatic tradition.

ABBREVIATIONS AND SHORT TITLES

NOTES

INDEX

Abbreviations and Short Titles

Journals

ELR	*English Literary Renaissance*
HLQ	*Huntington Library Quarterly*
JEGP	*Journal of English and Germanic Philology*
JMH	*Journal of Modern History*
MLN	*Modern Language Notes*
MLR	*Modern Language Review*
MLQ	*Modern Language Quarterly*
MP	*Modern Philology*
N&Q	*Notes and Queries*
P&P	*Past and Present*
PLL	*Papers in Language and Literature*
PMLA	*Publications of the Modern Language Association*
PQ	*Philological Quarterly*
SEL	*Studies in English Literature*
SP	*Studies in Philology*

Books

Akrigg, *Pageant* G. P. V. Akrigg. *Jacobean Pageant or the Court of King James I.* 1962. Rpt. New York: Atheneum, 1974.

Albright, *Publication* Evelyn May Albright. *Dramatic Publication in England, 1580–1640: A Study of Conditions Affecting Content and Form in Drama.* New York: Modern Language Association, 1927.

Bacon, *Works*	*The Works of Francis Bacon.* 15 vols. Ed. James Spedding, R. L. Ellis, and D. D. Heath. New York, 1872.
Bald, *Chesse*	R. C. Bald, ed. *A Game at Chess.* Cambridge: Cambridge Univ. Press, 1929.
Bentley, *Jacobean & Caroline Stage*	G. E. Bentley. *The Jacobean and Caroline Stage.* 7 vols. Oxford: Oxford Univ. Press, 1941–68.
Birch, *Court*	Thomas Birch, ed. *The Court and Times of James the First.* 2 vols. 1849. Rpt. New York: AMS Press, 1973.
Bradbrook, *Webster*	Muriel Bradbrook. *John Webster, Citizen and Dramatist.* London: Weidenfeld and Nicolson, 1980.
Butler, *Theatre & Crisis*	Martin Butler. *Theatre and Crisis, 1632–1642.* Cambridge: Cambridge Univ. Press, 1984.
Caputi, *Marston*	Anthony Caputi. *John Marston, Satirist.* Ithaca: Cornell Univ. Press. 1961.
Caspari, *Humanism*	Fritz Caspari. *Humanism and the Social Order in Tudor England.* New York: Teachers College Press, 1954.
Cassirer, *Philosophy*	Ernst Cassirer, Paul O. Kristellar, John H. Randall, Jr., eds. *The Renaissance Philosophy of Man.* Chicago: Univ. of Chicago Press, 1948.
Chamberlain, *Letters*	*The Letters of John Chamberlain.* 2 vols. Ed. N. E. MacClure. Philadelphia: American Philosophical Society, 1939.
Chambers, *Stage*	E. K. Chambers. *The Elizabethan Stage.* 4 vols. Cambridge: Cambridge Univ. Press, 1923.
Clarendon, *Rebellion*	Edward, Earl of Clarendon. *The History of the Rebellion and Civil Wars in England.* 7 vols. Ed. W. D. Macray. Oxford: Oxford Univ. Press, 1849.
Cohen, *Public Theater*	Walter Cohen. *Drama of a Nation: Public Theater in Renaissance England and Spain.* Ithaca: Cornell Univ. Press, 1985.
Cook, *Playgoers*	Ann J. Cook. *The Privileged Playgoers of Shakespeare's London, 1576–1642.* Princeton: Princeton Univ. Press, 1981.
CSPD, *James I*	*Calendar of State Papers, Domestic Series, of the Reigns of Edward VI, Mary, Elizabeth and James I, 1547–1625.* 12 vols. Ed. Robert Lemon and Mary A. Green, London, 1857–72.
CSPV	*Calendar of State Papers and Manuscripts . . . Existing in the Archives and Collections of Venice.* Vols. 10–21 (1603–25). Ed. Horatio F. Brown and Allen B. Hinds. London: His Majesties Stationery Office, 1900–16.
Dasent, *Acts*	John R. Dasent. *Acts of the Privy Council.* N.S. 32 vols. London, 1890.
DNB	*Dictionary of National Biography.* 22 vols. Ed. Leslie Stephen and Sydney Lee. Oxford: Oxford Univ. Press, 1937–38.
Dietz, *Finance*	F. C. Dietz. *English Public Finance, 1558–1641.* 2d ed. New York: Barnes & Noble, 1964.
Dollimore, *Radical Tragedy*	Jonathan Dollimore. *Radical Tragedy: Religion, Ideology and Power in the Drama of Shakespeare and His Contemporaries.* Chicago: Univ. of Chicago Press, 1984.

Edwards & Gibson, *Massinger*	Philip Edwards and Colin Gibson, eds. *The Plays and Poems of Philip Massinger.* 5 vols. Oxford: Clarendon Press, 1976.
Eliot, *Essays*	T. S. Eliot. *Selected Essays.* London: Faber & Faber, 1932.
Finkelpearl, *Marston*	Philip J. Finkelpearl. *John Marston of the Middle Temple: An Elizabethan Dramatist in His Social Setting.* Cambridge: Harvard Univ. Press, 1969.
Foucault, *Archaeology*	Michel Foucault. *The Archaeology of Knowledge.* Trans. A. M. Sheridan Smith. New York: Pantheon, 1972.
Gardiner, *England*	Samuel R. Gardiner. *History of England from the Accession of James I to the Outbreak of the Civil War, 1603–1642.* 10 vols. London: Longmans, Green, 1904–9.
Goldberg, *James I*	Jonathan Goldberg. *James I and the Politics of Literature.* Baltimore: Johns Hopkins Univ. Press, 1983.
Greenblatt, *Forms*	Stephen Greenblatt, ed. *The Power of Forms in the English Renaissance.* Norman, Okla.: Pilgrim Books, 1982.
Gregg, *Charles I*	Pauline Gregg. *King Charles I.* London: Dent, 1981.
Greville, *Sidney*	Fulke Greville. *The Life of Sir Philip Sidney.* 1652. Oxford: Clarendon Press, 1907.
Gurr, *Stage*	Andrew Gurr. *The Shakespearean Stage, 1574–1642.* 2d ed. Cambridge: Cambridge Univ. Press, 1980.
Harbage & Schoenbaum, *Annals*	Alfred Harbage. *Annals of English Drama, 975–1700.* Rev. by S. Schoenbaum. Philadelphia: Univ. of Pennsylvania Press, 1964.
Harington, *Nugae Antiquae.*	Sir John Harington. *Nugae Antiquae: Being a Miscellaneous Collection of Original Papers.* 2 vols. 1804. Rpt. New York: AMS, 1966.
Heinemann, *Puritanism*	Margot Heinemann. *Puritanism and Theatre: Thomas Middleton and Opposition Drama under the Early Stuarts.* Cambridge: Cambridge Univ. Press, 1980.
Herbert, *Records*	*The Dramatic Records of Sir Henry Herbert, Master of the Revels, 1623–1673.* Ed. Joseph Quincy Adams. 1917. Rpt. New York: Blum, n.d.
Herford & Simpson, *Jonson*	C. H. Herford, Percy & Evelyn Simpson, eds. *Ben Jonson: The Man and His Work.* 11 vols. Oxford: Clarendon Press, 1925–52.
Hibbert, *Charles I*	Christopher Hibbert. *Charles I.* New York: Harper & Row, 1968.
Hill, *Revolution*	Christopher Hill. *The Century of Revolution: 1603–1714.* 1961. Rpt. London: Cardinal, 1975.
Hillebrand, *Child Actors*	Harold N. Hillebrand. *The Child Actors: A Chapter in Elizabethan Stage History.* Univ. of Illinois Studies in Language and Literature. Vol. 11, no. 2. Urbana: Univ. of Illinois Press, 1926.
Houston, *James I*	S. J. Houston. *James I.* London: Longman, 1973.
Hunter, *Courtier*	G. K. Hunter. *John Lyly: The Humanist as Courtier.* Cambridge: Cambridge Univ. Press, 1962.

James I, *Works* Charles H. McIlwain. Introduction. *The Political Works of James I.* Rpt. of 1616 ed. New York: Russell & Russell, 1965.

Kenyon, *Stuarts* J. P. Kenyon. *The Stuarts: A Study in Kingship.* Glasgow: Fontana/Collins, 1958.

Levin, *Readings* Richard Levin. *New Readings vs. Old Plays.* Chicago: Univ. of Chicago Press, 1979.

Lockyer, *Buckingham* Roger Lockyer. *Buckingham: The Life and Political Career of George Villiers, First Duke of Buckingham.* London: Longman, 1981.

Lodge, *Illustrations* Edmund Lodge. *Illustrations of British History, Biography, and Manners, in the Reigns of Henry VIII, Edward VI, Mary, Elizabeth, and James I.* 3 vols. 2d ed. London, 1838.

Lucas, *Webster* F. L. Lucas, ed. *The Complete Works of John Webster.* 4 vols. London: Chatto & Windus, 1927.

Michel, *Philotas* Laurence Michel, ed. *The Tragedy of Philotas by Samuel Daniel.* New Haven: Yale Univ. Press, 1949.

Neale, *Elizabeth* J. E. Neale. *Queen Elizabeth I.* 1934. Rpt. Harmondsworth: Penguin, 1960.

Notestein, *Commons* Wallace Notestein. *The House of Commons, 1604–1610.* New Haven: Yale Univ. Press, 1971.

Ogg, *Europe* David Ogg. *Europe in the Seventeenth Century.* Rev. ed. London: Adams Charles Black, 1965.

Orgel, *Illusion* Stephen Orgel. *The Illusion of Power: Political Theatre in the English Renaissance.* Berkeley: Univ. of California Press, 1975.

Orgel & Strong, *Jones* Stephen Orgel & Roy Strong. *Inigo Jones: The Theater of the Stuart Court.* 2 vols. Berkeley: Univ. of California Press, 1973.

Ornstein, *Jacobean Tragedy* Robert Ornstein. *The Moral Vision of Jacobean Tragedy.* Madison: Univ. of Wisconsin Press, 1965.

Osborne, *Memoirs* Francis Osborne. *Traditional Memoirs of the Raigne of King James the First.* In *The Secret History of the Court of James the First.* 2 vols. Ed. Walter Scott. Edinburgh, 1811.

Parry, *Golden Age Restor'd* Graham Parry. *The Golden Age Restor'd: The Culture of the Stuart Court, 1603–42.* London: Manchester Univ. Press, 1981.

Patterson, *Censorship* Annabel Patterson. *Censorship and Interpretation: The Conditions of Writing and Reading in Early Modern England.* Madison: Univ. of Wisconsin Press, 1984.

Peter, *Complaint* John Peter. *Complaint and Satire in Early English Literature.* Oxford: Clarendon-Press 1956.

Petter, *Eastward Ho!* C. G. Petter, ed. *Eastward Ho!* London: Benn, 1973.

Peyton, *Catastrophe* Edward Peyton. *The Divine Catastrophe of the Family of the House of Stuarts.* In *The Secret History of the Court of James the First.* 2 vols. Ed. Walter Scott. Edinburgh, 1811.

Pocock, *Constitution* J. G. A. Pocock. *The Ancient Constitution and the Feudal Law: A Study of English Historical Thought in the Sev-*

enteenth Century. Cambridge: Cambridge Univ. Press, 1957.

Prestwich, *Cranfield* — Menna Prestwich. *Cranfield: Politics and Profits under the Early Stuarts.* Oxford: Oxford Univ. Press, 1966.

Prothero, *Documents* — George Prothero. *Select Statutes and Other Constitutional Documents, Illustrative of the Reigns of Elizabeth and James I.* Oxford: Clarendon Press, 1913.

Rebholz, *Greville* — Ronald A. Rebholz. *The Life of Fulke Greville, First Lord Brooke.* Oxford: Clarendon Press, 1971.

Rees, *Daniel* — Joan Rees. *Samuel Daniel: A Critical and Biographical Study.* Liverpool: Liverpool Univ. Press, 1971.

Ribner, *Jacobean Tragedy* — Irving Ribner. *Jacobean Tragedy: The Quest for Moral Order.* London: Methuen, 1962.

Russell, *Civil War* — Conrad Russell, ed. *The Origins of the English Civil War.* London: Macmillan, 1973.

Russell, *Parliaments, 1621–1629* — Conrad Russell. *Parliaments and English Politics, 1621–1629.* Oxford: Clarendon Press, 1979.

Sharpe, *Faction* — Kevin Sharpe, ed. *Faction and Parliament: Essays on Early Stuart History.* Oxford: Clarendon Press, 1978.

Smith, *James* — Alan G. R. Smith, ed. *The Reign of James VI & I.* London: Macmillan, 1973.

Stone, *Aristocracy* — Lawrence Stone. *The Crisis of the Aristocracy, 1558–1641.* Oxford: Clarendon Press, 1965.

Sullivan, *Court Masques* — Mary Agnes Sullivan. *Court Masques of James I: Their Influence on Shakespeare and the Public Theatres.* 1913. Rpt. New York: Russell & Russell, 1973.

Tanner, *Constitutional Conflicts* — J. R. Tanner. *English Constitutional Conflicts of the Seventeenth Century, 1603–1689.* Cambridge: Cambridge Univ. Press, 1971.

Tilley, *Proverbs* — Morris Palmer Tilley. *A Dictionary of the Proverbs in England in the Sixteenth and the Seventeenth Centuries.* Ann Arbor: Univ. of Michigan Press, 1966.

Weldon, *Court & Character* — Sir Anthony Weldon. *The Court and Character of King James.* In *The Secret History of the Court of James the First.* 2 vols. Ed. Walter Scott. Edinburgh, 1811.

Willson, *James I* — David H. Willson. *King James VI and I.* London: Jonathan Cape, 1956.

Wilson, *Apprenticeship* — Charles Wilson. *England's Apprenticeship, 1603–1763.* London: Longman, 1965.

Winwood, *Memorials* — Sir Ralph Winwood. *Memorials of Affairs of State in the Reigns of Q. Elizabeth and K. James I.* 3 vols. Ed. E. Sawyer, London, 1725.

Wood, *Athenae Oxonienses* — Anthony À Wood. *Athenae Oxonienses.* 4 vols. 1813–20. Rpt. New York: Johnson Rpt. Corp., 1967.

Zagorin, *Court & Country* — Perez Zagorin. *The Court and the Country: The Beginning of the English Revolution.* New York: Antheneum, 1969.

Zaller, *Parliament of 1621* — Robert Zaller. *The Parliament of 1621: A Study in Constitutional Conflict.* Berkeley: Univ. of California Press, 1971.

Notes

Preface
1. Orgel, *Illusion*, pp.56–58. See also idem, *The Jonsonian Masque* (Cambridge: Harvard Univ. Press, 1965) and Orgel & Strong, *Jones*.
2. Goldberg, *James I*, pp. 55–112.
3. Ibid., p. 31.
4. Ibid., pp. 165–66 on Roman plays; on Chapman's D'Ambois plays and *The Duchess of Malfi*, pp. 159, 274n. See also Goldberg, "Upon a Publike Stage: The Royal Gaze and Jacobean Theater," *Research Opportunities in Renaissance Drama* 14 (1981):17–22.
5. *The Works of Edmund Spenser*, 11 vols., ed. Edwin Greenlaw et al. (Baltimore: Johns Hopkins Univ. Press, 1932–49), 8:128–29 (ll. 891–906); *Donne: Poetical Works*, 2 vols., ed. Herbert Grierson (Oxford: Clarendon Press, 1912), 1:140.
6. Edward Guilpin, *Skialetheia or A Shadowe of Truth*, in *Certaine Epigrams and Satyres*, ed. D. Allen Carroll (Chapel Hill: Univ. of North Carolina Press, 1974), "Satire I," ll. 63–70.
7. *A Transcript of the Registers of the Company of Stationers of London: 1554–1660*, 5 vols., ed. Edward Arber (1875–1894; rpt. Gloucester, Mass.: Peter Smith, 1967), 3:677–78.
8. Unless otherwise noted, composition dates of plays in this study appear in text and are from Harbage & Schoenbaum, *Annals* except when modified by Gurr's more recent, but selective, *Stage*.
9. David Bevington, *Tudor Drama and Politics: A Critical Approach to Topical Meaning* (Cambridge: Harvard Univ. Press, 1968).
10. Peter, *Complaint*, pp. 9–13.
11. Ornstein, *Jacobean Tragedy*, ch. 1; Ribner, *Jacobean Tragedy*, ch. 1.
12. For a full statement of this older formalist dogma, see René Wellek and Austin Warren, *Theory of Literature* (New York: Harcourt Brace, 1956), pp. 148 ff.
13. Illustrative of Dollimore's approach in *Radical Tragedy* are pp. 231–46, which treat *The White Devil* in terms of such issues as "Sexual and Social Exploitation," "The Assertive Woman," and "The Dispossessed Intellectual."

14. Greenblatt, *Forms,* p.6.

15. Thematic interpretation appears to me indispensable in literary analysis, although I am mindful of Levin's strictures in *Readings,* pp. 11–77.

16 Foucault, *Archaeology,* pp. 135–40.

1. The Social Background: The Reign of James I

1. Weldon, *Court & Character,* 2:2.

2. Osborne, *Memoirs,* 1:271.

3. Gardiner, *England.*

4. Joel Hurstfield, "The Politics of Corruption in Shakespeare's England," *Shakespeare Survey* 28 (1975):15–28. See Russell, *Civil War,* pp. 1–31, and idem, *Parliaments, 1621–1629.* A monument to the quest for objectivity is the statistical method for establishing social trends as exemplified in Stone, *Aristocracy.*

5. Such views are prevalent in Weldon, *Court & Character;* Osborne, *Memoirs;* and Peyton, *Catastrophe.* Censorious modern treatments of the reign appear in William McElwee's, *The Wisest Fool in Christendom: The Reign of King James I and VI* (London: Faber & Faber, 1958), and G. M. Trevelyan's, *England under the Stuarts,* rev. ed. (London: Methuen, 1925).

6. Kenyon, *Stuarts.*

7. Prestwich, *Cranfield,* ch. 1; Willson, *James I,* reviewed in Smith, *James I,* p. 222.

8. See James I, *Works;* on James's poetry see B. M. Add. Ms. 24195. On James as philosopher and king, see Richard Martin, *A: Speach Delivered to the King's Most Excellent Majestie, in the Name of the Sheriffes of London and Middlesex* (1603), in J. Nichols, *The Progresses, Processions, and Magnificent Festivities of King James the First, His Royal Consort, Family, and Court,* 4 vols. (London, 1828), 1:132.

9. Ibid., 1:89.

10. Willson, *James I,* p. 163.

11. F. P. Wilson, *The Plague in Shakespeare's London* (Oxford: Clarendon Press, 1967), p. 114; Chambers, *Stage,* 4:350.

12. Wilson, *Plague,* pp. 36–40.

13. See Nichols, *Progresses,* 1:325–424.

14. The Gowry Conspiracy, most notably. See Willson, *James I,* pp. 126–30, 165.

15. *A Royalist's Notebook: The Commonplace Book of Sir John Oglander, Kt., of Nunwell,* ed. Francis Bamford (1936; rpt. New York: Blom, 1971), p. 197.

16. Harington, *Nugae Antiquae.*

17. *CSPV* (1607), no. 739, p. 513.

18. *Journal of Sir Roger Wilbraham,* ed. Harold S. Scott, in *Camden Micellany,* vol. 10 (London: Royal Historical Society, 1902), p. 59.

19. Lodge, *Illustrations* (Sept. 16, 1603), 3:27.

20. Willson, *James I,* p. 168.

21. Russell, "Parliament and the King's Finances," in his *Civil War,* p. 99.

22. R. H. Tawney, *Business and Politics under James I* (Cambridge: Cambridge Univ. Press, 1958), p. 139n.

23. Willson, *James I,* pp. 183–84.

24. Prestwich, *Cranfield,* p. 10.

25. Dietz, *Finance,* p. 105n. Wilson, in *Apprenticeship,* p. 91, puts James's cash gifts to Scotsmen, 1603–10, at £225,000.

26. Chamberlain, *Letters* (Feb. 6, 1607), 1:241. He cites the £44,000 figure referred to in the following sentence.

27. McElwee, *Wisest Fool,* p. 173.

28. *CSPV* (May 22, 1603), no. 55, p. 33.

29. Osborne, *Memoirs*, 1:150, 270.

30. Nichols, *Progresses*, 1:203. See the commentary in Stone, *Aristocracy*, p. 75.

31. Statistics throughout the paragraph are from Stone, *Aristocracy*, p. 75.

32. *CSPV* (July 30, 1603), no. 101, p. 70.

33. Lodge, *Illustrations* (Dec. 4, 1604), 3:108.

34. McElwee, *Wisest Fool*, p. 174; Willson, *James I*, pp. 191, 194, 388–89.

35. Osborne, *Memoirs*, 1:271; Akrigg, *Pageant*, p. 163.

36. Samuel Daniel, "Vision of the Twelve Goddesses"; Scott, *Journal of Wilbraham*, p. 66.

37. Chamberlain, *Letters* (Jan. 8, 1608), 1:252–53.

38. Sullivan, *Court Masques*, p. 147; cf. McElwee, *Wisest Fool*, p. 173.

39. *Diary of Lady Anne Clifford*, Intro. V. Sackville-West (London: Heinemann, 1923), pp. 16–17.

40. Akrigg, *Pageant*, pp. 240–43.

41. Alfred Harbage, *Shakespeare and the Rival Traditions* (Bloomington: Indiana Univ. Press, 1952), pp. 52–89.

42. The patent is reproduced in Chambers, *Stage*, 1:325.

43. On Anne's relationship with her husband and on their dwelling apart, see Willson, *James I*, p. 403, and Akrigg, *Pageant*, pp. 264–65.

44. Chambers, *Stage*, 1:325.

45. Brit. Mus. Ms. Birch 4164, f. 183r. & v. I have normalized the punctuation.

46. Winwood, *Memorials*, 1:271; Akrigg, *Pageant*, p. 163.

2. *Warnings for a New King: The Disguised Duke Play*

1. The first essay to draw attention to these plays as a group was David J. Houser's "Purging the Commonwealth: Marston's Disguised Duke and *A Knack to Know a Knave*," *PMLA* 89 (1974):993–1006. More recently, Leonard Tennenhouse, in "Representing Power: *Measure for Measure* in Its Time," in Greenblatt, *Forms*, pp. 139–56, has treated the political, sociopsychological ramifications of the group, which he calls "disguised ruler plays."

2. Fredson Bowers, ed., *The Dramatic Works in the Beaumont and Fletcher Canon*, 5 vols. (Cambridge: Cambridge Univ. Press, 1966–79), 1:157.

3. Alluded to in the induction to *The Malcontent*. See M. L. Wine, ed., *The Malcontent* (Lincoln: Univ. of Nebraska Press, 1964). All quotations are from this edition, and line references appear in text. On dates and auspices of production, see Caputi, *Marston*, pp. 265–67.

4. John B. Brooks, ed., *The Phoenix* (New York: Garland, 1980). All quotations are from this edition, and line references appear in text.

5. Thomas Heywood, *The Decoy Duck* (London, 1642), p. A1. See also Burton A. Milligan, "A Note on Knights of the Post," *MLN* 61 (1946):147–51.

6. Thomas B. Howell, ed., *Cobbett's Complete Collection of State Trials*, 34 vols. (London, 1809–28), 2:1. Most interpreters are concerned to treat Phoenix as James I. See Alan Dessen, "Middleton's *The Phoenix* and the Allegorical Tradition," *SEL* 6 (1966):291–308; Clifford Davidson, "*The Phoenix*: Middleton's Didactic Comedy," *PLL* 4 (1968):121–30; N. W. Bawcutt, "Middleton's 'The Phoenix' as a Royal Play," *N&Q* 201 (1956):287–88; Brooks, *Phoenix*, pp. 105–26.

7. See Levin's strictures on allegorical "James-figure" studies in *Readings*, pp. 189, 226–29, 242n.

8. See the discussion in Brooks, *Phoenix*, pp. 1–24.

9. *The Complete Works of George Gascoigne*, 2 vols., ed. John W. Cunliffe

(Cambridge: Cambridge Univ. Press, 1910), 2:152. See Ronald C. Johnson, *George Gascoigne* (New York: Twayne, 1972), pp. 115–16.

10. Peyton, *Catastrophe*, 2:369.

11. On Renaissance individualism, destructive and otherwise, see Jacob Burckhardt, *Civilization of the Renaissance in Italy,* 2 vols., trans. Ludwig Geiger & Walter Gotz (1929; rpt. Harper & Row, 1958), 1:143–47.

12. For a more general treatment of appetite, see Tennenhouse's "Representing Power," in Greenblatt, *Forms,* pp. 149–53. This essay shows how dramatists interpreted sexual desire in political terms as a form of selfishness and how, contrariwise, they elevated the chaste woman as being above selfish desire, and so the only fitting spouse for the true ruler. Tennenhouse also draws a fitting analogy between this dramatic phenomenon and Elizabeth's representation of herself as the virgin queen. See also Tennenhouse's *Power on Display: The Politics of Shakespeare's Genres* (New York: Methuen, 1986), pp. 106–22.

13. Howell, *State Trials*, 2:929–35, 951–66.

14. See William Slights, "'Elder in a Deformed Church': The Function of Marston's Malcontent," *SEL* 13 (1973):360–73, for a fine discussion of the religious issues in the play.

15. See, however, Finkelpearl, *Marston*, pp. 178–94, who champions the view that Altofronto is a "virtuous Machiavellian."

16. See Caputi, *Marston*, pp. 247–48.

17. Tennenhouse, "Representing Power," in Greenblatt, *Forms*, p. 145.

18. William Slights, "Political Morality and the Ending of *The Malcontent*," *MP* 69 (1971):138–39, reproduces the passage with exegesis.

19. I follow Chambers, *Stage*, 3:432, and Finkelpearl, *Marston*, pp. 223–24, who assign a 1606 date for revision.

20. Gerald A. Smith, ed., *The Fawn* (Lincoln: Univ. of Nebraska Press, 1961). All quotations are from this edition, and line references appear in text.

21. Edgar T. Schell & Irvine J. D. Schuchter, ed. *English Morality Plays and Moral Interludes* (New York: Holt, Rinehart, & Winston, 1969), p. v.

22. Finkelpearl, *Marston*, pp. 220–37, following, most notably, Morse Allen, *The Satire of John Marston* (Columbus, Ohio: F. J. Heer, 1920), p. 151, and Albert W. Upton, "Allusions to James I and His Court in Marston's *Fawn* and Beaumont's *Woman Hater*," *PMLA* 44 (1929):1048–65.

23. *Truth Brought to Light and Discouered by Times* (London, 1651).

24. Hunold Nibbe, ed., *The Fleire* (Louvain: Uystpruyst, 1912). All quotations are from this edition, and line references appear in text. I normalize the spelling of *Fleire* to *Fleer*.

25. Chamberlain, *Letters* (Jan. 8, 1604), 1:253. See also, Lodge, *Illustrations* (May 3, 1604) 3:138.

26. Chamberlain, *Letters* (Jan. 8, 1604), 1:253.

3. The Growth of Anti-Scot and Antiministerial Satire
1. On the date and position of *The Widow's Tears* and *Monsieur D'Olive* in the Chapman canon, see my "The Dates of the Plays of George Chapman," *ELR* 12 (1982):250–51.

2. For a fuller discussion of the social satire in the plays and Chapman's relationship to Tharsalio, see my "The Social Disorder of Chapman's *The Widow's Tears*," *JEGP* 72 (1973):350–59. For the view that Tharsalio's attitudes are Chapman's, see Samuel Schoenbaum, "*The Widow's Tears* and the Other Chapman," *HLQ* 23 (1960):334–35; and Thelma Herring, "Chapman and an Aspect of Modern Crit-

icism," *Renaissance Drama* 8 (1965):158; and the review by Ethel M. Smeak, ed., *The Widow's Tears* (Lincoln: Univ. of Nebraska Press, 1966), pp. xiii–xxi.

3. Alan Holaday, ed., *The Plays of George Chapman: The Comedies* (Urbana: Univ. of Illinois Press, 1970). All quotations are from this edition, and line references appear in text.

4. See Henry M. Weidner, "Homer and the Fallen World: The Focus of Satire in George Chapman's *The Widow's Tears," JEGP* 62 (1963):519–27.

5. Stone, *Aristocracy,* p. 755.

6. See Eugene M. Waith, *The Herculean Hero in Marlowe, Chapman, Shakespeare, and Dryden* (London: Chatto & Windus, 1962), pp. 16–59.

7. See A. P. Hogan, "Thematic Unity in Chapman's *Monsieur D'Olive," SEL* 11 (1971):295–306.

8. Albert H. Tricomi, "The Focus of Satire and the Date of *Monsieur D'Olive," SEL* 19 (1977):281–94.

9. In his edition, *The Plays of George Chapman: The Comedies,* 2 vols. (1914; rpt. New York: Russell & Russell, 1961), 2:773–74, Thomas M. Parrott argues that *Monsieur D'Olive* satirizes several ambassadorial expeditions, but see my findings supporting a single embassage in "Focus of Satire," pp. 288–91.

10. See Akrigg's account, *Pageant,* pp. 60–63.

11. Willson, *James I,* pp. 274–75.

12. Winwood, *Memorials,* vol. 2. Quotations are from this edition and page references appear in text.

13. See *Volpone,* 2.1.53–87, in Herford & Simpson, *Jonson,* vol. 5.

14. G. B. Harrison, *Jacobean Journal . . . 1603–1606* (New York: Macmillan, 1941), p. 195, dates the departure still later, April 6.

15. Notably, Alexander Leggatt's *Citizen Comedy in the Age of Shakespeare* (Toronto: Univ. of Toronto Press, 1973), pp. 47–51.

16. See Roscoe Small, *The Stage Quarrel between Jonson and the So-called Poetasters* (Breslau: M. & H. Marcus, 1899).

17. *Eastward Ho,* in Herford & Simpson, *Jonson,* vol. 4. All quotations are from this edition and line references appear in text.

18. On the geography of the play, see Petter, *Eastward Ho!,* pp. xxiii, 74n.

19. BM Add. Ms. 5832, fol. 205; printed in Petter, *Eastward Ho!,* pp. 123–24.

20. Herford & Simpson, *Jonson,* 4:496.

21. Akrigg, *Pageant,* p. 158.

22. *Conversations with Drummond,* in Herford & Simpson, *Jonson,* 1:140.

4. *An Antiroyal Satire Too Daring:* The Isle of Gulls

1. Winwood, *Memorials,* 2:54.

2. Birch, *Court,* 1:60–61.

3. Hillebrand, *Child Actors,* pp. 194–96.

4. Dasent, *Acts,* 37:338; 38:33.

5. R. E. Brettle, "*Eastward Ho,* 1605, . . . Bibliography, and Circumstances of Production," *The Library* 9 (1929):287–302; W. W. Greg, "Eastward Ho, 1605," *The Library* 9 (1929):303–4.

6. Raymond S. Burns, ed., *The Isle of Guls* (New York: Garland, 1980). All quotations are from this edition, and line references appear in text. I have normalized Burns's spelling of *Guls* in my text.

7. A. H. Bullen, ed., *The Works of John Day* (1881; rpt. London: Holland Press, 1963), p. xvi.

8. Finkelpearl, *Marston,* p. 223.

9. Bullen, *Day,* p. xvi.

10. Michael Shapiro, *Children of the Revels: The Boy Companies of Shakespeare's Time and Their Plays* (New York: Columbia Univ. Press, 1977), p. 52.

11. Burns, *Guls,* p. 15.

12. *CSPV* (July 30, 1603), no. 101, p. 70.

13. Lodge, *Illustrations* (May 3, 1604), 3:138; Harington, *Nugae Antiquae,* 1:393–94.

14. John Hacket, *Scrinia Reserata: A Memorial Offer'd to the Great Deservings of John Williams, D.D.* (London, 1692), 1:227.

15. Frederick G. Marcham, "James I of England and the 'Little Beagle' Letters," *Persecution and Liberty: Essays in Honor of George Lincoln Burr* (New York: Century, 1931), pp. 315–34.

16. Chamberlain, *Letters* (Jan. 26, 1605), 1:201.

17. See Notestein, *Commons,* pp. 125–40.

18. Tanner, *Constitutional Conflicts,* pp. 43–44. The issue came to trial on Robert Bates's refusal to pay an increased duty on currants (1605).

19. Osborne, *Memoirs,* 1:194–95.

20. *OED,* s.v. "put up."

21. See Alan G. R. Smith's biography, *Servant of the Cecils: The Life of Sir Michael Hickes, 1543–1612* (Totowa, N.Y.: Rowman & Littlefield, 1977).

22. Bullen, *Day,* p. xvi. Also put forward is Robert Carr, earl of Somerset, but this identification is impossible since James discovered Carr in 1607.

23. Willson, *James I,* pp. 175–76.

24. On Sackville, see Godfrey Goodman, *The Court of King James, the First,* 2 vols., ed. J. S. Brewer (London, 1839), 1:204, and Osborne, *Memoirs,* 1:280. On Cecil's career, see Houston, *James I,* p. 29, and especially, Lawrence Stone, "The Fruits of Office: The Case of Robert Cecil, First Earl of Salisbury, 1596–1612," *Essays in the Economic and Social History of Tudor and Stuart England,* ed. F. J. Fisher (Cambridge: Cambridge Univ. Press, 1961), pp. 89–116.

25. Akrigg, *Pageant,* p. 106.

26. Osborne, *Memoirs,* 1:238. Akrigg, *Pageant,* pp. 106–10, cites the Folger MS. 452.1 ditty on Robert Crookback, and other defamatory ballads and rhymes.

27. Akrigg, *Pageant,* pp. 107, 110.

28. Zagorin, *Court & Country,* pp. 74–118.

5. Suppression of the Satires of the Children of the Queen's Revels

1. Winwood, *Memorials,* 2:41; Neale, *Elizabeth,* p. 377.

2. Chambers, *Stage,* 1:327.

3. Neale, *Elizabeth,* p. 377.

4. Except perhaps for 1607. The company made up for the lapse in 1608, offending twice, with the Byron plays and the play of the mines.

5. The letter is reproduced in Chambers, *Stage,* 3:257–58.

6. Petter, *Eastward Ho!,* p. 32n.

7. See Albright, *Publication,* pp.19–59.

8. Ironically, Daniel was beset by financial difficulties, in part because of this appointment. See Rees, *Daniel,* pp. 96–97.

9. Dasent, *Acts,* 27:338.

10. Herford & Simpson, *Jonson,* 1:194–96; for Chapman's letters as well, see Petter, *Eastward Ho!,* pp. 126–28. On the Lord Chamberlain's role in regulating the drama, see Albright, *Publication,* pp. 23–27.

11. *STC*, 18582, Anthony Nixon, *The Blacke yeare* (London, 1606), p. 2br.

12. On these matters see Finkelpearl, *Marston*, pp. 195–97.

13. *CSPD, James I* (1604?), p. 182. Entries are listed by date and page.

14. The evidence would then square with Jonson's account in his *Conversations with Drummond*. See Herford & Simpson, *Jonson*, 1:140. All quotations from the *Conversations* are from this edition, and line references appear in text.

15. Chambers, *Stage*, 2:51.

16. Herford & Simpson, *Jonson*, 1:193; cf. 195, 198. All quotations from Jonson's letters are from this edition, and page numbers appear in text. All quotations from Chapman's letters are from Petter, *Eastward Ho!*, and numbers appear in text.

17. Birch, *Court* (Mar. 7, 1606), 1:61; Chambers, *Stage*, 3:286.

18. Chambers, *Stage*, 2:51–52, on whom I rely throughout the paragraph.

19. Ibid., p. 52.

20. Ibid., 4:338–39.

21. Ibid., 2:53. Chambers prints La Boderie's complaint.

22. Ibid., pp. 53–54. Abbreviations and superscripts have been written out in full.

23. Hillebrand, *Child Actors*, p. 199.

24. Thomas Heywood, *An Apology for Actors* (1612; rpt. New York: Garland, 1973), p. G3. v.

25. Hillebrand, *Child Actors*, p. 216.

26. Quotations throughout the paragraph are from Hillebrand, *Child Actors*, pp. 191–92.

27. Chambers, *Stage*, 2:55.

28. Ibid.

29. On Marston's biography see Caputi, *Marston*, pp. 247–48. On the erroneous attribution of political poems to Marston after he entered the clergy, see my "John Marston's Manuscripts," *HLQ* 43(1980):87–102.

30. Chambers, *Stage*, 2:55–56.

31. Greenblatt, *Forms*, pp. 4–5.

32. Neale, *Elizabeth*, p. 387.

6. The Political Background: Divine Right Kingship and the Ministry of Robert Cecil

1. Harington was knighted in Ireland by Essex and later appealed to Cecil for an appointment as archbishop of Dublin (where he would be no threat to Cecil), but to no avail. See Norman E. McClure, *The Letters and Epigrams of Sir John Harington* (1930; rpt. New York: Octagon, 1977), pp. 25–31, and Neale, *Elizabeth*, pp. 369–70. The careers of Daniel and Greville are treated below.

2. The material on the Essex circle is from Hugh Trevor-Roper, "The Elizabethan Aristocracy, an Anatomy Anatomized," *Economic History Review*, 2d ser. 3 (1951):279–98, and Vernon F. Snow, "Essex and the Aristocratic Opposition to the Early Stuarts," *JMH* 32 (1960):224–33.

3. Except where otherwise noted, the factual data on James's first Parliament are from Notestein, *Commons*, and Gardiner, *England*, vols. 1 & 2. See also Birch, *Court*, 1:114–32.

4. Tanner, *Constitutional Conflicts*, p. 29.

5. George Prothero, *Select Statutes and Other Documents, Illustrative of the Reigns of Elizabeth and James I* (Oxford: Clarendon Press, 1913), p. 289. All quotations from the Apology are from this edition, and subsequent references appear in text.

6. Foremost among those who hold that the *Apology* has been elevated out of all

proportion to its historical significance is G. R. Elton, "A High Road to Civil War?" in *Studies in Tudor and Stuart Politics and Government: Papers and Reviews, 1946–1972*, 2 vols. (Cambridge: Cambridge Univ. Press, 1974), 2:164–82.

7. Cited in Tanner, *Constitutional Conflicts*, pp. 43–44.

8. Ibid., pp. 22–24.

9. Sir Henry Finch, *A Summary of the Common Law of England* ([derived from 1613 Fr. ed.] 1654; rpt., New York: Garland, 1979), p. 2.

10. Houston, *James I*, p. 38; J. W. Allen, *English Political Thought, 1603–1644* (1938; rpt. Hamden, Conn.: Archon, 1967), pp. 10–17.

11. See Alan G. R. Smith, "Constitutional Ideas and Parliamentary Developments in England 1603–1625," in Smith, *James I*, pp. 160–64.

12. James I, *Works*, p. 62.

13. John Cowell, *The Interpreter* (1607; rpt. Menston, England: Scolar Press, 1972).

14. Houston, *James I*, p. 44.

15. James I, *Works*, pp. 306–25. Page references to this address appear in text.

16. Houston, *James I*, p. 38; cf. Gardiner, *England*, 2:71.

17. Chamberlain, *Letters* (May 24, 1610), 1:301.

18. S. R. Gardiner, ed., *Parliamentary Debates in 1610* (London: Camden Society, 1862 [vol. 81]), p. 40.

19. Leon E. Kastner and H. B. Charlton, eds., *The Poetic Works of William Alexander*, 2 vols. (Manchester: Manchester Univ. Press, 1921), 1:451n; 1:clxxxvii.

20. See Alexander M. Witherspoon, *The Influence of Robert Farnier on Elizabethan Drama* (1924; New York: Phaeton, 1968), pp. 84–180, and Matthew P. McDiarmid, "The Influence of Robert Farnier on Some Elizabethan Tragedies," *Etudes Anglaises* 11 (1958):289–302. Garnier's tragedies were the first to explore as a matter of principle the relationship between history and contemporary politics. See Gillian Jondorf, *Robert Garnier and the Themes of Political Tragedy in the Sixteenth Century* (Cambridge: Cambridge Univ. Press, 1969), pp. 26–46; Geoffrey Brereton, *French Tragic Drama in the Sixteenth and Seventeenth Centuries* (London: Methuen, 1973), pp. 22–24.

21. All biographical and chronological matters pertaining to Greville and his works are from Rebholz, *Greville*.

22. I rely on the biographical material in Rees, *Daniel;* on Daniel's relationship to Essex see pp. 62–65, 128–29, and Neale, *Elizabeth*, p. 89.

23. Chambers, *Stage*, 3:273.

24. *CSPD, James I* (1604?), p. 182.

25. Chambers, *Stage*, 2:51–52. See also R. E. Brettle, "Samuel Daniel and the Children of the Queen's Revels, 1604–5," *Review of English Studies* 3 (1927):162–68.

26. The quotation is from Michel, *Philotas*, pp. 98–99.

27. Greville, *Sidney*, pp. 217–19. All quotations are from this edition, and subsequent references appear in text.

28. For example, the falsely attributed *The Five Years of King James* by "Sr Foulk Greville, the late Lord *Brook*" (London, 1643).

29. I am here indebted to Snow, "Essex and the Aristocratic Opposition," pp. 224–33.

30. Lillian M. Ruff and D. Arnold Wilson, "The Madrigal, the Lute Song, and Elizabethan Politics," *P&P* 44 (1969):18n. This collection was published in 1630; most were contemporaneous with Greville and Cecil.

31. *STC* 21332; see Ruff & Wilson, "Madrigal," p. 41.

32. *DNB*, s.v. "Monson, William"; also, Rebholz, *Greville*, pp. 162–63; Ruff & Wilson, "Madrigal," pp. 41–42.

33. Chambers, *Stage*, 2:56.

34. Hillebrand, *Child Actors*, pp. 204, 237; Chambers, *Stage*, 2:56.

35. Ruff & Wilson, "Madrigal," p. 46.

36. Ibid., p. 45.

37. Patterson, *Censorship*, pp. 49–56.

38. See Phyllis Brooks Bartlett, *The Poems of George Chapman* (1941; rpt. New York: Russell & Russell, 1962), p. 479n. Essex evidently ignored Chapman's dedications.

7. The Not-So-Closeted Tragedies of Daniel and Greville

1. Michel, *Philotas*, pp. 37–39. All quotations from *Philotas* and these documents, including Daniel's letters, are from this edition and appear subsequently in text.

2. Greville, *Sidney*, p. 155. All quotations are from this edition, and subsequent references appear in text.

3. In *Censorship*, p. 57, Annabel Patterson makes it a principle of the "hermeneutics of censorship" that disclaimers of topical intention are not to be trusted. The social-historical evidence Patterson adduces is extremely pertinent to the case I am making with respect to an anticourt dramatic tradition in England.

4. Michel, *Philotas*, pp. 53–65. On Essex and Philotas, see Brent Stirling, "Daniel's 'Philotas' and the Essex Case," *MLQ* 3 (1942):583–94; and G. A. Wilkes's attempted refutation in "Daniel's *Philotas* and the Essex Case: A Reconsideration," *MLQ* 23 (1962):233–42.

5. See Geoffrey Bullough, ed., *Poems and Dramas of Fulke Greville, First Lord Brooke*, 2 vols. (New York: Oxford Univ. Press, 1945), 2:5–7. All quotations from *Mustapha* are from this edition, and subsequent references appear in text.

6. On Craterus as a shadow for Cecil, see Michel, *Philotas*, pp. 40 ff., and Cecil Seronsy, *Samuel Daniel* (New York: Twayne, 1967), p. 56.

7. In this assessment I agree with Michel, *Philotas*, p. vii; but see the less judgmental Seronsy, *Daniel*, pp. 55–56.

8. Michel, *Philotas*, pp. 42–43.

9. Interestingly, immediately following the section on *Sidney* in which Greville recounts his failure to gain access from Cecil to the state papers, Greville returns to the subject of drama to announce his allegiance to a species of political tragedy that seeks "to trace out the high waies of ambitious Governours, and to shew in the practice, that the more audacity, advantage, and good successe such Soveraignties have, the more they hasten to their owne desolation and ruine" (p. 221).

10. On Greville's plays, see Peter Ure, "Fulke Greville's Dramatic Characters," *RES*, n.s. 1 (1950):308–23, and Joan Rees, *Fulke Greville, Lord Brooke, 1554–1628: A Critical Biography* (Berkeley and Los Angeles: Univ. of California Press, 1971), pp. 139–81.

11. Eliot, *Essays*, p. 286.

8. Tacitean Republicanism in Jonson's Sejanus

1. Quotations from *Sejanus* and the *Conversations with Drummond* are from Herford & Simpson, *Jonson*, vols. 4 & 1, respectively, and line references appear in text.

2. Ibid., 9:592–93. On this subject the best essay is by Joseph Allen Bryant, Jr., "The Significance of Ben Jonson's First Requirement for Tragedy: 'Truth of Argument,'" *SP* 49 (1952):195–213.

3. Robert J. Lordi, ed., *The Revenge of Bussy D'Ambois* (Salsburg: Institut für Englische Sprache, Universität Salzburg, 1977), the Dedication, ll. 24–28.

4. B. N. De Luna's labored attempt to read Jonson's *Catiline* as "a classical paralleograph" of the Gunpowder Plot in *Jonson's Romish Plot: A Study of "Catiline" and Its Historical Context* (Oxford: Clarendon Press, 1967) has not won critical acceptance, nor has Norma D. Solve's interpretation of *Chabot* as an allegory on the earl of Somerset in *Stuart Politics in Chapman's "Tragedy of Chabot"* (Ann Arbor: Univ. of Michigan Press, 1929). See my critique in "Dates of the Plays of George Chapman," pp. 261–64.

5. Jonson names Lipsius's 1600 edition of *Tacitus* and Henri Estienne's 1592 edition of Dio Cassius, *History of the Romans,* as sources in "To the Readers" (ll. 39–41). See the corroboratory notes to *Sejanus* in Herford & Simpson, *Jonson,* 9:597–635.

6. See Snow, "Essex and the Aristocratic Opposition to the Early Stuarts," pp. 226–27, and Fred J. Levy, *Tudor Historical Thought* (San Marino, Calif.: Huntington Library, 1967), pp. 261–62. On the political use of Tacitus see Rebholz, *Greville,* pp. 294–95, and M. F. Tenney, "Tacitus in the Politics of Early Stuart England," *Classical Journal* 37 (1941):151–63.

7. See Annabel Patterson, "'Roman-cast Similitude': Ben Jonson and the English Use of Roman History," in *Rome in the Renaissance: The City and the Myth,* ed. P. V. Ramsey (Binghamton: Center for Medieval & Early Renaissance Texts, 1982), pp. 381–94. Patterson's *Censorship* appeared after the body of this present chapter was written. It offers important evidence on the political uses of Tacitus on the Continent and in England and also employs Jonson's *Sejanus* to explore the "hermeneutics of censorship" in the Renaissance (pp. 49–58). Patterson's interpretation of the theme of censorship in *Sejanus,* which anticipates mine, also helps to corroborate the claims I am making.

8. E. V. Lucas, ed., *The Works of Charles and Mary Lamb,* 5 vols. (1903; rpt. New York: AMS, 1968), 1:50.

9. See Daniel C. Boughner, "Sejanus and Machiavelli," *SEL* 1 (1961):81–100.

10. Tacitus, *The Annals of Imperial Rome,* trans. Michael Grant, rev. ed. (New York: Penguin, 1974), bk. 4, ch. 34. Subsequent citations, by book and chapter number, are from this edition and appear in text.

11. Informers in Rome hoped to inherit the property of those they informed upon. See Jonas Barish, ed., *Sejanus* (New Haven: Yale Univ. Press, 1965), p. 16. Informers were a grievance in Jacobean England; their activities were regulated in 1624. See Russell, *Parliaments, 1621–1629,* p. 68.

12. "The Discoveries" (ll. 1334–58), in Herford & Simpson, *Jonson,* 8:604–5.

13. Herford & Simpson, *Jonson,* 9:588–89. Pertinent to this view is Patterson's chapter "The Hermeneutics of Censorship," in *Censorship,* pp. 44–119, which establishes a Renaissance context for the writing and reception of politically sensitive texts. Patterson adduces eight hermeneutic principles. They include questions that contemporary readers continually asked, such as "'Why such a storie shold come out at this time.'" Patterson's arguments that there was a built-in indeterminacy in topical application and that disclaimers of topical intention cannot be trusted (pp. 47–48, 57–58) lay a firm foundation for the further study of politically sensitive texts. Two of Patterson's eight principles merit special notice. First, the idea that "it cannot be assumed that . . . [we can] depend on any crude opposition between a government and its critics" would surely apply to almost all Jacobean-Caroline dramatists. However, the very notion of loyal opposition in a country with a sovereign king is anachronous; what we should expect to find, and do, are playwrights who stake out

positions opposed to court or king on selected issues. Second, the inference that censorship is "ineffective in preventing the dissemination of prohibited news" since the censored work becomes notorious (p. 48) appears to me roseate. Distinctions between prepublication and postpublication censorship are important to observe, as is the distinction in the drama between licensing for performance and licensing for publication. In the drama the notoriety often attained by censored texts was frequently temporary; the ultimate act of censorship, suppression, was sometimes all too effective, as was the case with Jonson's *Isle of Dogs,* a play that no longer survives. Furthermore, I would urge that the persisting, routine practice of censorship suggests that it was not altogether ineffective. Indeed, the efficacy of the threats to suppress texts and punish authors manifests itself in the subtle kinds of oblique expression that necessitate the kind of interpretive strategies that Patterson's own hermeneutic principles seek to provide.

14. S. F. Bolton, ed., *Sejanus His Fall* (New York: Hill & Wang, 1966), p. xii.

15. For contemporary reactions, see Herford & Simpson, *Jonson,* 9:588–89.

16. See Arthur F. Marotti, "The Self-Reflexive Art of Ben Jonson's *Sejanus,*" *Texas Studies in Language and Literature* 12 (1970):197–220, and Ornstein, *Jacobean Tragedy,* pp. 84–97. For a more sympathetic interpretation of the structure, see Larry Champion, *Tragic Patterns in Jacobean and Caroline Drama* (Knoxville: Univ. of Tennessee Press, 1977), pp. 62–76.

17. Bacon, *Works* 12:206–9.

18. For connections to "the old Ideal Prince Traditions," see K. W. Evans, "*Sejanus* and the Ideal Prince Tradition," *SEL* 11 (1971):250.

19. See Gary D. Hamilton, "Irony and Fortune in *Sejanus,*" *SEL* 11 (1971):265–81, and Bolton, *Sejanus,* pp. xvii–xviii.

20. Boughner, "Sejanus and Machiavelli," p. 92n.

21. Renaissance historiography is being rewritten with attention to the fictions that accompany truthtelling endeavors. See Judith H. Anderson's *Biographical Truth: The Representation of Historical Persons in Tudor-Stuart Writing* (New Haven: Yale Univ. Press, 1984), esp. pp. 69–77.

22. Especially Hall. However, E. M. W. Tillyard's theory in *Shakespeare's History Plays* (London: Chatto & Windus, 1944) that Shakespeare's histories reflect this providential orientation has been discredited. See especially Henry A. Kelly, *Divine Providence in the England of Shakespeare's Histories* (Cambridge: Cambridge Univ. Press, 1970).

23. See Herford & Simpson, *Jonson,* 9:589.

24. See Allan H. Gilbert, "The Eavesdroppers in Jonson's *Sejanus,*" *MLN* 69 (1954):164–66.

25. See Christopher Ricks, "*Sejanus* and Dismemberment," *MLN* 76 (1961):301–7.

9. The Power of Princes and the Integrity of Subjects in Chapman's French Tragedies

1. On the date of *Caesar and Pompey* and all of Chapman's tragedies, see my "The Dates of the Plays of George Chapman," *ELR* 12 (1982), pp. 242–66.

2. This enduring interest in the liberty of subjects is as much evident in the Roman *Caesar and Pompey* as in the French tragedies. One of the pivotal precepts in *Caesar and Pompey* is, for example, "All just men / Not only may enlarge their lives, but must, / From all rule tyrannous, or live unjust," for "every just man [is] to himself / The perfect'st law" (4.5.57–72) (T. M. Parrott, ed., *The Plays of George Chapman: The Tragedies,* 2 vols. [1910; rpt. New York: Russell & Russell, 1961], vol. 2).

3. Both D'Ambois tragedies are set in the court of Henry III of France (ruled 1574–89), the Byron plays in the court of Henry IV (ruled 1589–1610). *The Revenge* presents a nonhistorical brother of Bussy, but Chapman's sources are historical—Pierre Matthieu's *Histoire de France* (1605) and Grimeston's *General Inventorie of the History of France* (1607).

4. Nicholas Brooke, ed., *Bussy D'Ambois* (London: Methuen, 1964), which is based on the original 1604 text. All quotations are from this edition, and line references appear in text.

5. The issue projects the Roman debate between the active and the private life, Chapman's beloved Cicero and Cato praising the active public life and Epictetus the virtuous private life.

6. "Of Revenge," *Essays or Counsels Civil and Moral,* in Bacon, *Works,* 12:92.

7. "Against Private Challenges" (Feb. 4, 1614), STC 8497; "A Publication . . . Against Private Combats" (1613), STC 8498; and *The Charge of Sir F. Bacon Touching Duells* (1614), STC 1125. Massinger and Field treat the dueling theme sympathetically in *The Fatal Dowry* (1615–20), Middleton somewhat satirically in *A Fair Quarrel* (1615–17).

8. André Joubert, *Louis de Clermont, sieur de Bussy D'Amboise, Gouverneur D'Anjou* (Paris, 1885), p. 110. See also Jean Jacquot, ed., *Bussy D'Amboise* (Paris: Aubier, 1960), pp. xxxvi–xxxvii.

9. The most influential example is Jean Bodin's *La République* (Paris, 1576).

10. Pocock, *Constitution,* p. 17. James himself appealed to the myth in his parliamentary address on Mar. 21, 1610 (*Works,* p. 309).

11. *Journals of the House of Lords* (n.d., n.p.), 3:761.

12. Ribner's formulation, *Jacobean Tragedy,* p. 29.

13. Seneca's emphasis, *Ad Lucilium Epistulae Morales,* 3 vols., trans. Richard M. Gummere (1917; London: Heinemann, 1953), 2:429–36. For a characteristic statement in Cicero, see *De Officiis,* trans. Walter Miller (London: Heinemann, 1947), bk. 3, ch. 17, p. 343.

14. Cicero, *De Finibus Bonorum et Malorum,* ed. and trans. Harris Rackham, 2d ed. (Cambridge: Harvard Univ. Press, 1914), bk. 4, ch. 12, p. 339. Cf. Seneca, above.

15. Joel Hurstfield's, "Political Corruption in Modern England: The Historian's Problem," *History* 52 (1967):16–34, shows that a degree of bribetaking was acceptable in seventeenth-century England; Bussy's speech demonstrates that bribetaking was, however, still a grievance.

16. Pico della Mirandola, "Oration on the Dignity of Man" (1486), trans. Elizabeth L. Forbes, in Cassirer, *Philosophy,* p. 225.

17. In this context I rely on Stephen Greenblatt's notion of self-fashioning in *Sir Walter Raleigh: The Renaissance Man and His Roles* (New Haven: Yale Univ. Press, 1973), pp. 37–38.

18. Thomas Greene, "The Self in Renaissance Literature," *Disciplines of Criticism: Essays in Literary Theory, Interpretation, and History,* ed. Peter Demetz et al. (New Haven: Yale Univ. Press, 1968), pp. 250–51.

19. This view would appear to be borne out by Comolot's concluding eulogy to Bussy (so placed in the 1604 text). Bussy's spirit will be "made a star," which by presiding over "a world of fire"—not just the French court—"and th' aged sky" may "Cheer with new sparks of old humanity" (5.3.269–74).

20. Consider Una Ellis-Fermor's conclusion that "irresponsible individualism" is broken by Chapman's "stern sense of public responsibility," in *The Jacobean Drama, an Interpretation,* 4th ed. (1957; rpt. New York: Vintage, 1960), p. 65.

21. George Ray, ed., *The Conspiracy and Tragedy of Byron,* 2 vols. (New York:

Garland, 1979). All quotations are from this edition, and line references appear in text.

22. Greville, *Sidney,* pp. 160–61.

23. See Howell A. Lloyd, *The Rouen Campaign, 1590–1592* (Oxford: Clarendon Press, 1973), pp. 117–22, 147–68.

24. On the D'Entragues conspiracy see the account of Paul F. Willert, *Henry of Navarr and the Huguenots in France* (New York: Knickerbocker Press, 1904), pp. 419–22.

25. Chapman had dedicated to Essex, then earl marshall, his *Achilles Shield* and *The Seaven Books of the Iliads* (1598).

26. Emil Koeppel, *Quellen-Studien zu den Dramen Chapman's, Philip Massinger's, und John Ford's* [*sic*] (Strassbourg: Trübner, 1897), pp. 24–26. See Parrott's critique in *Chapman: Tragedies,* 2:592.

27. Bertram Dobell, "Newly Discovered Documents of the Elizabethan and Jacobean Periods, III," *Athenaeum* 3832 (Apr. 6, 1901):433.

28. On *The Revenge* as setting forth a kind of heroism different from that of Bussy, see my "The Revised *Bussy D'Ambois* and *The Revenge of Bussy D'Ambois*: Joint Performance in Thematic Counterpoint," *English Language Notes* 9 (1972):253–62.

29. Best on Chapman's synthesizing use of Neoplatonic, Stoic, and Christian-humanist ideas is Jean Jacquot, *George Chapman, sa vie, sa poésie, son théâtre, sa pensée* (Paris: Les Belles Lettres, 1951), pp. 199–254. Other studies have over-emphasized orthodox stoic or Christian elements.

30. K. M. Burton, "The Political Tragedies of Chapman and Ben Jonson," *Essays in Criticism* 2 (1952):397.

31. Robert Lordi, ed., *The Revenge of Bussy D'Ambois* (Salzburg: Institüt Englische Sprache und Literatur, Universität Salzburg, 1977). All quotations are from this edition, and line references appear in text.

32. An increasingly common conception of the monarch in French political thought deriving from Jean Bodin. See, for example, the account in George L. Mosse, *The Struggle for Sovereignty in England, from the Reign of Queen Elizabeth to the Petition of Right* (New York: Octagon, 1968), p. 30.

33. By 1610 Englishmen perceived the French king to be absolute, as may be demonstrated by Sir Thomas Overbury's "Observations on the State of France, 1609, under Henry IV," in *Stuart Tracts, 1603–1693,* ed. C. H. Firth (Westminster: Constable, 1903), p. 223.

34. James I, *Works,* p. 310.

35. *The Politics of Aristotle,* trans. William Ellis (London: Dent, 1912), pp. 6–7.

36. Peter Bement, "The Stoicism of Chapman's Clermont d'Ambois," *SEL* 12 (1972):354–55.

37. Expounded in Ernst H. Kantorowicz, *The King's Two Bodies: A Study in Medieval Political Theology* (Princeton: Princeton Univ. Press, 1957).

38. Stephen Greenblatt, "Invisible Bullets: Renaissance Authority and Its Subversion," *Glyph* 8 (1981):57.

39. Goldberg, *James I,* p. 159.

40. Ibid., pp. 153 ff.

10. *Popular Anticourt Attitudes*

1. Gascoigne drew the miniature himself for his *Hermit's Tale.* The picture conveniently appears in Lacey Baldwin Smith, *The Horizon Book of the Elizabethan World* (London: Paul Hamlyn, 1967), p. 76.

2. H. R. Trevor-Roper, "General Crisis of the Seventeenth Century," in *Crisis in*

Europe 1560–1660, ed. Trevor Aston (London: Routledge & Kegan Paul, 1965), p. 81.

3. See the excellent discussion of the purposes of this work in Caspari, *Humanism,* pp. 145–209.

4. Sullivan, *Court Masques,* pp. 11–22.

5. This was especially true after 1605, when perspective settings were introduced. The king's seat was "the one perfect place" from which all lines of sight converged. The closer one sat to the king, the better one's lines of sight were and the more exalted one's position. See Orgel, *Illusion,* pp. 10–16.

6. Mary Susan Steele, *Plays & Masques at Court during the Reigns of Elizabeth, James, and Charles* (Ithaca: Cornell Univ. Press, 1926), pp. 135–42; Chambers, *Stage,* 1:196–97.

7. Akrigg estimates that by 1618 James was expending £4,000 a year for the Christmas masque alone (*Pageant,* p. 151).

8. Steele, *Plays & Masques at Court,* pp. 135–85, lists over twenty masques performed between Jan. 1, 1604, and Jan. 6, 1614. On the costs of masques, see Chambers, *Stage,* 1:211; Sullivan, *Court Masques,* pp. 144–49.

9. Chamberlain, *Letters* (Jan. 8, 1608), 1:252–53.

10. Edward F. Rimbault, ed., *The Old Cheque-Book, or Book of Remembrance, of the Chapel Royal, from 1561–1744,* n.s. 3 (London: Camden Society, 1872), pp. 164–65.

11. Chamberlain, *Letters* (Feb. 23, 1613), 1:427; see also, 1:255–56, 421, 425, 431.

12. Printed in Birch, *Court,* 1:43; also Chambers, *Stage,* 3:379.

13. Orgel & Strong, *Jones.*

14. Ibid., 2:442, 447; 1:190.

15. *Euphues and His England,* in *The Complete Works of John Lyly,* 3 vols., ed. R. Warwick Bond (Oxford: Clarendon Press, 1902), 2:103; see also, p. 105.

16. The anecdote is cited by Akrigg, *Pageant,* pp. 282–83, from Public Record Office, State Papers, 14/12/6.

17. Harington, *Nugae Antiquae,* 1:349–51; rpt. in Chambers, *Stage,* 1:172n.

18. Weldon, *Court & Character,* 2:3. Treated at length by Willson, *James I,* pp. 191, 194, 388–89.

19. William Ffarington, *The Ffarington Papers,* ed. Susan M. Ffarington (Manchester: Chetham Society, 1856), vol. 39 (Feb. 7, 1609), p. 151.

20. Peyton, *Catastrophe,* 2:369.

21. Osborne, *Memoirs,* 1:223.

22. Cook, *Playgoers,* pp. 16–17, 216–24.

23. The quotation is from Lucas, *Webster,* vol. 1.

24. On Italian forms, see Enid Welsford, *The Court Masque* (1927; rpt. New York: Russell & Russell, 1962), pp. 81–115.

25. Chambers, *Stage,* 1:206.

26. Inga-Stina Ekeblad, "The 'Impure Art' of John Webster," *Twentieth Century Interpretations of The Duchess of Malfi,* ed. Norman Rabkin (Englewood Cliff, N.J.: Prentice-Hall, 1968), pp. 52–56; R. W. Dent, *John Webster's Borrowing* (Berkeley & Los Angeles: Univ. of California Press, 1960), p. 230; Chambers, *Stage,* 1:173.

27. Brian Morris and Roma Gill, eds., *The Atheist's Tragedy* (London: Benn, 1976), p. vii.

28. Mary Edmond, "In Search of John Webster," *TLS,* Dec. 24, 1976; also, Bradbrook, *Webster,* pp. 10–27.

29. Bradbrook, *Webster,* pp. 11, 166, 180.

30. Richard H. Barker, *Thomas Middleton* (New York: Columbia Univ. Press, 1958), pp. 14, 20.

31. Lewis Einstein, *The Italian Renaissance in England: Studies* (New York: Columbia Univ. Press, 1902), pp. 161–63; Stone, *Aristocracy*, p. 700.

32. Written in the margin of a Folger Library copy of Raleigh's *Historie of the World* (London, 1634), sig. A1r, by Lord Stanhope. I am indebted for the quotation to Akrigg, *Pageant*, p. 41.

33. Tilley, *Proverbs*, E154.

34. Thomas Nashe, *The Vnfortvnate Traueller, Or, The Life of Iacke Wilton* (London, 1594), in *The Works of Thomas Nashe*, 5 vols., ed. R. B. McKerrow (Oxford: Basil Blackwell, 1958), 2:301.

35. Unique National Library of Scotland copy of John Marston, *The Insatiate Countess* (London, 1631), call no. EH1EW1.

11. *Economic and Social Alienation in* The Revenger's Tragedy

1. Lawrence J. Ross, ed., *The Revenger's Tragedy* (Lincoln: Univ. of Nebraska Press, 1966), p. xx. All quotations are from this edition, and line references appear in text.

2. On the use of Guicciardini, see Leo G. Salinger, "*The Revenger's Tragedy:* Some Possible Sources," *MLR* (1965):4–11; on the other Italian sources, see N. W. Bawcutt, "'The Revenger's Tragedy' and the Medici Family," *N&Q* 202 (1957):192–93; and Pierre Legouis, "Réflexions sur la recherche des sources à propos de la 'Tragédie du Vengeur,'" *Etudes Anglaises* 12 (1959):47–55. I name Tourneur rather than Middleton as author solely because of convention.

3. Dollimore, *Radical Tragedy*, p. 149.

4. Ibid., pp. 139–50.

5. For a discussion of this contractual lord-tenant relationship, see Paul S. Clarkson and Clyde T. Warren, *The Law of Property in Shakespeare and the Elizabethan Drama*, 2d ed. (New York: Gordian, 1968), p. 96.

6. Stone, *Aristocracy*, p. 766. On gentry selling, clearing, and marketing woodland, see Wilson, *Apprenticeship*, p. 111.

7. Prestwich, *Cranfield*, pp. 28–30. See also Dietz, *Finance*, p. 296.

8. Most notably, Eliot, *Essays*, pp. 189–90.

9. Thomas Bastard, *Chrestoleros: Seuen Bookes of Epigrames* (1888; rpt. New York: B. Franklin, 1967), bk. 7, no. 14. l. 8.

10. See Muriel Bradbrook's treatment of this pattern in *Themes and Conventions of Elizabethan Tragedy* (Cambridge: Cambridge Univ. Press, 1935), pp. 167–68. As *The Phoenix* also reveals, corruption of the judiciary was a long-standing English grievance, as was the bribery of state officials. Bacon's and Cranfield's fall (1621, 1624) illustrate the problem. See John D. Eusden, *Puritans, Lawyers, and Politics in Early Seventeenth-Century England* (New Haven: Yale Univ. Press, 1958), pp. 150–54.

11. Throughout the paragraph, I have refocused the general remarks on the humanist program of Hunter, *Courtier,* to interpret the subplot political farce of *The Revenger's Tragedy.*

12. The blazing star, associated with the Globe theater, offers a piece of corroboratory evidence that *The Revenger's Tragedy* was, like most Italianate tragedies, and as its title page suggests, a public-theater play. See Inga-Stina Ewbank, "A Note on 'The Revenger's Tragedy,'" *N&Q* 200 (1955):98–99.

13. John R. Hale, ed., *Guicciardini, "The History of Italy" and "History of*

Florence," trans. Cecil Grayson (New York: Twayne, 1964), pp. xxvii; Tilley, *Proverbs,* C718.

14. *OED,* s.v. "common."

15. See Samuel Schoenbaum, *"The Revenger's Tragedy:* Jacobean Dance of Death," *MLQ* 15 (1954):201–7.

16. See R. A. Foakes, ed., *The Revenger's Tragedy* (London: Methuen, 1966), p. xliv.

17. A. C. Bradley, *Shakespearean Tragedy* (London: Macmillan, 1904), pp. 23–29.

12. Spiritual Alienation and Anticourt Application in Webster's Tragedies

1. Those who wish to feel daunted will enjoy Don D. Moore's *John Webster and His Critics, 1617–1964* (Baton Rouge: Louisiana State Univ. Press, 1966).

2. William Slights reproduces the passage in "Political Morality and the Ending of *The Malcontent,*" *MP* 69 (1971):138.

3. For the view that Webster's tragedies lack moral vision, see Lacy Lockert, "Marston, Webster, and the Decline of the Elizabethan Drama," *Sewanee Review* 27 (1919):65, 78–81; Ornstein, *Jacobean Tragedy,* pp. 128–50, and J. R. Mulryne, " 'The White Devil' and 'The Duchess of Malfi,' " in *Jacobean Theatre,* ed. John R. Brown and Bernard Harris (1960; rpt. New York: Capricorn, 1967), pp. 201–25. I concur with Travis Bogard's view in *The Tragic Satire of John Webster* (Berkeley & Los Angeles: Univ. of California Press, 1955), p. 17, that Webster's tragedies are satiric but dissent from his conclusion that Webster was "apparently unable to discover an acceptable system for the evaluation of good and evil."

4. Quotations from *The White Devil* and *The Duchess of Malfi* are from Lucas, *Webster,* vols. 1 & 2, respectively, and line references appear in text.

5. See Gunnar Boklund's standard *The Sources of the White Devil* and *The Duchess of Malfi: Sources, Themes, Characters,* both from Cambridge, Harvard Univ. Press, 1957 and 1962, respectively.

6. Caspari, *Humanism,* pp. 217, 285, 288n, documents Padua's role as a center of learning for English humanists abroad, particularly for noninheriting sons of nobility and lesser landowners. Lawrence Stone, "The Educational Revolution in England, 1560–1640," *P&P* 28 (1965):41–80, records the rising entrance statistics in the universities and inns of court between 1600 and 1610. See also, Stone, *Aristocracy,* pp. 687–88, and J. H. Hexter, "The Education of the Aristocracy in the Renaissance," *JMH* 22 (1950):1–20.

7. Mark Curtis, "The Alienated Intellectuals of Early Stuart England," *P&P* 23 (1962):27.

8. Ibid., pp. 28–29.

9. Hunter, *Courtier,* p. 29.

10. Bradbrook, *Webster,* pp. 23–27; Wood, *Athenae Oxonienses,* 2:575.

11. For me the ineluctable theme, first explored by Bogard, *Tragic Satire,* pp. 119–31.

12. Hereward T. Price, "The Function of Imagery in Webster," *PMLA* 70 (1955):717–39.

13. Lucas, *Webster,* 1:269–70n; cf. allusions to Jacobean law and court life at 1:250n, 264n.

14. J. W. Lever, *The Tragedy of State* (London: Methuen, 1971), p. 87.

15. John R. Brown, ed., *The Duchess of Malfi* (Cambridge: Harvard Univ. Press, 1964), p. xxxix.

16. Brown's attempt to link Lady Arbella Stuart's ill-conceived marriage and

imprisonment to this play strains too much toward a *pièce à clef* to my mind, but see the treatment in Akrigg, *Jacobean Pageant,* pp. 227–28.

17. Along with the depiction of an odious court supported by informers' testimony, the speech establishes Antonio's reformist parliamentary perspective, which links *The Duchess of Malfi* to Chapman's and Webster's concerns in their Roman tragedies. In 1614 the French Estates General, or *Conseil D'Etat,* was meeting in what proved to be its last convocation before the French Revolution. See Ogg, *Europe,* p. 39.

18. Throughout the paragraph I am concerned to answer Joyce E. Peterson, *Curs'd Example: The Duchess of Malfi and Commonweal Tragedy* (Columbia: Univ. of Missouri Press, 1978), who salutarily places the tragedy in a "commonweal" tradition only to misconstrue the play's tonality, making the Duchess a "curs'd example" because she allegedly abrogates her responsibilities of state.

19. Caspari, *Humanism,* pp. 149–51.

20. See the excellent discussion in Frank Whigham's "Sexual and Social Mobility in *The Duchess of Malfi,*" *PMLA* 100 (1985): 167–86, which treats the tragedy as marking a painful transition in the kind of servants modern states require.

21. On these matters, and, particularly, on Elyot's *The boke named the Gouernour* (1531), see Caspari, *Humanism,* pp. 145–209.

22. See Middleton's poem praising *The Duchess of Malfi* as a masterpiece in Lucas, *Webster,* 2:34.

13. *The Anatomy of Court Culture and Jacobean Grievances in Middleton's* Women Beware Women

1. Two dates have been suggested—1613–14 and ca. 1621. The argument for the earlier date rests on insubstantial parallels between *Women Beware Women* and Middleton's masque of October 1613, "Triumphs of Truth." See Jackson I. Cope, "The Date of Middleton's *Women Beware Women,*" *MLN* 76 (1961):295–300. The weakness of the argument has been summarized by Roma Gill, ed., *Women Beware Women* (London: Benn, 1968), p. xiv. The later, preferred date is based on internal allusions. See Baldwin Maxwell, "The Date of Middleton's *Women Beware Women,*" *PQ* 22 (1943):338–42, and J. R. Mulryne's assessment of the evidence of his edition, *Women Beware Women* (London: Methuen, 1975), pp. xxxii–xxxviii. Quotations from Middleton's tragedy are from Mulryne's edition, and line numbers appear in text.

2. *The Second Maiden's Tragedy or The Tyrant* (ca. 1610–11), almost surely composed by Middleton, displays several such passages, which attack from a citizen's perspective, rack renting and heavy taxation (ll. 86–90, 134–36). I quote from Ann Lancashire's edition (Manchester: Manchester Univ. Press, 1978). The play, with no specific locale, is a near-cousin to the Italianate revenge play, depicting a lustful, usurping tyrant and his court.

3. Mulryne, *Women Beware Women,* pp. xxxviii-li, reviews the historical material underlying the play. Middleton's Cardinal and the Duke of Florence are based on the same historical personages that Webster presents in *The White Devil.* In real life Middleton's Duke Francisco was also the brother-in-law of Bracciano, Vittoria's lover in *The White Devil.* See F. L. Lucas, *Webster,* 1:71–73. On the historical basis for Bianca's and the Duke's poisoning, see Mulryne, who reproduces contemporary source materials (pp. 176–79). Middleton's nuptials masque, which brings about the bloody denouement, offers the clearest example of a reordering of authentic history. The revenge motif is wholly Middleton's invention, but the wedding masque for Bianca is fact. A. M. Nagler, *Theatre Festivals of the Medici, 1539–1637* (New

Haven: Yale Univ. Press, 1964), pp. 49–57, describes in detail this 1579 nuptials entertainment, called a "Sbarra."

4. Tilley, *Proverbs*, C721.

5. Sir Thomas Hoby, trans., *The Book of the Courtier From the Italian of Count Baldassare Castiglione* (1561; rpt. London: David Nutt, 1900), pp. 89–90.

6. Ibid., p. 140.

7. The anticourt imagery anticipates Middleton's technique in *A Game at Chess* (1624), in which the vicious courtly characters play the black pieces.

8. See Heinemann, *Puritanism*, pp. 18–36. On socioreligious attitudes in London, see Valerie Pearl, *London and the Outbreak of the Puritan Revolution* (London: Oxford Univ. Press, 1961).

9. Hibbert, *Charles I*, pp. 134–35; J. P. Kenyon, *Stuart England* (London: Penguin, 1978), p. 118.

10. See Ellis K. Waterhouse, *Painting in Britain: 1530–1790*, 4th ed. (Harmondsworth: Penguin, 1978), pp. 53–55. Arundel, Buckingham, and Charles amassed extensive art collections from the Continent. Note Daniel Mytens's portrait of Arundel with his gallery of sculptures (p. 54), and see the excellent account of these collections in Parry, *Golden Age Restor'd*, pp. 113–16.

11. See E. Engelberg, "Tragic Blindness in *The Changeling* and *Women Beware Women*," *MLQ* 23 (1962):20–28.

12. Tilley, *Proverbs*, C724.

13. Hill, *Revolution*, pp. 133–34. On enforced marriage in the drama, see Glenn H. Blayney, "Enforcement of Marriage in English Drama," *PQ* 38 (1959):459–72.

14. Notestein, *Commons*, pp. 85–96. For a full account of the corruption of the system, see Joel Hurstfield, *The Queen's Wards: Wardship and Marriage under Elizabeth I* (Cambridge: Harvard Univ. Press, 1958), pp. 181–217.

15. On the need for abolishing wardship, see Wilson, *Apprenticeship*, pp. 91–92, and Hill, *Revolution*, p. 133.

16. Hill, *Revolution*, p. 133.

17. Notestein, *Commons*, pp. 86–87.

18. Dietz, *Finance*, records that the revenues from wardships and other licenses fluctuated between £15,000 and £20,000 per year in Elizabeth's reign, but during the Stuart reign reached £81,000 by 1640 (p. 303; cf. pp. 176–77).

19. Hurstfield, *Queen's Wards*, p. 72.

20. Ibid., citing Brinklow, p. 25.

21. M. R. Golding, "Variations in the Use of the Masque in English Revenge Tragedy," *Year's Work in English Studies* 3 (1973):44–54.

22. Pico della Mirandola, "Oration on the Dignity of Man," in Cassirer, *Philosophy*, p. 225.

23. Cited in Hunter, *Courtier*, p. 141.

24. John Potter, "'In Time of Sports': Masques and Masquing in Middleton's *Women Beware Women*," *PLL* 18 (1982):381. For its implicitly anticourt orientation this is an important essay.

25. The quotation is from A. L. and M. K. Kistner, "Will, Fate, and the Social Order in *Women Beware Women*," *Essays in Literature* 3 (1976):17, who invoke this point of view in order to refute it. See also their discussion in *Middleton's Tragic Themes* (New York: Peter Lang, 1984), pp. 85 ff. On Middleton as an environmentalist or social determinist, see David Holmes, *The Art of Thomas Middleton* (London: Oxford Univ. Press, 1970), pp. 162–65, and Inga-Stina Ewbank, "Realism and Morality in *Women Beware Women*," *Essays and Studies* 22 (1969):59.

26. On Middleton's steady viewpoint, see John F. McElroy's admirable "*The*

White Devil, Women Beware Women, and the Limitations of Rationalist Criticism," *SEL* 19 (1979):295–312.

27. "The Hesperides," in *The Poetical Works of Robert Herrick,* ed. L. C. Martin (Oxford: Oxford Univ. Press, 1956), p. 255; cf. Tilley, *Proverbs,* "Like Prince, like people," K70.

28. I allude to Parry's title, *Golden Age Restor'd.*

29. Dollimore, *Radical Tragedy,* pp. 17–19.

30. The Italianate Globe tragedy *The Devil's Charter* (1607) luridly depicts the papal court as a temporal institution. Like Middleton's and Webster's Italianate tragedies, Barnabe Barnes's offers a biographical chronicle, drawing from Guicciardini's *La Historia D'Italia* to dramatize sensationally the career of Pope Alexander VI.

14. *Crisis of Confidence: The Buckingham Era*

1. Except where otherwise noted, I rely for the political background of the 1620s and for England's involvement in the Thirty Years War on the accounts of Gardiner, *England,* vols. 4–6; Ogg, *Europe,* pp. 118–82, and Willson, *James I,* pp. 378–447. Key details and interpretive points are cited in the text.

2. S. L. Adams, "Foreign Policy and the Parliaments of 1621 and 1624," in Sharpe, *Faction,* pp. 148–50.

3. Ibid., p. 150. Houston, *James I,* p. 78, and Conrad Russell, "Parliament and the King's Finances," in Russell, *Origins,* p. 103, cite rounded figures between £900,000 and £1,000,000 per annum.

4. Prothero, *Documents,* p. 310; Tanner, *Constitutional Conflicts,* p. 48.

5. Prothero, *Documents,* p. 310; Tanner, *Constitutional Conflicts,* p. 48.

6. John Rushworth, ed., *Historical Collections of Private Passages of State,* 8 vols. (London, 1721–22), 1:53. See Zaller, *Parliament of 1621,* p. 178.

7. Ogg, *Europe,* p. 132; Lockyer, *Buckingham,* p. 126. Massinger dramatized this event allegorically in *The Maid of Honor.*

8. On Mompesson's shakedown of inns, see Zaller, *Parliament of 1621,* pp. 56–56. On the proliferation of monopolies, see Hill, *Revolution,* pp. 37–40.

9. Russell, *Parliaments, 1621–1629,* p. 102.

10. I rely throughout the paragraph on Robert Hamilton Ball, *The Amazing Career of Sir Giles Overreach* (Princeton: Princeton Univ. Press, 1939), pp. 6–8.

11. On Buckingham's relationship to Mompesson and on the complicity of Kit and Edward Villiers in the offensive monopolies, see Lockyer, *Buckingham,* pp. 90–94, and Russell, *Parliaments, 1621–1629,* pp. 105–9.

12. Zaller, *Parliament of 1621,* pp. 56–65, 116–22, offers a detailed account of the parliamentary inquiry and of Yelverton's testimony.

13. On Michell, see Akrigg, *Pageant,* p. 237. On Bacon's fall and the king's posture through the parliamentary inquiry, see Russell, *Parliaments, 1621–1629,* pp. 110–13, and Zaller, *Parliament of 1621,* pp. 82–85.

14. On Buckingham's titles, see Charles R. Cammell, *The Great Duke Buckingham* (London: Collins, 1939); Lockyer, *Buckingham,* pp. 25–52. The quotation is from Sir Henry Wotten, "A View of the Life and Death of George Villiers, Duke of Buckingham," in *Reliquiae Wottonianae* (London: 1672), p. 219.

15. Cammell, *Buckingham,* p. 100.

16. Dietz, *Finance,* p. 198.

17. Throughout the paragraph I rely on R. E. Ruigh, *Parliament of 1624* (Cambridge: Harvard Univ. Press, 1971), pp. 303–81.

18. Lockyer, *Buckingham,* p. 230.

19. For a concise account of Charles's tactics and the rising opposition to Buck-

ingham, see J. P. Kenyon, *Stuart England* (Harmondsworth: Penguin, 1978), pp. 94–98; for a fuller account, see Russell, *Parliaments, 1621–1629*, pp. 269–303.

20. Gardiner, *England*, 6:106.

21. P. M[atthieu], *The Powerful Favorite, or, the Life of Aelius Sejanus* (Paris, [London?], 1628); STC 17664. The STC entry notes, "*Tr.* as a satire on the Duke of Buckingham" (2:146).

22. See Frederick W. Fairholt, *Poems and Songs Relating to George Villiers, Duke of Buckingham* (London: Percy Society, 1851), vol. 29.

23. *CSPV* (June 30, 1628), no. 208, p. 157.

24. Clarendon, *Rebellion*, 1:14; Russell, *The Crisis of Parliaments: English History 1509–1660* (Oxford Univ. Press, 1971), p. 286; Willson, *James I*, p. 389.

25. Lockyer, *Buckingham*, p. 474.

26. Ibid.

27. Kevin Sharpe, "The Earl of Arundel, His Circle and the Opposition to the Duke of Buckingham, 1618–1628," in Sharpe, *Faction*, pp. 232–33.

28. On these constitutional matters, see Tanner, *Constitutional Conflicts*, pp. 60–61.

29. G. E. Aylmer, *A Short History of Seventeenth-Century England: 1603–1689* (New York: New American Library, 1963), p. 79.

30. Zagorin, *Court & Country*, pp. 74–118; Heinemann, *Puritanism*, pp. 200–203.

15. Censorship, Citizen Opposition Drama, and A Game at Chesse

1. *CSPD, James I* (Dec. 24, 1620), p. 202; *STC* 8649; cf. Zaller, *Parliament of 1621*, p. 27.

2. *CSPD, James I* (July 26, 1621), p. 278; *STC* 8668.

3. *CSPD, James I* (Sept. 1621), p. 83; *STC* 8714.

4. Michael Drayton, *Elegies Upon Sundry Occasions* (1627), in *Works*, 5 vols., ed. J. W. Hebel (Oxford: Shakespeare Head Press, 1961), 3:206–9, ll. 9–16.

5. Robert Burton, *Anatomy of Melancholy*, 3 vols., ed. Holbrook Jackson (London: Dent, 1932), 1:87.

6. Burton, *Anatomy*, 1:121.

7. Quotations from *The Roman Actor* are to Edwards & Gibson, *Massinger*, vol. 3, and line references appear in text.

8. See the excellent accounts of Louis B. Wright, "Propaganda against James I's 'Appeasement' of Spain," *HLQ* 6 (1943):149–72, and Heinemann, *Puritanism*, pp. 155–59.

9. Thomas Scott, *The Second Part of Vox Populi* (Holland, 1624), STC 22104. See also Scott's *Vox Regis* (1623), STC 22162.

10. Samuel Calvert to Buckingham, Nov. 28, 1620, *The Fortesque Papers*, ed. S. R. Gardiner (London: Camden Society, n.s., 1871), 1:143; E. K. Chambers and W. W. Greg, ed., *Dramatic Records from the Privy Council Register, 1603–1642*, in Malone Society, *Collections* (Oxford, 1911), 1:379–81. See also Albright, *Publication*, pp. 164–68.

11. *CSPD, James I* (Aug. 12, 1624), p. 325. Henry Herbert *had* licensed the play for production; only after its long run was it suppressed. See Bald, *Chesse*, p. 159. All quotations are from this edition, and line references appear in text.

12. On the royal language of representation, see Goldberg, *James I*, pp. 55 ff. See also his, "The Poet's Authority: Spenser, Jonson, and James VI and I," in Greenblatt, *Forms*, pp. 81–99.

13. The ambassador's letter is translated in Edward M. Wilson and Olga Turner, "The Spanish Protest against *A Game at Chesse*," *MLR* 44 (1949):480–82.

14. Chamberlain, *Letters* (Aug. 21, 1624), 2:578.

15. John R. Moore, "The Contemporary Significance of Middleton's *A Game at Chesse*, *PMLA* 50 (1935):761.

16. Chamberlain, *Letters* (Aug. 21, 1624), 2:578.

17. *CSPD, James I* (Aug. 12, 1624), p. 325; Chamberlain, *Letters*, 2:578.

18. *CSPD, James I* (Aug. 12, 1624), p. 325; (Aug. 14, 1624), p. 327; (Aug. 21, 1624), pp. 329–330; (Aug. 27, 1624), p. 331. Bald, *Chesse*, pp. 159–66, reprints the pertinent documents. See also Bernard M. Wagner, "New Allusions to *A Game at Chesse*," *PMLA* 44 (1929):827–34.

19. See Sullivan, *Court Masques*, p. 176, on the anti-Jesuit bias in plays of the period.

20. See J. W. Harper, ed., *A Game at Chesse* (New York: Hill & Wang, 1966), pp. xxii–xxiii.

21. Zaller, *Parliament of 1621*, p. 146.

22. Roussel Sargent, "Theme and Structure in Middleton's *A Game at Chesse*, *MLR* 66 (1971):729.

23. By 1610 these ideas had been fully formulated. See Pocock, *Constitution*, pp. 48, 51. On fundamental law the most pertinent study is J. W. Gough, *Fundamental Law in English Constitutional History* (Oxford: Oxford Univ. Press, 1955), esp. ch. 4 on James I. See also the discussion of Sir Henry Finch's ideas on the subject in J. P. Cooper, "Differences between English and Continental Governments in the Early Seventeenth Century," in *Britain and the Netherlands*, ed. J. S. Bromley and E. H. Kossmann (London: Chatto & Windus, 1960), p. 65.

24. On England's fear of cryptopapists, see the cover of *A Scourge for the Pope*, which depicts "a disguised Iesuite," reproduced in Bald, *Chesse*, between pp. 94–95. On Middleton's last-minute additions, completed between July and Aug. 12, 1624, see George R. Price, "The Huntington MS of *A Game at Chesse*," *HLQ* 17 (1954):83–88, and Harper, *Chesse*, pp. xiv, 51n. The Fat Bishop (Spalato) was an entirely new addition.

25. Willson, *James I*, p. 416.

26. Wilson and Turner, "The Spanish Protest," p. 480.

27. Heinemann, *Puritanism*, pp. 164–65; Harper, *Chesse*, p. 84n; Lockyer, *Buckingham*, p. 153. For contemporary views of Buckingham's lechery, see Weldon, *Court & Character*, 1:446–47, and Clarendon, *Rebellion*, 1:52.

28. Ruigh, *Parliament of 1624*, pp. 244–45, 300.

29. Quotations from *The Staple of News* are to Herford & Simpson, *Jonson*, vol. 6, and line references appear in text.

30. Harbage & Schoenbaum, *Annals*, pp. 132–33. The conjecture 1629 for the original date of performance is my own.

31. *DNB*, s.v. "Lamb, John"; Lockyer, *Buckingham*, p. 451.

32. Quoted in Gregg, *Charles I*, p. 174.

33. Fairholt, *Poems and Songs Relating to George Villiers, Duke of Buckingham*, vol. 29, p. xv. See also Bentley, *Jacobean Caroline Stage*, 1:267–68, on the ineverent ballad "The Tragedy of Dr. *Lambe*."

34. Published accounts of Mrs. Bodenham's activities postdate the lost play on Lambe. See Nathaniel Crouch, *Kingdom of Darkness* (London, 1699), pp. 16–18.

35. *A Briefe Description of the Notorious Life of Iohn Lambe* (Amsterdam, 1629), pp. 4–6, 15–19.

36. Harbage & Schoenbaum, *Annals,* p. 126, list the play c. 1628–1634. The issues raised by the Five Knights Case in November 1627 make the earlier limit more likely.
37. Joyce O. Davis, ed., *King John and Matilda* (New York & London: Garland, 1980). All quotations are from this edition, and line references appear in text. See Heinemann, *Puritanism,* pp. 224–26, for a fuller treatment of the play than mine.
38. *Magnetic Lady,* Chorus, Inter-Act, 3:23–25, in Herford & Simpson, *Jonson,* 6:564.
39. Herbert, *Records,* pp. 18, 27.
40. Ibid., p. 19. A. H. Bullen rediscovered the *Barnavelt* ms. in the early 1880s. See Charles J. Sisson's "Introduction to *Believe as You List,*" in *The Seventeenth-Century Stage: A Collection of Critical Essays,* ed. G. E. Bentley (Chicago: Univ. of Chicago Press, 1968), pp. 170–95.
41. Harbage & Schoenbaum, *Annals,* pp. 120–21, and Herbert, *Records,* pp. 20–21.
42. See also *The Game at Chesse, a Metaphorical Discourse* (London, 1643), which analyzes the proceedings of the parliamentary and royal parties.

16. The Patrician Opposition Drama of Philip Massinger
1. Heinemann, *Puritanism,* pp. 166–69; Bald, *Chesse,* p. 21.
2. In fact, there are strong links between the erstwhile Essex supporters and the opposition aristocrats of the 1620s. See Snow, "Essex and the Aristocratic Opposition to the Early Stuarts," pp. 224–33.
3. A disputed point. See Donald S. Lawless, *Philip Massinger and His Associates,* Ball State Monograph no. 10 (Muncie, Ind.: Ball State Univ., 1967), pp. 1–2.
4. Edwards & Gibson, *Massinger,* 1:313. All quotations from Massinger's poems and independently composed plays are from this edition, and line references appear in text. On Massinger's relationship to Philip Herbert, see ibid., 1:xviii, 4:389–91.
5. *CSPD, James I* (Aug. 14, 1619), p. 71.
6. Chamberlain, *Letters* (May 8, 1619), 2:236, 236n, and Arthur Wilson, *The History of Great Britain, Being the Life and Reign of King James The First* (London, 1653), p. 127.
7. Bullen published *Barnavelt* in *A Collection Old English Plays* (London, 1882–1885), vol. 2.
8. On the scenes composed by Massinger, see the attribution of Wilhelmina P. Frijlinck, ed., *The Tragedy of Sir John Van Olden Barnavelt* (Amsterdam: H. G. van Dorssen, 1922), p. xcvi. All quotations are from this edition, and line references appear in text. Superscripts have been normalized.
9. Albright, *Publication,* pp. 185–86; V. C. Gildersleeve, *Government Regulation of the Elizabethan Drama* (New York: Columbia Univ. Press, 1908), p. 114.
10. See Pocock, *Constitution.*
11. *Debates in the House of Commons in 1625,* ed. Samuel R. Gardiner (London: Camden Society, 1873 [vol. 6]), p. 110.
12. Cf. *The Bondman,* which reports of tyrannous insurrection "To change the Aristocracie of *Corinth* / Into an absolute Monarchy," stamping "Vpon the Cities freedome" (1.3.131–37).
13. Lockyer, *Buckingham,* pp. 50, 76, and Alan P. McGowan, "The Royal Navy under the First Duke of Buckingham: 1618–1628," Ph.D. Diss., Univ. of London, 1967. From 1619 the situation improved.
14. Kenyon, *Stuarts,* pp. 54–55; Zaller, *Parliament of 1621,* pp. 26–30.
15. Nicholas Tyacke, "Puritanism, Arminianism and Counter-Revolution," in

Russell, *Origins*, p. 131. Buckingham had in fact appointed William Laud to a bishopric in 1621. See Willson, *James*, p. 400.

16. See S. L. Adams, "Foreign Policy and the Parliaments of 1621 and 1624," in Sharpe, *Faction*, pp. 139–40.

17. S. R. Gardiner, "The Political Element in Massinger," *Contemporary Review* 28 (1876):495–507. This important essay overstates the case in two important respects. Believing that *The Maid of Honour* was composed in the 1630s, Gardiner argues that the play reproduces the military situation in England in 1621–22 (which it does) and the parallel situation Charles I faced in 1631. Gardiner also allegorizes (with a heavy hand) *all* the elements he treats, thereby confining Massinger's plays to a single plane of significance.

18. Essential to an understanding of the hortatory use of examples is John M. Wallace, " 'Examples Are Best Precepts': Readers and Meanings in Seventeenth-Century Poetry," *Critical Inquiry* 1 (1974):273–90.

19. Contrary views: Edwards & Gibson, *Massinger*, 1:106, assert, "The idea that [Massinger] was conducting political propaganda [is] an absurdity," and Allen Gross, "Contemporary Politics in Massinger," *SEL* 6 (1966):279–80, who allows that these plays treat "vital issues" but denies the presence of personal satire. On latter-day plays lauding Elizabethan militarism, see Butler, *Theatre & Crisis*, pp. 198–203.

20. See my "Philip Earl of Pembroke and the Analogical Way of Reading Political Tragedy," *JEGP* 85 (1986):332–45.

21. This depiction of the lustful favorite fits Buckingham, who was known as a womanizer and seducer of court ladies. See Lockyer, *Buckingham*, p. 153, and Peyton, *Catastrophe*, 2:354–55.

22. On the connections between Overreach and Mompesson, see Ball, *Giles Overreach*, pp. 3–25.

23. See Akrigg, *Pageant*, p. 237.

24. Edwards & Gibson, *Massinger*, 2:278. This view continues to exert its influence in recent criticism. See, for example, Nancy S. Leonard, "Overreach at Bay: Massinger's *A New Way to Pay Old Debts*," in *Philip Massinger: A Critical Reassessment*, ed. Douglas Howard (Cambridge: Cambridge Univ. Press, 1985), p. 192n.

25. Chamberlain, *Letters* (July 12, 1623), 2:506; *CSPD, James I* (Feb. 8, 1624), p. 161. See Russell, *Parliaments*, 1621–1629, pp. 399–400.

26. Gardiner, *England*, 4:41; Russell, *Parliaments*, 1621–1629, p. 234.

27. Gardiner, *England*, 4:44.

28. *DNB*, s.v. "Herbert, Philip" and "Mompesson, Giles"; Ball, *Giles Overreach*, p. 6.

29. See my "*A New Way to Pay Old Debts* and the Country-House Poetic Tradition," *Medieval and Renaissance Drama in England* 3 (1986):177–87.

30. Quotations to "To Penshurst" are from Herford & Simpson, *Jonson*, 8:93–96, and line references appear in text.

31. C. A. Gibson, "Massinger's Use of His Sources for 'The Roman Actor,' " *Journal of the Australasian Language and Literature Assoc.* 15 (1961):65; W. D. Briggs, "The Influence of Jonson's Tragedy in the Seventeenth Century," *Anglia* 35 (1912):311–22. On the Tacitean background in Massinger's plays, see Martin Butler, "*The Roman Actor* and the Early Stuart Classical Play," in Howard, *Massinger*, pp. 140–46.

32. Massinger evidently reacted to "A Short Treatise against Stage-Playes," dedicated to Parliament in 1625. See the account by William Sandidge, Jr., ed., *The Roman Actor* (Princeton: Princeton Univ. Press, 1929), pp. 17–24. Parliament did not approve the recommendation to prohibit stage plays but did prohibit plays on the

Sabbath. See Russell, *Parliaments, 1621–1629*, p. 234. On representation in *The Roman Actor*, see the fine discussion in Goldberg, *James I*, pp. 203–9. On the censorship of Massinger's plays, see Herbert, *Records*, pp. 17–23.

33. Butler, "Roman Actor," in Howard, *Massinger*, p. 150.

34. Important in this regard is the discussion of "necessity of state" in *Believe as You List* by Douglas Howard, "Massinger's Political Tragedies," in Howard, *Massinger*, pp. 129–34.

35. John Aubrey reports in *The Natural History of Wiltshire*, ed. J. Britton (London, 1847), p. 91, that William Herbert sent Massinger £20 or £30 per annum. On Herbert's aiding the players of *A Game at Chess*, see Bald, *Chesse*, p. 21.

17. The Dispersion of Opposition Conceptions of Governance

1. Alfred Harbage, *Cavalier Drama: An Historical and Critical Supplement to the Study of the Elizabethan and Restoration Stage* (New York: Modern Language Assoc., 1936), pp. 22, 23, 40, 45. See also Jefferson B. Fletcher, "Précieuses at the Court of Charles I," *Journal of Comparative Literature* 1 (1903):120–53, and George F. Sensabaugh, "Love Ethics in Platonic Court Drama 1625–1642," *HLQ* 1 (1938):277–304. A corollary recently expressed by Cohen in *Public Theater*, p. 280, is that "Caroline absolutism" engendered an "extreme" crisis in the public theaters after 1629.

2. Butler, *Theatre & Crisis*, pp. 181–250, 25–54. On the survival of popular drama, see Heinemann, *Puritanism*, pp. 237–57. Cook's emphasis in *Playgoers* on privileged versus plebeian audiences works against my concern to piece out the gradations of opposition attitudes and audiences.

3. See Foucault, *Archaeology*, pp. 31–39, 227–29, on discursive formations and the coercive power of language.

4. For the history of the period of prerogative government, I rely on Gardiner, *England*, vols. 7–10; Clarendon, *Rebellion*, vol. 1; Roger Lockyer, *Tudor and Stuart Britain, 1471–1714* (London: Longman, 1964), ch. 12; Hibbert, *Charles I*; and Gregg, *Charles I*. For Laud's ecclesiastical policies I rely particularly on Nicholas Tyacke, "Puritanism, Arminianism and Counter-Revolution," in Russell, *Origins*, pp. 119–43. I have cited only outstanding or pivotal historical points. Other kinds of evidence are documented below. Esther S. Cope's *Politics without Parliaments, 1629–1640* (London: Allen & Unwin, 1987), appeared after this study was in press, but its view that the absence of Parliaments deprived the English, who were an informed people, of an important means of airing grievances and raised apprehensions at the local level about England's heritage and religion, is important to the views I have expressed in this chapter.

5. See Elizabeth Hamilton, *Henrietta Maria* (New York: Coward, McCann & Geohagen, 1976), pp. 100, 136, 169, and on the incessant rumors of conversion, pp. 142–58.

6. Christopher Hill, "Literature and the English Revolution," *Seventeenth Century* 1 (1986):20. Hill contends that "something like two cultural traditions were forming, at least from the time of Elizabeth." However, I wish to exphasize the gradations of opposition expressed in the Caroline drama.

7. William Prynne, *Histriomastix*, ed. Arthur Freeman (New York: Garland, 1974), Index, s.v. "Women-Actors"; "Dancing." Shirley also attacked Prynne in his dedicatory verses to Ford's *Love's Sacrifice* (1632?).

8. By 1635 a French troupe touring England with its female actors (supported by the queen) opened at the Phoenix. See Bentley, *Jacobean & Caroline Stage*, 1:233–

35; 3:452–53; 6:45–47. On the queen as Chloridia, see Orgel & Strong, *Jones,* 2:442, 447.

9. For the chronology of events pertaining to Prynne's imprisonment and Shirley's satire, see Frances F. Senescu, ed., *James Shirley's The Bird in a Cage* (New York: Garland, 1980), pp. lv–lviii. On Prynne's sentence see William M. Lamont, *Marginal Prynne, 1600–1669* (London: Routledge & K. Paul, 1963), p. 33.

10. Herbert, *Records,* pp. 22–23, 54–55.

11. Hibbert, *Charles I,* pp. 134–35.

12. Bentley, *Jacobean & Caroline Stage,* 5:1154–63.

13. Quotations from Shirley's masque are from Orgel and Strong, *Jones,* 2:546–53, and line references appear in text.

14. For example, Orgel, *Illusion,* pp. 80–83.

15. Bentley, *Jacobean & Caroline Stage,* 5:1155–56.

16. See Thomas Clayton, ed., *The Works of Sir John Suckling: The Non-Dramatic Works* (Oxford: Clarendon, 1971), p. lxvi.

17. On the circle at Great Tew, see Kurt Weber's *Lucius Cary, Second Viscount Falkland* (New York: Columbia Univ. Press, 1940), pp. 66–68, 82.

18. Clayton, *Suckling: Non-Dramatic Works,* pp. xxxiii–xxxiv.

19. Dates of Suckling's plays are from L. A. Beaurline, ed., *The Works of Sir John Suckling: The Plays* (Oxford: Clarendon Press, 1971), pp. 244, 253, 288, 289. All quotations are from this edition, and line references appear in text.

20. Suckling's personal relationship with Charles and Henrietta-Maria appears, along with the deference, in the prologue "To the King" (l. 16.1) in *Aglaura* (1637) and in Suckling's account of his audience with Charles in Clayton, *Suckling: Non-Dramatic Works,* pp. 126–29.

21. Elliott M. Hill, ed., *The Tragedy of Nero* (New York: Garland, 1979).

22. Letter to Henry German, 1640, in Clayton, *Suckling: Non-Dramatic Works,* pp. 163–67.

23. Kenneth Allott, ed., *The Poems of William Habington* (London: Univ. of Liverpool Press, 1948). All quotations are from this edition, and references, by title and page number, appear in text.

24. Quotations from *The Queen of Arragon* are from *A Select Collection of Old English Plays,* ed. W. C. Hazlitt, 4th ed. (1874–76; rpt. New York: Blom, 1964), pp. 329–416.

25. Wood, *Athenae Oxonienses,* 3:224–25.

26. Quotations from *The Royal Slave* are from *The Plays and Poems of William Cartwright,* ed. G. Blakemore Evans (Madison: Univ. of Wisconsin Press, 1951), pp. 193–253, and line references appear in text.

27. See Butler's fine discussion of *The Queen of Arragon* and, specifically, of Magna Carta in *Theatre & Crisis,* pp. 62–76, 72–74.

28. *Aubrey's Brief Lives,* ed. Oliver L. Dick (Harmondsworth: Penguin, 1982), p. 183.

29. Quotations from Denham's works are to *The Poetical Works of Sir John Denham,* ed. Theodore H. Banks, 2d ed. (n.p., Archon, 1969), and line references appear in text.

30. Herbert, *Records,* p. 64.

31. Ibid., p. 64n; *Calendar of State Papers, Domestic Series . . . Charles I, 1639,* vol. xiv, ed. William D. Hamilton (London, 1873) (May 8, 1639), p. 140.

32. *Vox Borealis* (London, 1641), n.p. See the discussion by George F. Byers, ed., *The Valiant Scot by J. W.* (New York: Garland, 1980), pp. 83–85.

33. *CSPD, Charles I* (Sept. 29, 1639), pp. 529–30.
34. Ann Haaker, ed., *The Antipodes* (Lincoln: Univ. of Nebraska Press, 1966), Prologue, l. 20. The play's date is from Haaker.
35. Butler, *Theatre & Crisis*, p. 220. Butler's reassessment of Brome as a major opposition dramatist is important, and my disagreement with his interpretation of *The Court Beggar* as a major subversive play does not extend to his penetrating analysis of Mendicant as a monopoly beggar (pp. 220–29).
36. Quotations from *The Court Beggar* are from *The Dramatic Works of Richard Brome*, 3 vols., ed. R. H. Shepherd (1873; rpt. New York: AMS Press, 1966), vol. 1, and page references appear in text.
37. Ralph J. Kaufmann, "Suckling and Davenant Satirized by Brome," *MLR* 40 (1960):332–44.
38. Bentley, *Jacobean & Caroline Stage*, 1:333; Herbert, *Records*, p. 66.
39. Butler, *Theatre & Crisis*, pp. 222–23.
40. *CSPD, Charles I* (Apr. 9 & 23, 1639), pp. 30, 71.
41. *DNB*, s.v. "Fane, Mildmay." See also, Alfred Harbage, "An Unnoted Caroline Dramatist," *SP* 31 (1934):28–34.
42. Clifford Leach, ed., *Mildmay Fane's Reguaillo D'Oceano 1640 and Candy Restored, 1641* (1938; rpt. Vaduz, Germany: Kraus, 1963), in *Materials for the Study of the Old English Drama*, ser. 2, vols. 44–46. All quotations are from this edition, and line references appear in text. Superscripts have been normalized.
43. In 1639 Charles demanded 3,000 trained men from the City bands and a £100,000 loan. See Robert Ashton, *The City and the Court* (Cambridge: Cambridge Univ. Press, 1979), p. 198. On the decline of royal credit see idem, *The Crown and the Money Market, 1603–1640* (Oxford: Clarendon Press, 1960), pp. 154–84.
44. Herbert, *Records*, pp. 22–23.
45. Parry, *Golden Age Restor'd*, pp. 190, 203, 221–22, 242, 249.
46. Edwards & Gibson, *Massinger*, 1:xxvii, xxxix.
47. Herbert, *Records*, p. 23.
48. Patterson, *Censorship*, pp. 21–23.
49. Herbert, *Records*, p. 38.
50. In this view I exclude the much more coercive regulation, such as the fining of the Red Bull-King's company for £1,000 in 1639 (see n. 31, above), that prevailed in London's open-air theaters.

Epilogue
1. Bentley, *Jacobean & Caroline Stage*, 2:690.
2. Heinemann, *Puritanism*, pp. 18–47.
3. Ibid., pp. 235–39; Cohen, *Public Theater*, pp. 277–78.

Index